John Kay

Theo De Vos

John Kay

From Barbed Wire to Steppenwolf

Not Always an Easy Ride

Aspekt Publishers

John Kay, not always an easy ride

© Theo de Vos
© 2023   Aspekt Publishers | Amersfoortsestraat 27
              3769 AD Soesterberg
              info@uitgeverijaspekt.nl | www.uitgeverijaspekt.nl

Cover: Lisa Dijkhuizen
Inside: BeCo DTP-Productions, Epe

ISBN: 9789464870039
NUR: 662

All rights reserved. No part of these pages, either text or image may be used for any purpose other than personal use. Therefore, reproduction, modification, storage in a retrieval system or re-trans-mission, in any form or by any means, electronic, mechanical or otherwise, for reasons other than personal use, is strictly prohibited without prior written permission.

"So many times when young people have a dream, they are often told how unrealistic their dreams are. And so, we often kill something in the spirit of those young people when we try to talk them out of things that are important to them. In my case, even if it was a long shot and it had risk involved, I'm one of the lucky ones who saw his dream come true. So yes, I realize how fortunate I am ..."

John Kay, Brussels, Belgium, April 30, 1998

Introduction	Page

- Changing Plans 11
- Disappointment Number on May 23, 1969. 19

Part 1. German Thorns and Tears
- East Prussia, a Lost Heritage 25
- A War, a Wedding and a Farewell 29
- Fleeing the Russians 51
- "Heimatvertriebenen" and Aftermath of May 8, 1945 77
- Through a Hole in the Barbed Wire 99
- Between the Ruins in Hannover. 119

Part 2. The New World
- Under the Leaf of the Maple Tree. 135
- California Horizon Blue(s) and Sparrow 147
- Steppenwolf 169
- A Crack in the Iron Curtain 249
- Feed the Fire. 273
- Arnstadt 2022* 303
- The Maue Kay Foundation 323

Epilogue 335

*Only in the English edition.

A 25-year-old John Kay in Belgium on May 23, 1969.

John Kay as a wildlife advocate, fighting for all creatures who have no voice of their own. (See chapter The Maue Kay Foundation)

A few important people:

– Waquin Krauledaitis = Joachim Fritz Krauledat (John Kay) an East Prussian/German war fugitive who becomes a music icon.

– Jutta Maue: a lady from Hamburg, Germany who moves to Toronto, Canada in 1962. Five years later, she marries John Kay.

– Fritz Krauledaitis (Krauledat): an *Oberfeldwebel* of Lithuanian descent in the German Army.

– Elsbeth Zimmermann: a brave war widow and war fugitive from Tilsit, East Prussia.

– Frau Kranz: a guardian angel from Arnstadt, Germany.

– Gerhard Kyczinski: John's handy stepfather, who moves with Joachim and Elsbeth to Toronto, Canada in 1958.

Introduction

Changing Plans

A global lockdown, panic buying of groceries and a mandatory wearing of face masks. Protests against and violation of the imposed Covid rules all over the world. Relaxations of those rules and masks off, then tightening of the rules and masks on again. During all this, we had that very strange case in Western Europe with a Belgian soldier, called Jürgen Conings. Totally on the loose, he openly rebelled against one of our virologists and cried out loud that *"he would cut that man's throat"*. In 2020 and 2021 we lived through some extremely unusual circumstances.

So to say that this whole Covid 19 pandemic seriously undermined the normal course of life even for law-abiding citizens is -to put it mildly- on the one hand a considerable understatement, but on the other hand, could it also be that many people got more of a sense of reality and resignation? This is at least the impression I have *myself* sometimes. This extremely bizarre situation has made many people realize how quickly things can change and how transient things in life are. While some people concentrate on the far-reaching limitations and often feel bad about themselves, others easily find satisfaction in the many (simple) things that are still possible. Or they suddenly get bright ideas and see opportunities they otherwise would not have thought of. At a time when the healthcare sector was walking its legs off, the idea of writing this story emerged somewhat out of the blue.

Honestly, I had no intention of drafting *this* story in the first place. I was only busy sketching the situation of German war refugees and all the deportees from the zone occupied by the Soviet Union during and just after the Second World War. In Germany they are better known under the name *"Heimatvertriebenen."* Their story is not very well known by the descendants of the Allied Forces of that time.

In fact, most people did not care too much about the fate of the Germans way back then. In itself, that is completely understandable, given the misery they had caused here for us in the Netherlands, Belgium, France and the rest of the world. So, it was my intention to clarify a little more the strange story of those many millions of German refugees and expelled (ethnic) populations in the zone occupied by the Soviet Army. Starting with the situation in 1943/44/45, covering the political East-West differences and the Cold War, I ended up with the fall of the Berlin Wall and the tearing open of the Iron Curtain. In the process, the escape story of Joachim Fritz Krauledat from East Germany in 1949 (see chapter *Through a Hole in the Barbed Wire*) was only supposed to be the *introduction* to the whole story.

However, when I made plans to go to Germany (once again) for further investigations, Covid struck hard, and people were no longer allowed to travel. When finally travelling became possible again, there was already a waiting list for more than a year for people who wanted to do some research in the German National Library at Leipzig. Moreover, an important contact of mine over there (in Jena) suddenly passed away. These unforeseen circumstances inspired me to change the plans somehow by linking most of the things I had already collected, straight to John Kay's story and to bring it all on from another point of view. AND- obviously- also from a totally different point of view than his own biography. Still in an attempt to write an interesting story but not precisely *the one* I first had in mind …

The book itself I like to dedicate to all my good childhood friends. Too many of them are unfortunately no longer with us. I cherish all those beautiful memories in such a way that I want to mention them here in general. Our interest in music at the end of the '60s/early '70s and the beautiful childhood we had way back then, are the additional reasons for writing this story. Furthermore, I dedicate the book to my own sister Irena, who passed away at the very beginning of the Covid Crisis in March 2020. And last but not least, writing this story gave me the opportunity to link two totally different subjects that have fascinated me throughout my whole life. One of the subjects is general (war) history and the other one is the striking hard rock and blues music of the American/Canadian/German group Steppenwolf.

After my previous books *In the Claw of the Eagle* about the First World War and *Steel Splinters and Shadow Heroes* about the Second World War (both only available in Dutch), I am now uncovering again a big chunk of (German) war history. The reason for this is that from the turbulent times of the Second World War a very strange story emerges of an ordinary East Prussian boy named Waquin (= Lithuanian for Joachim). This Waquin was almost blind as a child and besides all the other inconveniences the Germans went through at the time, he obviously had a very hard time during his entire childhood because of this physical handicap. Born in the middle of the war in Tilsit, East Prussia, he is only nine months old when his mother Elsbeth Zimmermann and he went on the run in extremely hard winter conditions for the advancing Russian Army. In January 1945 they both end up as refugees in the bombed-out German state of Thuringia. Partly on foot, partly on a horse-drawn sleigh and partly by train, his mother Elsbeth finally gets to Arnstadt with him. However, the damaged train tracks prevent them from going any further West. Completely bewildered and desperate, Elsbeth no longer knows where to go. While she's staring dazed and apathetically around her, she is standing in the middle of the night between the ruins of Arnstadt, with her crying toddler in her arms. Thanks to the generosity of a very kind lady who happens to be passing by, she is able to find shelter for herself and little Joachim for the night. Things will turn out differently however, because Elsbeth and her son will stay there for another four years ...

To write down the whole life story of this Joachim, you need at least ten times as many pages. Joachim also wrote an autobiography *Magic Carpet Ride* (in English only) together with John Einarsson, which was initially written in 1994 and "updated" in 2020. I never read it yet myself, because I didn't want it to influence my own description and especially because -as a not perfect English-speaking person- I don't like reading with a dictionary in my hand.

But a lot of old magazines, together with numerous interviews throughout the decades, have given me enough material to give a clear picture of his lifeline. Although, as a complete outsider, I have to admit I can't give full guarantee about *every* detail. Even John Kay isn't always quite sure...

In the first place, I am focusing very strongly -even mainly- on the historical background and the situation of the Germans at the end *of* and just *after* the Second World War. So, it is certainly *not* just about John Kay. Many other elements are added to outline the general situation in which refugees and expelled people (mainly Germans, but also others) then find themselves. Tough times lay ahead for these people and especially in the zones occupied by the Russians after the war, this is very noticeable. In the Western zones, the expected pattern of life for the Germans is indeed more favorable. After all, a comforting hand is immediately extended by American, British (and French to a somewhat lesser extent) authorities quite forgivingly to all (Western) Germans to build a new world together and engage fully in the rapidly reviving Western economic situation.

But in the eastern part of Germany, communism is dictating the rules from now on and this regime does not lend itself to far-reaching freedom anyway. Moreover, the Soviet Union is also not at all inclined to allow any mercy or easing in the rigid pattern of life of the German people, who had recently terrorized the Soviet people so horribly. Shamelessly and terribly brutally, indeed, the Nazis went to war against Russia a few years ago. German soldiers caused many millions of deaths of Soviet citizens and soldiers in the process. The rigid, repressive Russian attitude toward (East) Germans after the cessation of hostilities of May 8, 1945, may not be entirely excusable, but certainly explains their rigid attitude in part. To get out of the squeeze, many East Germans living in the Russian zone try to escape to the much freer West. They know, however, that in doing so they are also risking their lives. Anyone attempting to escape would be shot immediately by the border guards without any excuse. While many East Germans seem resigned to their unenviable fate behind the Iron Curtain, others are intent on fleeing the Russian encirclement and Communist influences at all costs.

And so did Elsbeth Zimmermann-Krauledat and her little boy Joachim, yes indeed! In the period between the blockade of Berlin and the official founding of the GDR in 1949 (and the complete souring of East-West relations), she and her five-year-old toddler Joachim flee again, and this time to the free West. Near the East German town of Eisenach, at the border, they crawl through a hole in the barbed wire during a very risky nighttime action, hearing the barking of dogs and machine gun fire from East German border guards who are hot on their heels. Joachim flees from East Germany to West Germany with his mother and an aunt. He first lives in Hannover for about nine years before emigrating with his mother (and the stepfather he will have by then) to Canada. From then on, Joachim is determined to build up his own future. And despite his severe visual handicap and the fact that he ends up in a strange country where he barely understands the people, he will succeed. His life in Canada starts out as that of an insecure and lonely immigrant, but it increasingly becomes the story of a focused and self-confident man.

Part 1 of this book tells the amazing and thrilling story of his early childhood in the former Germany, from the mid-'40s to the late '50s. The rest of the story in Part 2 sounds -in retrospect- somewhat like a fairy tale. Yet not everything was a rosy heavenly experience for him. The American dream it *did* become in the end. However, it was mainly *his* dream and even though it was preceded by a difficult period and involved a lot of risk, he was one of the lucky ones who finally made it. Throughout his life, Joachim has shown his extreme gratitude, because he has always realized how lucky he was. But he did not get it all for free and especially in his youth, Joachim had to fight hard for some respect. At a noticeably youthful age he absorbed the fact that nothing is just handed to you if you are not born in the right place under a good sign. Because of his visual handicap, it was sometimes extremely difficult for him at school and when playing, because children can be ridiculously hard on each other, and his bad eyes were often mocked.

Bullying because of physical imperfections is nowadays fortunately detected a bit faster at school than in the past, but eliminating it completely seems to be impossible. Joachim must therefore develop some character and learn how to stand up for himself. No one will help him doing that and he will learn to fend for himself. It is also this trait of character that will help him (much) later, as the leader of a world-renowned music band, to make decisions that may seem unpopular in the eyes of the larger crowd, but which have sometimes been unavoidable in order to continue functioning in a serious way. John Kay, as Joachim Fritz Krauledat is called by that time, has in all likelihood throughout his life indeed not been the easiest person to work with. But that is most likely a consequence of the fact that he has always fully realized that the road to success was long and very difficult and that is something that was not always sufficiently felt by some of his fellow musicians in the band. It is thanks to his extreme drive that his whole story can serve as an example for *all* migrants who end up somewhat orphaned in a totally foreign country. A few critics on the sidelines will dare to argue, from their comfort zone and from behind their laptops, that he had every chance anyway, only ... because he was white. This cliché argument, however, is in our opinion too often used today as an excuse when someone doesn't want to seize his own opportunities. Moreover, it is diametrically opposed to the fact that Joachim undoubtedly had to deal with other, possibly even worse prejudices than his skin color. After all, as a German, he had not long ago belonged to the enemy's camp, and many Canadians and Americans had died under German fire in Europe during the war. And despite the outstretched hand of Western countries in general toward the Germans, that was certainly not simply forgotten by everyone on the other side of the Atlantic in the 1950s. In Canada, the inhabitants were slightly more moderate than the Americans in their attitude towards the Germans after the war. So, it was a lot easier to emigrate to Canada than to the USA. Therefore, this was the main reason the Kyczinski-Zimmermann family first moved to Canada before migrating to the USA...

In this English version of the book, we have changed the title in *"John Kay, not always an Easy Ride"*. But the original Dutch version, with Plectrum & Prikkeldraad (*Plectrum and Barbed Wire*) as a title, may appeal to the imagination on the one hand, but on the other hand it may also be taken literally to some extent. Given his severe visual handicap, there were virtually no possibilities for Joachim to spend his free time on group sports or other physical commitments. As a consequence, his choice of playing guitar in Toronto, Canada was more than obvious. But the barbed wire is also a justified allusion to him and his tumultuous history for the following reason: he could freely put forward his political views as a musician in the free Western world. This is something he amply did over several decades, by the way. In many of his lyrics he often took a very militant stance on politics. This was not always and everywhere gratefully received (and certainly not by everyone in the US). That he able to enjoy total lyrical freedom to express his political views in the Western world, was of course largely thanks to his mother Elsbeth. Just after the war she managed, in the interest of her son Joachim, to battle her way literally and figuratively through difficult circumstances…and the barbed wire, so that he could fully enjoy this freedom. What if she had stayed put in East Germany in 1949 and remained in Arnstadt? Then there would indeed have been -again literally and figuratively- nothing but that barbed wire that would have curtailed both his physical and lyrical freedom and all his musical ambitions. Joachim would then have been a prisoner of the GDR regime for the rest of his life and therefore would have been doomed to swallow all political messages and forced to keep his mouth shut …

"Everyone belongs to the world and the world belongs to everyone" sang Dutch singer T. Lau once upon a time and Joachim Fritz Krauledat has clearly proved that. In any case, a land border did not stop his dreams and ambitions …

For this author, however, writing this story is primarily a tribute to this special, somewhat mysterious man. For there is something that, for me personally, rises far above all the other reasons.

Despite the fact that Waquin Krauledaitis, aka Joachim Fritz Krauledat aka John Kay since his birth to this day, is still almost 100% color blind, he did, after all, color my childhood in the late '60s to mid-'70s musically in a very rich way. And I thank him so much for that!

In our youth club at the time, 't Schureke (Dutch for "The Shed) in Walem near Mechelen, Belgium, he and his Steppenwolf reverberated through the speakers for many years, alternating with other great artists we loved during that beautiful period of our youth: Deep Purple, Jimi Hendrix, Cream, Cat Stevens, Golden Earring, Crosby Stills Nash & Young, Yes, Black Sabbath, Santana, Chicago Transit Authority, Blood, Sweat & Tears, Slade, Iron Butterfly, Ten Years After, Blue Cheer, Grand Funk Railroad, Led Zeppelin, Pink Floyd, Beatles, Rolling Stones, Simon & Garfunkel, Jethro Tull, Uriah Heep, CCR, etc. ...

Steppenwolf always sounded the loudest through the speakers. Coincidence? Not at all! Of course, along with John Fogerty and Ian Gillan, John Kay certainly did have by far the most powerful voice of all. The real truth, however, was that *someone*(!) always secretly pumped up the volume when Steppenwolf was played.

Disappointment Number, May 23, 1969

Belgium, Walem near Mechelen at 5 p.m.

A sparkling spring sun is spreading its pleasant afternoon warmth and it seems to become a very enjoyable evening. At least as far as *the weather* is concerned, because it won't be a pleasant evening for everyone ...

At that very moment, at the back of the small porch of the house where he's living, a (nearly) fourteen-year-old young man sits in quiet solitude listening to the radio. He feels incredibly sad, because he would rather jump on his rickety bike and ride to the sports hall at the Winketkaai in Mechelen. After all, he really wants to attend the performance of an internationally renowned rock group that is performing there tonight. But he is in a dark mood because there are two reasons why he cannot go there. First of all, his parents do not allow him to go. They believe that he is still too young "for such things". Of course, he could have slipped away without their approval, regardless of the hefty slaps on the ears and the house arrest he would have been guaranteed to receive afterwards. At that moment, he really didn't give a damn about that. He would also have spent his very last penny to be able to go anyway, together with some of his friends whose parents *did* allow them to go. But that's also the second reason he will have to stay at home: he doesn't have any money! Even if his parents give him permission to go, he will never be able to get those 200 old Belgian francs (6 $) to buy an entry ticket. So deeply disappointed and completely isolated from the rest of the world, he is listening to the wailing radio. Out of sheer frustration, he would even like to smash that grey, creaking, primitive portable "Optalux" with batteries and all on the floor ...

The Flemish/Belgian weekly magazine HUMO had already announced it a few weeks ago. Steppenwolf, the band with those five rough men from the United States of America; those men from *Sookie, Sookie, Born to be Wild, Magic Carpet Ride, Rock Me*, is coming to the Netherlands and to Belgium. And they are even coming to Mechelen, right here in our backyard! Wildly enthusiastic the message goes around in our local circle of friends, and everyone wants to go and see those guys. Wildly enthusiastic the boy also tells his mother about it ... and we already know how excited *she* was, not to mention his father ...

Coincidence or not, but it seems as if that stupid, stubborn radio wants to sprinkle some salt in the wounds at this very moment. Just then, suddenly on Radio 2 East Flanders, we hear Steppenwolf with the song: *Happy Birthday*, as a foretaste of the music that the group in question will bring that evening in Mechelen. Spontaneous tears appear in this young man's eyes. He first listens very attentively to that song, then sits down even more disillusioned next to his primitive 2-watt mono record player and puts on a 45-rpm record. Very softly, almost inaudibly, because his father is coming home from work, and he doesn't want to hear "all that screaming"...

One second later *Everybody's Next One* (= the flipside of the hit *Born To Be Wild*) sounds through the speaker. What a clever piece of music this is too! Still, this is only a very meager consolation prize knowing that the highest possible prize in the lottery could be won tonight. Rock group Steppenwolf is playing not even five kilometers from here, and without him being able to be there. Especially that mysterious singer, John Kay, the man with the powerful, gravelly, abrasive voice and dark glasses, he would have loved to have seen him at work.

At that time, the boy in question had no idea how hard the singer had worked and what risks he had to take to get where he stands today.

More than 52 years later (even 54 years for the English version), that disillusioned boy of long ago will draft this book, split up in two totally different parts, somewhat independent of each other. They could even be two totally separate books. But in the end, it will turn out that these two separate parts of this sociological and political-historical story with its distinct musical reverberations, do carry a clear link.

The life story of the mysterious singer with dark glasses begins on April 12, 1944, in the middle of the Second World War. On that day, a certain Waquin Krauledaitis is born in the Prussian town of Tilsit, East Prussia ...

Part 1

German Thorns and Tears

East Prussia, a Lost Heritage

"My birthplace would be hard to find. It changed so many times I'm not sure where it belongs."

East Prussia is a place name that sounds rather mysterious. Somewhere far at the back of our minds, we realize that we have seen, read or heard that name somewhere at some point. But what do we actually know about it? Fully justified, younger generations today may ask the question: *"Where is this legendary-sounding place mentioned so often in this story actually located?"* When we try to locate it on the map of Europe today, we won't even find it, at least not under its original name. The age-old German Prussian pride has faded away and the name *Ostpreußen* has completely disappeared from the world scene.

Nowadays, it is partly located in what is known today as Kaliningrad, a small Russian exclave on the Baltic coast, wedged between present-day Lithuania and Poland. It is separated from the actual, large homeland of Russia by Belarus. Is this destiny final?

At the end of the Second World War in Europe in May 1945, Soviet party leader Joseph Stalin had his own plans for the part of Europe he occupied. This included *his* part of Germany, to which East Prussia then still belonged integrally. He was convinced that the Germans and the Lithuanian Prussians who still lived there, would not accept their destiny just like that. After all, such a proud people would not simply agree to live under the yoke of the Soviet Union. Because he did not want history to repeat itself, he had deported all the very last Germans and German-supporting Prussians at once from both German East Prussia itself and from the three Baltic states of Estonia, Latvia and Lithuania (which had already been absorbed by Russia in 1940). At least those people who were still there at the time, because by the end of the war, many of them had already died, while more than two million others had fled their own region for the approaching troops of the Red Army. Those who had nevertheless remained there and survived the horror of the war, were all dispersed without recourse to other areas of the Soviet Union between 1945 and 1947 at the hands of the Stalin regime. Often, they found themselves forced to the homeland of Germany itself ... or to Siberia. From then on, the ancient German region of East Prussia itself was populated exclusively by native Russians, professional soldiers of the Soviet army or Stalin-minded sympathizers who in turn had moved up from elsewhere to that ancient German region. All German accents in East Prussia disappeared completely, the names of cities and towns were given Slavic-sounding names, and names were spelled exclusively in the Cyrillic script. The ancient German city of Memel became Klaipèda, which sounds better in Russian, Tilsit became Sovetsk and Königsberg became Kaliningrad. The Memel River, along whose banks descendants of old medieval German knights and nobles had lived for several centuries, would henceforth only be called Njemen. In that old, proud German East Prussia, only Russian is spoken today, indeed. In the Kaliningrad Oblast (as most of the former East Prussia is called today), German is only spoken when nostalgia-sensitive German tourists want to visit that beautiful region of their ancestors. Is all this really forever? Who is to say? Even in our humble opinion it is impossible to say with certainty where this region actually belongs and whether it will remain forever as it is today ...

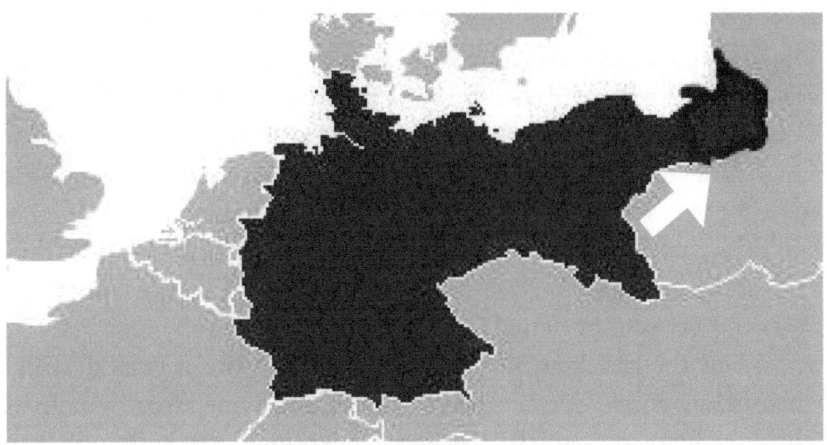

East Prussia situated in the German Empire of 1914.

This black area on the map represents the gigantic German empire as it was between 1871 and 1919. The German state of East Prussia (surrounded here with a black border and marked with a white arrow) still directly bordered Russia in the East. The state of Poland and the Baltic States of Latvia, Estonia and Lithuania did not exist at that time.

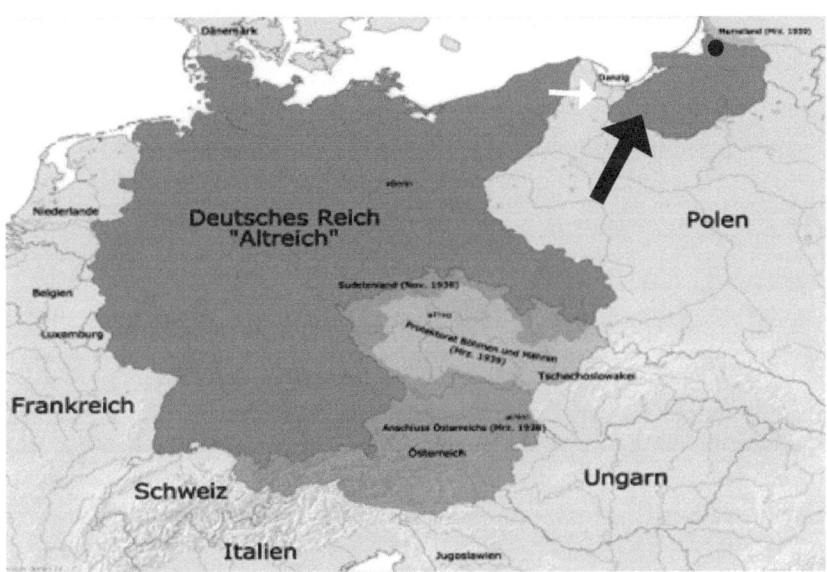

East Prussia situated in the Germany of 1939.

Details on picture page 27 below: East Prussia (the small dark grey area marked with a black arrow) was disconnected from the actual German homeland after the German defeat in the First World War. On this map, Memelland (exceedingly small, narrow, and almost invisible strip above the black dot on the right), Sudetenland (Czechoslovakia) and Austria were already annexed by Germany on the initiative of the Nazis and ever new concessions by France and Great Britain. Between the actual German homeland and the East Prussian state, only the Free State of Danzig and a small part of Poland, which once belonged to German West Prussia and Pomerania, remained. Hitler wanted to open the passage -a corridor it was called- to East Prussia by force (see small white arrow) and therefore he invaded Poland on September 1, 1939. The German soldiers were considered liberators by many residents. The black dot with white border itself, at the top on the right, is Tilsit, the birthplace of Joachim Fritz Krauledat.

A War, a Wedding and a Farewell

"Joachim, your father won't be home again. He died during the war one or two months before you were born. Some pictures, his golden ring and a lot of good memories are all what 's left for us."

July 1943. At the Russian front, the war between Germany and Russia has been raging in full force for just over two years now. German troops had to abandon the siege of the Russian capital Moscow at the beginning of this sizzling summer month. Although the Russian troops which had been set up as a protective shield around that Stalin bastion have suffered very heavy losses, they have not succumbed to the heavy German pressure. Adolf Hitler is furious, yet he has wisely decided to temporarily suspend the offensives of his German armies all along the front line. Some order must be restored first. The landing of American troops in Sicily, moreover, oblige him to rethink his entire strategy. Despite the not very encouraging situation for his armies, some German soldiers who had recently accumulated great merits during the fighting can finally enjoy a few days of hard-earned leave. One of the boys who is allowed to go home for a few days, is **Fritz Krauledaitis** *-alias Krauledat- a Lithuanian Prussian who wears a German uniform ...*

Tilsit, East Prussia, July 1943. Despite the war, the situation in the German state of East Prussia is noticeably quiet for the time being. The German/Russian front line is still far away from here. The summer sun reflects brightly on the surface of the Memel River, which winds through the small town of Tilsit* like a ribbon of glittering

---

* *The then (German) East Prussian town of Tilsit is now called Sovetsk and is located today in the Russian exclave of Kaliningrad, between Klaipèda and Kaunas.*

light. It is exceptionally hot this summer and because of the high outside temperatures, there is truly little movement on the streets. In any case, there are hardly any men to be seen, except for a few older men who, because of their age or physical condition, are no longer fit to be sent to the front in the service of Nazi Germany. And if you *do* see a younger man, it is most likely a wounded soldier who is hobbling along on some makeshift crutches, trying to rehabilitate the best he can from some serious injury sustained during the horrific fighting. Some children are playing in the shadow of the ornamental brick towers of the Queen Louise Bridge or have thrown out their self-made fishing rods in an attempt to replenish the food supply, which has become very scarce. A self-caught freshwater fish -carp, pike or barbel, it doesn't matter- from the Memel River would be very welcome. But it is too hot and therefore the fish stay quiet, just like the people. Most of the inhabitants therefore prefer to cool off in the nearby *Tilsiter Stadtwald* or just sit on a wooden bench in their garden under a tree, having a chat and drinking a cup of water …

But this is not just a hot summer's weekday for everyone. Not far from the city center, on this sunny afternoon, a very modest party is going on. From the speaker of a manually activated gramophone sounds *Einmal Wirst du Wieder bei Mir Sein,* a song by the extremely popular German singer Rudi Schüricke. It is a song that was often played and sung along loudly in German domestic circles when highly motivated German soldiers went to war in Poland in September 1939 and later, from May 10, 1940 onwards, also trampled all over Western Europe.

A young couple who just got married in the local Lutheran church a bit further down the road, are enjoying their just-concluded life commitment and are now initiating a dance to the tune of this song. On the first notes of the romantically compelling music, newlyweds Elsbeth and Fritz drown in each other's eyes. They smile at each other and try to fully take in this unique moment. Although this song clearly suggests that they will see each other again soon, in reality both their futures are very doubtful, to say the least. It is even possible that this is their very last dance and that these moments are possibly the last moments they can spend together. How's that? Newly married and still have to say goodbye? Yes! Fritz Krauledat is on duty, and he wears the uniform of an *Oberfeldwebel* in the German Wehrmacht. He realizes that tomorrow he will have to leave for the front again and that puts a damper on the atmosphere. The chance that he will ever return to his wife Elsbeth Zimmermann in perfect health, is rather small given the ongoing war …

"Now imagine you're pregnant, and it's already such hard times,"

Says Fritz in a very gentle way to his brand-new wife Elsbeth, as he continues to lead the dance.

"Well, then I see this as a gift from God. And if it turns out to be a girl, I don't know yet what her name will be. But if it's going to be a boy, that's why I'll probably call him 'Waquin',"*

Elsbeth answers, very emotionally, while she tries to wipe the tears from her eyes with a handkerchief.

"And Fritz will be his second name; like his father," she adds.
Fritz whispers in the ears of his brand-new bride:

"Please, feel free to call him Joachim. Waquin still sounds too Lithuanian, don't you think?"

Slowly the feet of a few dancing people slide across the floor. They are trying to forget the misery of the war here and now, at least for a moment, by doing a romantic dance. Exuberant partying is, as a matter of course, not the thing to do and neither is having fun at weddings in Germany today, as was the case before and even at the beginning of the war. The unbridled euphoria from the period of the great German military successes at the very beginning of the war has

---

* Waquin literally means "created by God."

faded too much today. Among the guests present here and throughout the region, by the way, there are plenty whose relatives have already lost their lives during this damn war. They were able to put their dejection aside for a brief time on this occasion, but the loss of those beloved people obviously keeps people from celebrating and being cheerful in all spontaneity. Yet, at the party, they are indeed happy for the newlyweds, and they wish them all the happiness. However, everyone also fully realizes that Elsbeth could soon be yet another young war widow. Indeed, it does not look as if Nazi Germany will abandon the struggle without having secured a total victory, and that victory seems further away at this very moment than ever before. Indeed, the Germans have suffered yet another profoundly serious blow recently (at Moscow) and a little earlier this year (at Stalingrad). At Moscow, the Germans were forced to abandon the siege and withdraw, and at Stalingrad even the entire German 6th Army under the command of Field Marshall Friedrich Paulus was forced to surrender earlier this year, 1943. So many thousands of German soldiers had died in battle in the process, but almost as many died of sheer deprivation. Thousands died without even ever having seen the enemy. Hunger and the persistently murderous freezing cold clearly played to Stalin's advantage here. After all, the Red Army was much better hardened against the extremely harsh Russian winters.

Hitler was furious because of Marshall Paulus' surrender. Hadn't he just promoted him to field marshal to point out that from this capacity he couldn't even *consider* surrendering to the Russians? Sorry? What are you saying? He was completely hemmed in there at Stalingrad? Well, then he still would have had to first sacrifice every German soldier under his command to death and then shoot himself through the head. To win or to die, that was the Nazi spirit and that was what Hitler and his totalitarian regime expected of every German!

However, there was much more to it. Hitler was also very agitated because the American army had landed on the island of Sicily at the beginning of the month. The Italians, who were gradually feeling the heat, showed increasingly that they actually wanted to change sides.

Benito Mussolini faced increasing opposition on the home front to the continued propagating of his fascist views. The Italian king and government also seemed to be turning away from him. In all this, Mussolini no longer felt safe, and even in his beloved workplace of Milan he was no longer at ease. When he drove through the streets in his fast Alfa Romeo sports car, he hardly dared to open the roof of that beautiful and powerful eight cylinder with 2900 cc engine anymore. After all, at times he was totally unexpectedly confronted with very harsh reproaches. Hitler felt let down because his main ally failed. Great Britain, with still that stubborn bastard of a Churchill as their master chief, was still not defeated either, by the way. And hadn't Hitler had that huge sobering up before that at some of the major Soviet cities like Kharkov, Smolensk, Kiev and Kursk? On top of all that and the earlier (and surprising) fiasco in their attempt to starve Leningrad (St Petersburg), this was yet another deep disappointment for the German troops and a heavy blow to that fiendishly ambitious *Führer*. In Leningrad a million Russian civilians had starved and tens of thousands of Russian soldiers were killed. And still the siege had not led to a surrender of that garrison. Each time, the heavy Russian losses at the front had been supplemented just in time with reserve troops. And a rickety lifeline, built up in the rear, still provided supplies of some foodstuffs.

It was a superhuman sacrifice for the Russians to save Leningrad. Russian truck drivers who had tried to supply the city with food and fuel via frozen Lake Ladoga in the 1941/42 winter of famine, had sometimes sunk (with their truck and all the goods) through the nearly two-meter-thick ice, never to surface again. Russian women who were literally starving to death, managed to build a narrow-gauge railroad along the north-eastern edge of the city in freezing temperatures of -5°(Fahrenheit). All this was done in order to get as many supplies and medicines as possible into the city and its suburbs, which had been brought in by the American aid plan via the port of Vladivostok throughout Siberia or by the British via the frost-free port of Murmansk. Some workwomen suddenly died of complete deprivation in the icy mud and frozen snow, at the place where they were working. But the women who could still remain somewhat upright, continued to toil the whole time. Leningrad did not fall, and the self-confidence of the German army in the east of Europe was already given a first serious blow; something that would only get worse from then on. As of today, July 1943, things were looking worse and worse for the German troops, and motivation was dwindling. However, at the start of the Russian Barbarossa campaign, on June 21, 1941, Hitler had confidently said:

"Kick in the front door and that entirely rotten Russian system will collapse."

Fritz Krauledat, the man who is marrying Elsbeth Zimmermann here today, has realized that making such nonsensical statements at the time had been nothing more than some boastful propaganda talk on behalf of the Nazi party. But Fritz too would probably have believed such things without questioning in the past. He was, after all, fully motivated and, like 98% of the Germans, supported their *Führer* at the start of the campaign against the Soviet Union. In the meantime, however, the average German soldier has become much wiser.

After all, the Russian soldier is much tougher than expected and their people are willing to make the greatest sacrifices, determined and persistently stubborn to the death! In spite of the much better war material of the Germans and their better combat training, the Russians had innumerable reserves in terms of manpower. Moreover, they were more hardened against the extreme winter conditions and Stalin had always been able to keep the Russian war industry running by immediately starting up again his production lines that threatened to fall into German hands, always far behind the front line. The Germans had never expected such a flexibility in their dealings and such fanatical determination to fight back. Moreover, during the first winter war of 1941/42 on the Russian front, the German soldiers themselves were still walking around in their summer clothes, with nothing on their heads but a green-gray cotton field cap. No winter clothing was available to them! It was all deemed *nicht notwendig* by the German

Nazi authorities to produce it, for the war against the Russians would be over before that coming winter. But hadn't Napoleon Bonaparte, in all his arrogance, declared something similar in 1812? History would indeed largely repeat itself. There was a desperate call to the German people to send warm civilian clothes to the Russian front. A few weeks later, Fritz Krauledat and tens of thousands of other German soldiers at the front were walking through their frozen positions, dressed in the musty and para-dichlorobenzene (mothballs) smelling fur coats from the closets of -in most cases- well-to-do German women. By now, the German soldiers had lost so much weight from months of deprivation that those women's coats easily fitted them.

For many thousands of German soldiers and foreign SS volunteers, however, that extremely bizarre support came much too late. Besides, winter clothing alone does not satisfy the needs if there is not a sufficient supply of primary basic needs, such as food ...

But today, on this special summer day of leave in July 1943, Fritz Krauledat is trying awfully hard not to think about that. After all, normally you only get married once in your life, however short or long that life may be. He is already enjoying these unique moments on the occasion of his marriage to Elsbeth. And he also fully enjoys the music; something he -as a passionate music lover- had been missing almost all the time on the front line. The charming Marika Rökk also passes by on the gramophone here this afternoon with her version of *Eine Insel aus Träumen geboren*. A little later, Lale Andersen will be heard, first with *Es geht Alles vorüber, es geht Alles vorbei* and then with her own version of *Lili Marlene*. No, this is NOT the original and so famous version by Marlene Dietrich! This afternoon we will certainly not play any songs by that pretentious superstar! The once so popular Maria Helena Dietrich, who rolled into the German film world in fashionable Potsdam behind the Wannsee, had lost much of her prestige with many German fans by choosing America in 1930. Her mega success in the film *Der Blaue Engel* had gone straight to her head. When Hitler begged her to return to Germany, she not only shrugged her shoulders, but also expressed her deep dissatisfaction with the situation in Adolf Hitler's Nazi Germany. That totally wrong attitude of hers had not done her image any good at the end of the thirties with Hitler's supporters (which most Germans were at the time).

A little later Rudi Schüricke again chimed through the gramophone; this time with *Du bist ein Engel*. Every time Schüricke sings the first line of the chorus, Fritz whispers the same words *Du bist ein Engel* into Elsbeth's ears with a smile. He says:

"Did you know, mein liebe Schatz, that Rudi Schüricke grew up in Königsberg; a good 100 kilometers from here? He was born in Brandenburg and came here for economic reasons. But so, he also became a bit of an East Prussian; just like us, in other words ..."

Elsbeth and Fritz's wedding party turns out to be a quiet and relaxing event, where everyone can put aside their greatest worries, at least for a little while until they have to return home that evening. That beautiful day, however, is over far too quickly. Sad on the one hand, but dutiful and without grumbling on the other, Fritz will have to put on his military uniform again tomorrow ...

German Evangelical church in Tilsit, where Protestant believers could go for the blessing of the marriage. (Bundesarchiv)

... The day after the wedding ... All the guests have now returned home safely. Elsbeth and Fritz are trying to enjoy the few hours they can still spend together, but the newly-married couple is now suddenly very depressed. Fritz will soon have to return to the unsteady front line in the north of Russia, because his short leave is over.

In July 1943, Fritz Krauledaitis is a 30-year-old Lithuanian Prussian and he's on duty as an *Oberfeldwebel* in the German Wehrmacht during the Second World War. Fritz was born as the oldest of nine children in 1913 in Papegen (Papègiai), a small provincial town in the beautiful, flat land region of Memelland and located just a few miles north-east of the Memel River. He felt responsible for his six younger brothers and two younger sisters, and so he helped his parents as much as he could by raising them all. Despite his former Lithuanian origins, Fritz really does feel like a German in his heart today. This is only logical, because when he was born, his native Memelland was still an integral part of East Prussia and was by definition also part of the great German Empire of Kaiser Wilhelm II. The kinship and connection between Memelland with the rest of East Prussia, and with the actual German motherland, was intensely experienced and it was completely mutual. The wide Memel River had never been an obstacle for this, rather on the contrary. Throughout that region lived descendants of prestigious old, medieval German knights, German nobles with aristocratic backgrounds, former Teutonic dukes, German large landowners and even some descendants of Frederick the Great. Throughout the centuries, this Prussian region had been an example of mutual tolerance among the various population groups. Origin had always been subordinated to brotherhood. No laws needed to be drawn up, because every Prussian took it for granted. The choice of one's own religion was also peacefully tolerated. Catholics, Orthodox and Protestants (Lutherans) lived peacefully side by side all the time. Even the Jews were left in peace there (at least until 1938). Also, many descendants of Protestant Huguenots who had previously been persecuted in France, Austria and Germany had fled there in all their desperation and survival instincts and they also finally found peace and tranquility there. The ethnicity problems for Memelland and essentially for the entire German-Prussian territory actually began just after the First World War, namely in 1919. The Treaty of Versailles then suddenly called into question all the firmly gathered life wisdom in that entire vast region.

Suddenly the cohesion among the population groups was largely lost. This situation is preceded by a number of factors ...

... Despite all the efforts of the wise Chancellor Otto von Bismarck to finally unite all the small German states into one large German empire in 1871, Kaiser Wilhelm II's megalomania and the German defeat in the First World War resulted in the division of this proud, strong and unified Germany in 1919. Pomerania, Silesia, and a large part of West Prussia were torn from Germany and promptly given to the (re)founded state of Poland, while Danzig (Gdansk) became an independent Free State on the Baltic coast. The protests of the very many German-minded citizens were to no avail. After all, Germany had lost the (First) World War and every German would suffer the consequences. East Prussia itself remained German, but it became also totally orphaned. So far removed and physically completely cut off from the actual homeland with the new Polish state and the Free State of Danzig right in between, it was almost completely on its own. The (new) Germany after the Treaty of Versailles in 1919 again resembled that patchwork it had been before the founding of the German Empire in 1871. In addition, transport of foodstuffs and all sorts of goods over land from the homeland to East Prussia was prevented by the new Polish administration. At a time when Germany was already suffering enormously from a devastating economic and financial recession, this was felt even more acutely in East Prussia than elsewhere. And there were even more elements at play that made East Prussian citizens felt increasingly more discriminated. Suddenly, blatant ethnic problems surfaced in East Prussia itself as a result of the unforeseen whims of the new administration, which functioned somewhat like a willing puppet of the League of Nations and ... the domination of France. Never before that peaceful, freshwater Memel River had been a hindrance to mutual Prussian solidarity. But that honest and spontaneous sense of belonging between Memelland and the rest of East Prussia was deliberately thwarted from 1919 onward. The Memel River was suddenly considered a border, and Memelland was even severed from East Prussia at institutional level. This well-defined narrow strip of land to the north-east of the Memel River was suddenly no longer under direct Prussian control, thanks to a provision in the Treaty of Versailles. French politician Georges Clemenceau arranged that Memelland came under Lithuanian and ... French rule. It seemed as if a needy child was being deliberately and ruthlessly snatched from its mother's breast just when it needed some affection. The residents of Memelland were also suddenly urged to stop feeling German and start feeling (and behaving) a bit more Lithuanian again. The fact that in a general referendum most Memelland residents would spontaneously choose the conservative German-minded *Deutsches und Litauischer Heimatbund*, was a setback for the pro-Lithuanian/French administration. This choice made it very clear that more than 80% still felt distinctly German and wanted to *remain* German. France and Lithuania weren't too pleased about this, and a clear form of bias and discrimination against the German-minded population of Memelland, although in the majority, was introduced. In 1923, Lithuania even occupied Memelland. This Lithuanian occupation came out of pure frustration, because the Lithuanian Prussians chose to live as *Germans* and not to deny the close connection they felt with Germany. Fritz Krauledaitis' own ancestors had already experienced several identity transformations since the collapse of the old Polish-Lithuanian state in 1795. They, too, had for some time been resolutely drawing their own conclusions and choosing to go on living as German and not as Lithuanian citizens. After 124 years they had lost touch with the old Lithuanian background culture. In the referendum of 1923, they had clearly indicated that they did not want the Lithuanian invasion of their Memelland, and they had also promptly opted for the *Deutsches und Litauischer Heimatbund*. Fritz's family had already changed his name officially from the unmistakably Lithuanian sounding "Krauledaitis" to a more Germanic "Krauledat".

But a complete reunification with East Prussia itself -the dream of many Lithuanian Prussians- was not yet forthcoming for the German-minded inhabitants of Memelland.

... This was one of the reasons why Fritz had already sought a better life on the other side of the Memel River during the interwar period. He often stayed on the west side of the river, and he liked that very much. There he could feel himself German without being ashamed ... and then one day he met a certain Elsbeth Zimmermann in a tailor's workshop in Tilsit. Love knows no bounds and his feelings strengthened his conviction to stay on the western side of the Memel River forever. The consequence, however, was that as a German citizen, he had to fight for the ideals of the fatherland, which in his case was Adolf Hitler's Nazi Germany. If he had gone up to Lithuania, only a few miles further northeast, he might eventually have been conscripted into the Red Army of the Russians after that country had become part of the Soviet Union. Consequently, in that case, he would have to fight on the other side. Life's destiny sometimes depends on intricate details and sometimes the difference lies in a small place, figuratively and literally. As Soviet influence in the Baltic States of Estonia, Latvia and Lithuania grew more and more towards the end of the 1930s, the Lithuanian Prussians of Memelland felt threatened by Stalin and they turned to the distant homeland for moral and tangible assistance. One person in Germany would absorb this Prussian message very well. It was an Austrian Bavarian with small, sparkling blue eyes, a long lock of hair and a somewhat bizarre rectangular mustache under his nose. That mysterious man, who as a born Austrian had volunteered to serve in a *German* Bavarian infantry regiment in the First World War, had taken over all power in Germany, and that man had listened with very benevolent ears to all those German-Prussian pleas. Adolf Hitler, therefore, would now gladly answer the entreaties of many Prussians and German-minded inhabitants of East Prussia, West Prussia, Memelland, Pomerania and Silesia ... and not only at a moral level.

He would put in the necessary energy at physical level as well ... And that had been one of the (false?) reasons for invading Poland on

September 1, 1939. Germany wanted a corridor to remote East Prussia via Danzig and it would also reclaim the part of East Prussia called Memelland, cut off in 1919, for itself and for Germany. So, Hitler got Stalin's approval and the Germans were allowed to occupy that narrow strip of land called "Memelland." As compensation, Stalin in turn was allowed by Hitler to absorb the three Baltic states of Latvia, Lithuania and Estonia. For both Stalin and Hitler, it was a fair deal at the time.

Hitler as the great liberator of Memelland. We can read: "This land will remain German forever." Less than six years later, there would be no German left in that region which had become part of the Soviet Union.

Those German soldiers were very warmly welcomed when they entered Memelland, because the narrow strip of land northeast of the Memel River could once again be considered German. Good news for the many German-minded inhabitants, but from then on, the German Jews were no longer safe ...

... But let's go back first to Fritz and Elsbeth in Tilsit in July 1943. We are a little further in time and the war is now in full swing. Fritz Krauledat, after two years of war in Eastern Europe, proudly wears the coveted German Iron Cross. Moreover, as a reward for his exemplary behavior in general, he had been given a few days leave. What a surprise it was for his fiancée Elsbeth when he suddenly and unannounced appeared at her door. Everything was immediately prepared so that they could get married quickly and have a small party for a few invited guests. However, the holiday ended much too soon. Just married and already we have to say goodbye. It's hard ...

Fritz and Elsbeth continue listening to some music on this summer afternoon. Once again, the famous Rudi Schüricke sounds through the loudspeaker; this time with his version of the beautiful and romantic *Eine Insel aus Träumen geboren* ...

"I still prefer the version of Marika Rökk, which we heard just yesterday on our wedding day. You know, the version from that beautiful, romantic movie." *

"It would only be truly romantic if the two of us could someday travel together to that beautiful, faraway Hawaii," was Fritz' reply.

"That would be very difficult, since we have been at war with the Americans for eighteen months now!" says Elsbeth.

Music is softly playing and both their minds become full of emotions and melancholy. This bloody war, why doesn't it stop?

"Please don't look so glum, Elsbeth. To cheer you up, shall I bring out my violin or accordion and play a nice tune myself?"

"No, please don't! I'm not in the mood. Another time perhaps."

---

* *From the German cinema film* Eine Nacht im May, *from 1938.*

Fritz Krauledat would give anything to stay here a bit longer. However, duty-bound as he is, he doesn't even want to think about that. With great pain in his heart, he leaves his wife Elsbeth and that beautiful little house in the quiet suburb of the -as yet- peaceful town of Tilsit that very same evening. He walks to the station, where he will take the train together with some other leave takers to the north of the German/Russian frontline. The laughter fades from him completely. On the way, he notices how the flowers of the tuberous plants are blooming so beautifully just now. He casts a glance at all those graceful yellow, red, and white dahlias, the peonies and the rows of slender orange and red gladioli that are everywhere in the little gardens delineated by wooden posts. A little further on in the spacious, flat fields in the area, the many thousands of sunflowers look straight into the eyes of the setting sun, followed by fields of mixed wildflowers; primroses, cornflowers, buttercups and dandelions ... so simple and yet so beautiful!!!

Fritz thinks by himself, *"My God! How difficult it is to leave again, just when nature looks so peacefully beautiful."*

Unconsciously, a faint smile appears on his face for the sake of those trite thoughts, because in the past, he didn't even notice those flowers. Men who think about flowers the way women do? Come on! But on this very moment and to his own surprise, it makes him a little melancholic. Quite unusual, because living at the frontline has transformed him into a hard, ruthless and in a way even emotionless man.

He has seen people being killed in terrible conditions and dozens of executions of civilians, sometimes Russian partisans but at least as often innocent civilians. He has also seen Jews taken away to be killed and he has also seen so many things happen, that he is no longer concerned about anything. That great victory, which, according to their *Führer*, would have come two years ago, is still extremely far away today, by the way. Fritz has now mainly learned to survive. So, there is no more room for any sentimentality. But now, at this very moment, Fritz is filled with melancholy and all those beautiful flowers are suddenly among the most beautiful things in life, even for him. What a contrast indeed with the cursed region he is about to visit again. Not a single flower has grown there for some time and not even a bird flutters in the air. Even the grass doesn't get the chance to grow properly anymore. Time after time the earth is turned upside down by the explosion of tens of thousands of bombshells. Everywhere along that very long front line, you can stumble over those many dead bodies. Some unburied bodies of unfortunate people were flattened by passing tanks. Not to mention the stench of human bodies in a state of decomposition in the summer heat. Terrible! And when winter comes again soon, everything will freeze over again, and all of this will just get buried under the snow. Most of all those killed people too, because there is hardly ever enough time to bury the bodies of the many unfortunate. And when there is a break between battles, the ground is so frozen that no one can get a spade or other digging tool into the ground ...

All those beautiful flowers that Fritz was able to behold for a moment just now will surely grow back next year. But his farewell from home will be final, for it is possible -and even probable- that he himself will not return in one piece. He arrives at the Tilsit railway station and, after registering his presence, he can almost immediately board the train. Half an hour later and together with a few other (un)fortunate vacationers, he rides across the Memel River via the railroad bridge in an easterly direction, back to the unstable Eastern Front.

He's shivering at the sight of the beautiful Queen Louise Bridge. In the depths of his wounded and bleeding soul, Fritz feels that he will never cross that Memel River in the other direction again. After all, the overall German loss figures already exceed 900,000 on the Eastern Front. So why should he, Fritz, be able to escape the worst fate that awaits someone on a front line? Then possibly all those beautiful dahlias and lilies he saw here could serve to adorn his tombstone. Lilies? Again, he smiles to himself when he thinks of those beautiful lilies in Elsbeth's garden. He also suddenly remembers that cheerful tune, *Drei Lilien* that he and his mates sang at the top of their voices two years ago on that infamous twenty-second of June 1941, when they attacked the Soviet Union from East Prussia via Libau in Lithuania. Barely a few days later, they were already standing in front of Leningrad. It was originally a Dutch folk song, to which a German text had been composed. The German soldiers of the Wehrmacht sang it when they went to war in Poland in 1939 and throughout Western Europe in 1940. On the way on the train, he runs over the entire tune, with the intention of being able to turn his thoughts to something else than his beloved wife Elsbeth, whom he has just said goodbye to ...

"Drei Lilien, drei Lilien verblüh'n am Wegesrand
Weil mein Lied zu deinem Herzen den Weg nicht fand
Juwifalleralalalalaa-Juwifalleralalalalaa-a
Weil mein Lied zu deinem Herzen den Weg nicht fand

Drei Lilien, drei Lilien - allein steh' ich am Tor
Wie ein Kind, das nacht im Regen den Weg verlor
Juwifalleralalalalaa-Juwifalleralalalalaa-a
Wie ein Kind, das nacht im Regen den Weg verlor

Drei Lilien, drei Lilien, zu früh seid ihr verblüht
Weil die Nacht in meinem Herzen den Tag nicht sieht
Juwifalleralalalalaa-Juwifalleralalalalaa-a
Weil die Nacht in meinem Herzen den Tag nicht sieht

Drei Lilien, drei Lilien wiltken in der Hand
Und die Spuren uns'rer Träume verweh'n im Sand
Juwifalleralalalalaa-Juwifalleralalalalaa-a
Und die Spuren uns'rer Träume verweh'n im Sand ...

... That very evening, after Fritz's departure, Tilsit once again seems completely deserted. Despite the beautiful orange-red setting sun on the western horizon, the world seems bleaker than ever for Elsbeth Zimmermann, who remains behind. After Fritz's farewell, she feels totally orphaned and miserable. She cries bitter tears constantly. She also sensed what was going on in her husband's head when he said goodbye to her earlier this day. As if she already had strong feelings that she would never see him again. That long and heartfelt hug with which he had just overspread her in tenderness, was wrapped in a mysterious veil. Elsbeth had never felt anything so extremely awkward. There was indeed something very mysterious going on at that very moment; something tragic even. It seemed to her as if he wanted to tell her something and could not find the words. It even seemed for a moment as if there was an invisible third person standing between them who had deliberately caused some spiritual confusion at this strange moment. Fritz indeed added no more words to his warm embrace. But at such a moment, women don't need any words to understand such deep emotions. Fritz's fiery, desperate embrace indeed radiated cold drama. Women can feel when there is something wrong in the heart or head of their beloved, especially if that feeling is well meant ...

Elsbeth already feels at that very moment that she will most likely never, ever see her Fritz again.

Typical idyllic scene in East Prussia in the late thirties.

Meanwhile and after a long, nightly train ride, *Oberfeldwebel* Fritz Krauledat reaches the station of his final destination. Once he arrives back at the German-Russian front line, he immediately wants to know how the others are doing. No one answers this clearly "unnecessary" question. After all, almost everyone over there has become totally indifferent to these things. When things were still going well at the front line, all the German soldiers and their allies were still full of enthusiasm, but today's indifference means unwelcome news in all cases. The odds on the front line are now clearly turning against the Nazis. Moscow has not fallen, nor has Leningrad, and since the German fiasco at Stalingrad, the trend has now clearly definitely been reversed to Germany's disadvantage. It is the Russians who are now beginning to advance in turn.

Moreover, after the recent beating, Germany's Romanian, Hungarian, Italian, Ukrainian and Finnish allies (and even some French, Belgian and Dutch SS volunteers) have largely lost faith in German victory. When things were going well and they saw opportunities to benefit themselves, they had still been fairly reliable as Adolf Hitler's allies in battle. Now that things are going worse and worse, they refuse more stubbornly to continue fighting "Hitler's war" on Germany's side. So, from now on the Germans are practically on their own. Despite the temporary suspension of the German offensives on the orders of the *Führer* himself (after the recent debacle near Moscow), it appears that in the brief period of Fritz's absence, many familiar persons have once again perished in the horrific and never-ending battles. Butchered, dismembered, crushed by the murderous and never-ending artillery fire from those famous and all-destroying Russian *Katyushas** across the river ...

"Ich hatte eine Kamerade," sighs Fritz, as he makes a sign of the cross and recites a short prayer to remember and honor the fallen (who until recently had been his friends) for one small moment anyway.

---

* *In the vernacular also often called "Stalin organ" ...*

"*Eine*" *Kamerade*, Fritz? Meanwhile, more than one million German soldiers have already fallen on the Eastern Front. All perished in a German uniform to fulfill the diabolical ambitions of their great *Führer* over there. But no one has come even one step closer to victory! And how in God's name could it have come to this. Hadn't the Russians and Germans concluded a mutual "non-aggression pact" in 1939? …

For a long time, people in both Germany and Russia thought that the treaty concluded on August 23, 1939, would guarantee a lasting peace for the two countries.

Both their ministers of foreign affairs von Ribbentrop and Molotov, had concluded that agreement in the name of Hitler and Stalin. It also stated that Poland would vanish again, and they would divide the Polish territory neatly between them.

They want to return to -roughly- the same situation as it had been before 1919. After all, between 1795 and 1919, all of Poland had been part German and part Russian territory, so they thought it only logical that Poland should simply disappear from the map again. Beyond that, their ambitions towards each other would not reach.

But this was beyond that devilish Hitler. The *Führer* had already built up so much power, that he was no longer satisfied with his earlier political and military achievements. On the contrary, the hunger for even more power compelled him to claim hegemony over all of Europe. In order to realize his diabolical ambitions, only the relentless Great Britain and … his temporary "pseudo-ally", namely Joseph Stalin's Soviet Union, stood in the way. Because he absolutely wanted to bring home his big battle before winter and inflict a strategic defeat on the Soviet Union, in the summer of 1941 he sent his troops across the Curzon Line* previously agreed upon between Molotov and von Ribbentrop. At the time, the German soldiers all sounded happy and cheerful. Morale was high. They were going to very quickly overrun the red communists over there. They were not afraid of the Soviet soldiers. Their own morale was rock solid, and they felt superior by definition.

---

* *Agreed demarcation line between Nazi Germany and the Soviet Union. The eastern part was occupied by the Soviets and the western part by the Germans.*

Fritz himself often thinks back to those beautiful early days of the summer of 1941. He also remembers, in addition to the marching song *Drei Lilien*, that other, beautiful, and rousing German marching song *10,000 Man* that sounded loudly and incessantly from the mouths of those many thousands of advancing German soldiers full of conviction:

"Zehntausend man ... die zogen ins Manöver
Zehntausend man ... die zogen ins Manöver
Wàrum dideldum ... wàrum dideldum
Die zogen ins Manöver

Da komen sie beim Bauer im Quartiere
Da komen sie beim Bauer im Quartiere
Wàrum dideldum ... wàrum dideldum

Der Bauer hat 'ne wunderschöne Tochter
Der Bauer hat 'ne wunderschöne Tocher
Dàrum dideldum ... Dàrum dideldum ...

Today, two years after the start of the German attack on Russia, only the Horst Wessel song* is still heard in the German ranks, and then only among the ultra-fanatical supporters of the *Führer*: his own SS troops, who against all odds, still believe in a positive result.

"Die Fahne hoch, die Reihen fest geschlossen ..."

But the average *Wehrmacht* fighter sees that the situation is gradually becoming hopeless and that the ranks are no longer closed. One by one, the allies are also pulling out. Romania, Hungary, Italy, Ukrainian SS volunteers ... and soon also Finland. The Germans are completely on their own.

... And the other fierce German battle songs also sounded almost nowhere in this summer of 1943. A bad sign ...

---

* *Horst Wessel song: the unofficial anthem of the Nazi party.*

The Queen Louise Bridge in Tilsit in 1941. The way to the Northern frontline in Eastern Europe for so many German soldiers, including a certain Fritz Krauledat. (Bundesarchiv)

Fleeing the Russians

"My mother took me as a nine-month-old infant and she left East Prussia, just before the Russians came ..."

January 1945. After nearly four years of heavy fighting, Red Army soldiers are ready to launch their final offensive against the Nazis. The Germans have to retreat everywhere from the Baltic coast in the north, across the Visla line (Weichsel) to the Black Sea in the south of Europe. But the German army refuses to surrender, and some units will continue to defend themselves stubbornly. In the process, most SS remain loyal to their Führer and will fight to the death. But the millions of killed people are not only soldiers. Some fifteen million Russian and Polish civilians have also perished in terrible conditions. Tens of thousands die of starvation and total deprivation. Jews who fall into German hands are still sent by those Germans to the extermination camps. Where that "process" fails, they are executed on the spot. People who have nothing to do with the whole war, are often mistaken for German or Russian spies and they are killed in one way or another by both the retreating and the advancing armies. Houses are destroyed, men and children are often shot for no reason and women are living the worst possible nightmares. Many of those women are brutally murdered after being raped several times. Throughout the area where horny, murderous soldiers from both armies pass, people experience hell. But the war itself is irrevocably lost for the Germans. The Russians are coming, and they want to go straight to Berlin. Everything in their path is shot to pieces. German citizens flee by tens of thousands, but they don't all get away ...

January 1945. Just like the Baltic states and much of the Soviet Union, the German state of East Prussia is covered by a three-feet deep carpet of snow. A razor-sharp, icy wind is blowing over the vast

A typical image from January 1945 in East Prussia. These fleeing people hope to get a place on a horse-drawn sleigh. (Bundesarchiv)

Baltic and Russian plains and bleak grassy peaks. From the coast in the far north, to the Caucasus Mountains in the very south of the Soviet Union, freezing temperatures of around -15° Celsius are recorded during the day. At night, temperatures of -35° to -40° are very normal.

Russian General Chernyakhovsky is pounding the Germans in the Northeast of East Prussia. The whole region of Memelland and both cities Tilsit and Memel (still "liberated" by Hitler in 1939) are soon in Russian hands. In a rush, those Russians cross the Memel River. But the Russian offensive along the Baltic coast doesn't go as they hoped. The sturdy resistance of the Germans in the region around Königsberg, makes Russian Commander-in-Chief Zhukov decide to split up General Rokossovsky's army, which is active a little further south, and to send some units northward in support.

This puts a higher pressure on the last German resistance, but it also leaves large gaps in the tight Russian positioning pattern. Many German soldiers and refugees seep through the hesitating Russian lines. The over-aged, but certainly brave German *Volkssturm* guard in East

Prussia will do its part to give as many Prussian citizens as possible the opportunity to slip away by land or sea. But the noose around the neck of the remaining piece of East Prussia that is still in German hands is being drawn ever closer.

On January 22, the Russian troops of Marshal Rokossovsky are able to occupy the Prussian town of Allenstein from the south. The local hospital was stormed at once, and all bedridden German patients, often wounded soldiers, were silenced for good with a bullet in the head. The order from Soviet Party leader Stalin is "Get rid of them." Not only the patients, by the way, because all the German female nursing staff in that hospital are also bluntly killed after first being brutally raped. Even their own Russian nurses who had previously been captured by the Germans are shot along with them without any recourse. Some of those Russian nurses had dared to offer their services to the German medical service in the local hospital. They saw no friend or foe in any wounded soldier, but only a victim in need of help, and only wanted to help where they could. They are therefore mercilessly executed as "betrayers" of the Red Army along with the German nurses and doctors. Furthermore, anyone wearing a German uniform or who is a German citizen may fear for his life. Not only soldiers and old *Volkssturmers*, but also men who wear a uniform of the railroads or postal services. In a Russian revenge for the numerous and terrible massacres committed against innocent civilians, especially by SS troops, all soldiers of any nationality in the service of the German SS are executed immediately.

But the Russian overrunning war machine does not run everywhere and against everyone in such a ruthless manner, for some captured German soldiers of the regular *Wehrmacht* do remain partially spared from direct execution after the surrender modalities.

However, the fact that some regular German *Wehrmacht* soldiers are spared for the time being, does not immediately mean good news. For them it is just the beginning of a new ordeal. They are led away on foot to the faraway Gulags or penal camps in Siberia and they have to travel many hundreds of kilometers on foot through the high snow and the icy cold. Food is barely provided for them, if at all. The conditions they will encounter are terrible and most of them would not survive. It is not until the late 1940s and even the early 1950s that the remaining survivors will gradually be released. Only a few are left by then ...

Amber stones and boulders along the Berstein beach on the Baltic coast. This setting near the town of Palmnicken was the scene of the massacre of 7,000 Jews by fanatical Nazis at the end of January 1945. (Bundesarchiv)

On January 23, 1945, Marshal Rokossovksy's Soviet army also reaches the town of Elbing on the "Frisches Haff" bay on the Baltic coast. A little later, they penetrate the port of Tolkemitt. Once the bay is under control, Chernyakhovsky further expands his own offensive, making the situation much scarier for the remaining Germans in East Prussia. But a small triangle of Prussian territory on the Baltic coast is still fanatically defended by Germans*. And despite the enormous

---

* *That little strip of land will even hold out until after the fall of Berlin.*

pressure from the Russians, the fanatical SS there are still doing what they think they have to do. Loyal to their *Führer* to the death, they will still try to eliminate all the Jews who are still alive. Now that the Russian siege prevents the Jews from being sent to the extermination camps in Poland, they are immediately executed on the spot. On the Baltic coast near Palmnicken, just north of Königsberg, a mass murder on thousands of Jews is taking place at the moment the Germans are almost completely surrounded …

A few days ago, Elsbeth Zimmermann has closed the front door of her home in Tilsit. For good! She is fleeing, just like many others. Her choice is drastic, but it is the only choice she has if she wants to have a serious chance of survival. Indeed, given the Russian threat, there is no reason for her to stay here any longer. And she was only just in time to leave! But despite her firm decision, she is afraid. Very much afraid that she won't get away in time and far enough, because the much-feared "Russian hordes" are hot on the heels of the refugees. She is also afraid for the future and especially for the future of her nine-month-old son Joachim. The stories circulating everywhere about advancing Russian soldiers, do not sound genuinely nice. These Russian soldiers go on a rampage like wild animals against everything that is German, everything that has ever been German and everything that -for some reason- even sounds a little German. From severely injured soldiers returning from the front, the inhabitants of Tilsit and the whole surrounding area had previously learned that the Russians behave like bloodthirsty monsters everywhere they pass.

Many ordinary men, women and children are often bluntly slaughtered on the spot. Those who escape direct liquidation are deported to some distant, unknown destination, probably even to Siberia. And no woman is safe from the horny and vengeful Russian soldiers. Only the words "*Frau, kom!*" are about enough to realize what someone is planning to do to a defenseless woman who had not fled in time. Resisting only makes things worse and it increases the chance that she will not survive at the end. There are also rumors that the East Prussian (so German) women are not only all brutally raped, but -being completely naked- also crucified at stable doors. The Russian motto in front of German women and children was:

"We will do exactly the same to you, as your fathers, husbands and brothers have done to our women and children before."

So Elsbeth has no choice and just like so many thousands -mostly women and children and here and there a single grandparent- she flees.

Of course, it is ridiculously hard for all these people being forced to leave this beautiful region. Life had always been very peaceful in this fertile land, until now, with all those tanks and soldiers arriving here in this flat green area …

Once upon a time, Elsbeth's own ancestors -Austrian/French Huguenots- had moved up here, because they had been expelled from several other places in Europe. The persecution those Huguenots had suffered in the later Middle Ages, which had been ushered in by Bartholomew's Night*, must have been horrible indeed. But there in East Prussia, as alleged late medieval "heretics," they were finally left in peace. Now again, however, they are all in danger of experiencing another tragedy.

Here, in this God-chosen place, they are now no longer safe either. And even though the persecution is not directly of a religious nature this time, she must now leave here again and this time probably for good …

Elsbeth is having an exceedingly tough time on her way out. In her arms she carries her nine-month-old son Joachim. The little fellow is wrapped in a warm blanket, so that he is somewhat protected from

---

* Bartholomew's Night is the beginning of a black page in history. The massacres began on August 23, 1572, in Paris and continued for several months throughout Western Europe. Huguenots were hunted down and exterminated. Only a minority of them were able to escape the witch-hunt set up by Catholics. Many of them migrated eastward and ended up in Prussia …

the icy wind. On her back she carries a bag with a few small items and the most necessary things for Joachim. At her former neighbor's, she had been able to quickly grab some milk for the road.

"Take it with you before the Russians take it all," said her neighbor.

From a compassionate fellow citizen, Elsbeth got a seat on a horse-drawn sleigh for a little while. She wants to go to the railway station, where she hopes to catch a train that will take her as far as possible away from the rapidly approaching Russian armies. On the way where? As long as my little Joachim ends up well. It doesn't matter for the rest, but absolutely away from those Russians! So, off to the West then! For her husband Fritz, she doesn't have to wait anymore. Fritz Krauledat, the man she married in the summer almost two years ago, will never come home again. As she had feared all along and what had happened to so many: *Oberfeldwebel* Fritz was killed on the Eastern Front near Pleskau, on the road from Riga to St- Petersburg. In March of last year, she had received that terrible news at home. Just as she was rubbing her bulging, pregnant belly and while she felt her unborn baby pounding in the womb, there was an unexpected knock at her door. Instinctively, she immediately sensed what was going on. A delegation from the *Sicherheitspolizei* brought her the terrible news. And notwithstanding she knew very well that this could happen, the news of Fritz's death still came as a bolt from the blue. She realized that from now on, she was on her own and, moreover, that her baby would come into the world without ever being able to see his father. She had only a few pictures to show him, because the love of her life would never come home again.

The man who had captured her heart and regularly moved her to tears by playing "Schubert" songs with his alto violin or cheered her up when he brought out his accordion and played some rhythmically cheerful songs, she would never see him again. He was only 31 years young and already he was on his way to a place in heaven, instead of returning to those people who needed him so badly. It is so hard and unfair. Her entire world collapsed, just at the moment she was about to give birth and could have used all the moral support she could get ...

Barely a few weeks later, on April 12, 1944, Elsbeth gave birth to a healthy son. She immediately recognized in this newborn baby the striking facial features of her recently deceased Lithuanian-Prussian husband Fritz. While she shed tears as a result of all the emotions of the past few months, she remembered those last moments together with Fritz about nine months ago. As she had whispered to him when she saw him for the last time, she named her son Waquin (which would officially become Joachim). However, her state of mind became totally distraught after that terrible news and for days, she did nothing but cry lots of bitter tears. They had not been married for long and she did indeed become pregnant during a truly brief period of leave of her fiancé. Once they got married, Fritz had to return pretty soon to the German front. But somewhere in her mind, she already knew -and feared- that the possibility of her Fritz ever coming back alive, was extremely small. And as she feared the whole time, he didn't come back indeed. In all honesty, she admitted to herself that in those summer days of July 1943, they both had already felt this in their hearts.

A few days after his death, Fritz's golden ring was sent to her, practically the only tangible element she now still has of him. She would cherish it and pass it on to Joachim at the appropriate time.

But there was no time or space to fall into a postpartum depression. She recovered quickly, and she had to, because the war was still going on and everyone had to deal with their own problems. Moreover, she -and she alone- had the full responsibility for a newborn baby. But at the same time, that little Joachim gave her the perspective to hold on. That little boy was now her main reason to keep fighting for survival. He was now her only consolation, her footing, her reason to exist, her everything ...

Meanwhile, along with Elsbeth, from January 1945 on, an ever increasing flow of German citizens fled from East Prussia to the actual German homeland. Along the way many Polish citizens of German origin from Pomerania and Silesia join the flow of refugees. All of them, everywhere, are fleeing from the approaching Russian army. Even though they have been Polish and not German citizens since 1919, they know very well that the Russians will still consider them as Nazi sympathizers and/or potential traitors or partisans. Sometimes these people no longer feel any connection with the Germans, but they are even more afraid of the Russians than of the Germans, and so they flee west with them. And Germans living near the Polish-German border on the Oder and Neisse rivers also move further inland. Many ethnic Germans from Sudetenland in Czechoslovakia also join the refugees. Everyone tries in every way possible to stay ahead of the Russians.

Reaching the homeland for people who were still behind the Russian lines at the end of January 1945, however, becomes almost impossible. From then on, all escape routes over land are hermetically sealed off by those Russians. Not a single Prussian or Polish refugee can still escape overland. Fortunately, the sea still offers some possibilities. There are many ships moored and others are still on their way to deliver war material and food for the remaining and still fanatically defending German soldiers and *Volkssturmers* in Prussia. However, that war material can no longer be used everywhere in time. The Russian pressure becomes too heavy, and, in some places, people abandon the relief supplies (except for the frugal food) and join the refugees. Hundreds of thousands of Germans have already fled East Prussia by land, and now tens of thousands of refugees are pouring into the Baltic ports in the hope of finding a place on some ship that can take them to safer places by sea as quickly as possible.

They want to go to Germany, if possible, but also Denmark (as yet occupied by the Germans) or perhaps Sweden (neutral, but Nazi-friendly) are OK. But by all means: far away from those Russians! There is a huge influx of refugees at every docking bay. But it is not easy to evacuate so many thousands of people just like that. It is a hard winter and the inlets in the "Frisches Haff" are all covered with thick ice. Because the water on the Baltic coast is -naturally- a bit brackish, the sea freezes there much more easily in these extremely cold temperatures than elsewhere. Icebreakers often have to be deployed and everything is done to get the ships moored in order to evacuate as many refugees as possible via the Baltic Sea.

A German troopship docks in the town of Pillau, one of the few places where the sea is not already completely frozen. Fleeing Prussians are waiting to be evacuated by sea. (Bundesarchiv)

But the German people have to be very patient. Getting a place on a ship is not just an option for everyone. The fanatical members of the Nazi party are demanding priority, and they themselves assume that this is totally normal. However, the starving and freezing refugees do not care at all about this favoritism toward their own party leaders. Many lose their composure in the scorching freezing wind, that constantly blows through the harbor channel, and they try to force their way onto a ship. Sometimes they are firmly called to order by the security guards and are forced to wait their turn. Elsewhere, their rebellion is successful, and they forcefully gain access to some ship. Many will succeed and will leave their beloved East Prussia behind by sea. But nothing will pass smoothly. One of the evacuations, part of the "Hannibal evacuation plan" of German Admiral Dönitz, will on January 31, 1945, turn into -by far- the biggest disaster at sea in human history. In terms of the number of victims, even much worse than the disaster with the Titanic ...

... Also, in the bay of Danzig (Gdansk) German ships are ready to evacuate the freezing people. One of the larger evacuation ships, the Wilhelm Gustloff, takes on board some 10,000 German refugees on January 31 and seems to be safely on its way to the German motherland by sea. The ship had been converted into a hospital ship at the beginning of the war and it was equipped with all possible medical equipment and other useful material. On every tween deck, the refugees are now literally crammed together, but the people don't care at all about the lack of basic comfort. They are extremely glad to have the possibility to escape ... at least that's what they think. Because deep below the surface of the icy Baltic Sea, Russian submarines patrol incessantly like bloodthirsty sharks in search of defenseless prey. The submarines are attracted by the sound of the heavy engines of the German transport ships. Once in the open sea, the enormous ship Wilhelm Gustloff, which was launched by Adolf Hitler in 1937, is hit by three torpedoes from a Russian submarine.

Thousands of people are engulfed by the icy water at the very moment of impact and the abrupt cooling kills many people in one blow by hydrocution or cold shock. Many still try to make it to the deck, but they usually fail and those few who finally *do* reach the deck, are spontaneously forced to jump into the water themselves in order not to be sucked into the depths along with the sinking ship. They hope that they will still be picked up by another German ship. Indeed, a German torpedo boat escorting the Gustloff immediately comes to rescue. But understandably, that crew is also worried to death because they fear another torpedo attack on their own ship. Nevertheless, their ship's commander gives the formal order to hoist as many unfortunates on board as possible, no matter what happens next. However, hypothermia sets in very quickly among the helpless people who cannot be hauled aboard immediately. Thousands of lifeless bodies are soon bobbing in droves on the icy surface of the sea. The approximately 1,200 survivors who are picked up, are put ashore by a rescue ship in Denmark, which at that time is still under German occupation. Nearly 8,000 others lose their lives in the bleak, freezing Baltic Sea.

Meanwhile, many hundreds of thousands of refugees who are still ahead of the Russian vanguard, are also making their way overland in many different ways to the actual homeland. By train for those who are somewhat lucky, sometimes by horse and cart and others often on foot. The horse-drawn sleighs, which were first used massively on the wide expanses of snow, are no longer able to get through the thick mud and frozen snow in some places. For lack of food, in many cases the horses are slaughtered and eaten on the spot. Some people feel sorry for those brave horses who had worked extremely hard all their lives and who, moreover, brought many people to safer places, away from the Russian advance. They actually deserve a better fate, but when people threaten to perish from hunger and misery, such difficult choices always have to be made.

Together, the refugees in the central part of Germany are still hoping to find a small place where they can survive. Many are heading for Berlin, but they realize that the Russians are likely focused on that city. That is why they often choose a slightly more southerly escape route and arrive first in the federal state of Saxony. Together with hundreds of thousands of Sudeten Germans who fled from Czechoslovakia, many Prussians and Poles of German origin ended up in the historic center of Dresden.

For many, the city of Dresden still looks like a safe haven at first. It is assumed that British and American soldiers are milder in their behavior than the Russians, and so they hope the bombers will spare this beautiful old medieval part of the city along the Upper Elbe. Nowhere in the whole area is there any (war) industry. The thousands of civilians seeking temporary asylum there, therefore hope for understanding from the Allies out of respect for humanity and the historic

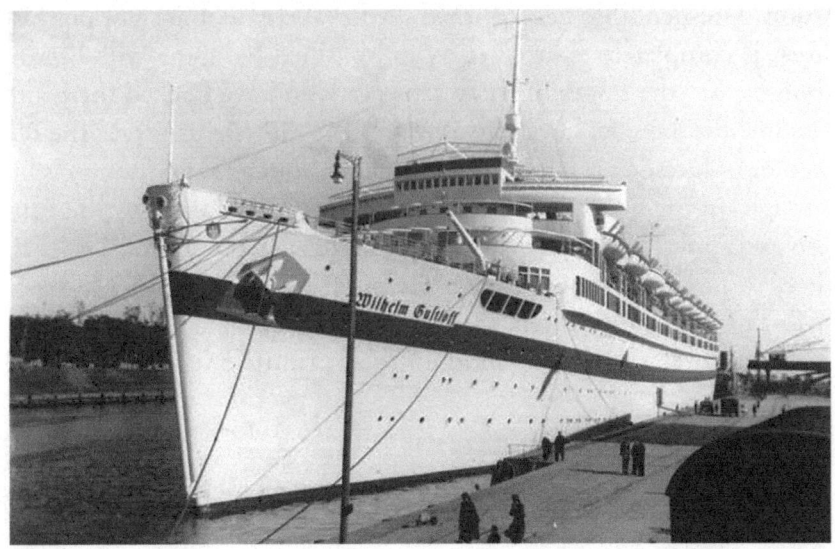

The German evacuation ship Wilhelm Gustloff, here in better times, when it was still a cruise ship. In 1939, it brought back German volunteers of the "Condor Legion" from Spain who had fought there for dictator Franco. The ship was sunk by three Russian torpedoes in Dantzig Bay (Dantziger Bucht) on February 1, 1945. Almost 8,000 people (the sources contradict each other) who were on board perished. Among them also a thousand wounded German soldiers. Never in history has a shipwreck in such a short time resulted in so many victims.

architecture in that city center.

However, British Air Force General Arthur Harris thinks otherwise. Just like Winston Churchill, Harris believes that the Germans have neither shown any respect for centuries-old buildings or innocent people in Great Britain or elsewhere in the world in recent years. Their vision is crystal clear and offers no room for sentimentality:

"We are going to flatten everything down there! The Germans terrorized us day after day for about five years. So why should we always let them be "the bad guys"?"

Viewing the destruction in and around the state of Saxony makes everyone hopeless. As far as you can see, almost all buildings lie in ruins. Dresden, that beautiful old medieval city with its glorious history, is completely reduced to ashes by Allied bombing with brisant bombs. So, the hopes of those refugees who have flocked there and assumed to be safe, have proved vain. The disbelief is great. The old center of Dresden is targeted by the heavy bombers and the city is hit straight in the heart. In the terrible havoc wreaked there by the British and American bombing raids, more than 25,000 people lost their lives in just a few hours during the night of February 13-14, 1945. Most of the fatalities were among the refugees. Some local residents were just able to go into hiding in their primitive self-made air-raid shelters.

Dresden, February 13, 1945, the day after: death, misery and despair everywhere....

Many years later, the question has often been raised whether it was still necessary to carry out such heavy bombardments on German cities, knowing that Germany was already on its knees and that there would be many innocent victims. Not everyone agrees, but in our opinion, there are two causes which could explain that those large-scale Allied actions are somewhat justified. First, the Allied Forces (and especially their politicians) think it is fair that the German people finally feel for themselves what the murderous German war machine has done elsewhere in Europe in all those years. Belgium, Great Britain, France, Norway, the Netherlands and the Soviet Union (and Denmark to a lesser extent): all these countries were heavily bombed in order to achieve the planned German hegemony over Europe. The Russians and British therefore think that now nothing or no one from that German nation should be spared.

It is now their turn to experience and feel the horror of the war. Women, children, the elderly, handicapped and invalids. No mercy; for no one! For the record: there are not that many severely handicapped people left in Germany, for they have already largely exterminated them through their own "purification program." So even the people who have always stayed far away from the misery of war may, as far as the British are concerned, finally realize what others went through when the German hordes threw everything into the battle to mercilessly overwhelm other nations. Americans are a bit more moderate in their stance than the Russians and the British for the time being, but they also know that the Nazis need to be confronted head on*.

A second reason why it is suspected that the incessant bombing of cities like Dresden is necessary: the Nazi top still does not want to know about capitulation. They even want to start a counter-offensive against the advancing Russian army in order to bring about an ultimate turnaround.

According to the official British version, British General Harris sees in the city of Dresden (just as before in Hamburg) an important railroad junction along which the Germans want to send reinforcements to the eastern frontline. Dresden would now -reportedly- be the strategic hub for logistical support to the impending German

---

* *So far, no one knew exactly what had happened in the extermination camps. When the Americans found out they were enraged and executed several SS volunteers on the spot, without any prior trial.*

Operation Solstice (*Unternehmen Sonnenwende*), which, with General Hanz Guderian at the helm, was to usher in another desperate German counteroffensive. So, to maximally sabotage support for that operation, the entire railroad infrastructure there must be completely disabled. Guderian's ultimate offensive will consequently be unsuccessful. Due to the general chaos, his planned breakout of February 15, 1945 is already over after barely three days. He is hopelessly stuck in the snow, ice and mud for lack of supplies with his heavy armor.

From then on, the entire German army is going completely down the drain. Just like in the Battle of the Bulge in Belgium and Luxembourg barely two months ago, any possible German initiative is now surely doomed to failure. The means to force something more, are no longer there and the troops necessary for this have already been decimated. The German army has indeed completely fallen apart. Although now even the older German men who still have some strength left in them, are being sent, without any shame, into the gun smoke of the shaky German front line. Every older man who can still somehow hold a gun or a *Pantserfaust* is mobilized to help keep the approaching Americans, British and French in the west and the Russians in the east of Germany out of their regional *Kreis*. And there are real patriotic fighters among all those over-aged elements of the *Volksturmers*. Emaciated and worn out, they are still bravely fighting on. Some of these elderly veterans are completely toothless, or they cough the phlegm from the lungs of their sick, frail bodies because they suffer from a terminal form of tuberculosis as a result of total deprivation. Even if they do not die immediately, some of them will most likely not be alive three weeks on, due to their ill health. But the Nazi philosophy reasons as follows:

"What do we care if they drop dead of misery in about three weeks. Surely, they will be able to hold a gun for three more days first, right?" ...

Although, discouraged, sick and totally exhausted, most of the old German *Volksturmers* will wisely surrender to the Allies. Not everyone is willing to sacrifice themselves for a lost cause.

Hitler is also playing his very last trump card. Incredibly young members of the Hitler Youth are put into a military uniform, equipped with weapons of war, and start fighting fanatically. Everything is thrown into the (desperate) fray with the aim of strengthening the tottering front line near their homes in order to protect their collapsing *Heimat* and their *Führer*.

These brainwashed boys of barely fourteen years old will also fight very fanatically. They are still convinced that they can turn the tide. So now it is up to the old men and those much too boys to try and save the moribund *Third Reich* from final destruction ...

While on the one hand the Hitler Youth and many old *Volkssturmers* are prepared to sacrifice themselves for their *Führer*, on the other hand there are more soldiers of the *Wehrmacht* who want to give up. That regular German army, by the way, has practically ceased to exist. Some soldiers secretly put on civilian clothes and try to escape to the American lines. But desertion is always punishable by the death penalty and the fanatics of the SS, and the Gestapo carry out murderous raids and executions on a regular basis. The Gestapo also watches the population very suspiciously and anyone who openly shows signs of defeatism by expressing the wish that "the war should be over soon" is arrested and promptly executed for treason. On the streets it comes to open confrontations -life-and-death fights- between those still fanatical Hitler followers and ordinary people who no longer saw any point in denying that the whole bloody war is long lost. So, the Gestapo continues to execute people for defeatism or defamation of the Reich Chancellor through summary justice (well, justice?). In the streets, many fanatical SS who have the Americans or Russians in their sights are still firing their last cartridges and shoot themselves through the head with the very last bullet. Surrender? Never! They want to spare Hitler and themselves the same dishonor as in 1918, and many do not want to relive a second heavy military defeat with such "unfair" consequences as in that "dictated" Treaty of Versailles. Germany shudders and trembles, but still refuses to surrender. Either win the war or go down together. That was the only option and that was the philosophy according to Nazi doctrine. But if the Nazis don't want to admit they have already lost the damn fight, the bombing will continue. Therefore, in the spring of 1945, any link to the German war industry or to military actions, is further targeted and destroyed by the Allies.

One consequence, however, of that fanatical German fighting is that not only Saxony, but also the rest of Germany, has become an unprecedented mess by the spring of 1945.

Meanwhile, ground troops are pushing the last remnants of German armies further and further back. Many civilians want it to finally stop, and they silently beg to be allowed to fall quickly into American or British hands, but they do not dare to make this statement.

So, from the Allied military point of view, the bombing of cities such as Dresden is more or less understandable. The question can then simultaneously be asked why, in addition to so many tons of fragmentation bombs, thousands of incendiary brisant bombs had to be used. It is therefore clearly about more than just destroying a strategically important or sensitive point. Since the Germans (by mistake, by the way) had flattened a part of London in complete darkness during the night of 25 to 26 August 1940 instead of the planned fuel depots along the Thames, followed by the later -and indeed deliberate- flattening of among others the industrial cities of Coventry, Bristol, London, Birmingham and Liverpool, there is no longer any British "fair play". The bombing of Dresden can therefore be labeled as an outright war crime. But actions that can be labeled as war crimes have occurred on both sides and by the hundreds, even thousands ...

However, according to the Russians, who are allies of the British and the Americans in the fight, the real reason for the flattening of cities such as Dresden, among others, lies elsewhere and is rather political in nature. It is certainly not the case that the Russians give a damn about the many thousands of German dead. On the contrary: the only good German for them at this moment is indeed a *dead* German. But on the other hand, according to Stalin, the British would indeed have deliberately chosen to destroy as much terrain and infrastructure as possible which they suspected would be occupied by the Soviets afterwards. Thousands of incendiary and fragmentation bombs do indeed destroy over several square kilometers just about everything that rises above the surface of the earth ...

For one small group of people in Dresden, the flattening of the city ironically means their salvation. They are the 90 Jews (out of a total of 200) trapped there to be deported to one of the extermination camps. They now happen to be able to escape by coincidence, after the entire Gestapo building in Dresden collapses. Initially, those Jews were all locked up there, waiting for their transport to the camps of death. Forty of them did get crushed by the collapsing concrete blocks and perished instantly, but the others were able to get away as if by miracle. Despite the unsettled situation that Nazi Germany has found itself in, and the considerable number of Gestapo operatives who are now trying to get themselves to safety by bluntly murdering someone, stealing their identity, and fleeing, the logistical arrangements for murdering undesirable elements of all categories of *Untermensch* are still going on as usual at the same time. And even though their *Sicherheitsdienst* itself has already lost quite a few employees in the incessant bombing, there are still plenty of fanatical Jew-hunters who immediately go after those escapees from the moment the gory dust of the prickly cement mists has cleared up. Even in the utter chaos of blackened and red-hot concrete chunks lying around everywhere and the many piles of dead bodies being counted, that same day some 70-odd of those Jews who had fled, were rounded up again and put to death. Even in the hour of their own demise, the fanatical Nazis still consider it their honorable duty to continue in the name of their *Führer* with the "final extermination" program.

Since Dresden is now no longer a place to stay, the refugees move deeper and deeper into Germany. Driven by the human survival instinct, people are driven further and further west. In this way they now also end up in the state of Thuringia in large numbers, hoping to fall into American or British hands there. But even in Thuringia there are still no British or American ground troops to be seen.

Airplanes, however, are all over the place and they arrive by many hundreds in the air above the larger cities such as Jena, Arnstadt, Erfurt, Gera, Gotha and Weimar. British and Americans bombers are indeed everywhere. The American commanders have decided to throw their bombs -as much as possible- on military targets only. But the British are bombing about everything. And they are now throwing tons of bombs in Thuringia too. It was a vain hope for the many refugees who arrived here, that they would finally be safe, because the bombing raids with heavy Lancasters, B-17s and B-24 Flying Fortresses over the whole German state doesn't stop here either.

All German refugees are now completely worn out and their hearts have sunk into their boots. Because those boots are literally worn through, they also have injured feet. They are dirty and filthy, sick and hungry. The weak simply die in the streets from exhaustion. Underneath the huge piles of rubble of steel, wood and concrete, there are still people who had already been killed by the previous bombings. Concrete blocks thrown around by the new explosions or dislodged from dilapidated buildings are relentlessly making new victims. People sometimes can no longer tell the difference between the masses of pulverized concrete and human remains lying everywhere in between. There is a pungent smell of decomposition, and the survivors still desperately search for a last more or less safe place. It is a terrible sight, but all well considered, they are still among the lucky ones, for they have survived for the time being. But how much longer? ...

The war itself has long been lost for the Germans, and only the most fanatical party members do not yet realize that. Those unscrupulous collaborators of the devil, however, are convinced in all their diabolical imagination that it is better to drag that entire German empire into the deepest damnation, than to try to save what can be saved.

In fact, there is no point at all in the Germans fleeing, because nowhere is safe now. Packed in large crowds, homeless, cramped from the cold, practically without clothes or food and with constantly weeping babies in their arms: people are desperate. Some of them have recently been overwhelmed by the sad news that their husband, son, father or brother has been killed in the fighting a little further away. At least insofar as reliable information is still being provided. Because of the precarious military situation of the Germans, it is no longer a priority to keep statistics. Most people therefore remain for the rest of their lives in the dark about what exactly happened to their fighting relatives who were still at the front. Most of the war correspondents who crawl around the front lines reporting are in danger of being killed themselves if they don't get out of the way quickly. Moreover, there is no need anymore to estimate, let alone *know*, the exact numbers and names of the soldiers killed. German reporters, like all Germans, may fear Russian revenge. People are moving further and further west in the hope of meeting American ground troops very soon.

For Elsbeth and her little son Joachim, survival and not falling into Russian hands is also still the most important message at the moment. They too have now arrived in Thuringia. For the time being, they have been able to stay ahead of the approaching Russians, because they were lucky enough to be able to travel a large part of the route in one of the trains that could still run. However, there was no heating in that rickety train. The transparent white ice flowers stood out on the window glass because of the freezing cold, but the cold was the least of Elsbeth's worries. Little Waquin is still wrapped in his warm blanket. Her consolation is that she herself knows that the little boy obviously doesn't realize what is happening. But the train ride progresses very sluggishly. Sometimes it goes so slowly that it seems that even on foot, the Red Army can still catch up with all the refugees here on the train.

Elsbeth did manage to get further than the burning city of Dresden and ruined Jena. But since the train tracks in Thuringia are also largely bombed further to the West by American B-17, B-24 and British Lancaster aircraft, the train driver is suddenly forced to stop in the middle of nowhere. The railway tracks are completely destroyed, and sharp pieces of deformed steel are pointing out in all directions. It is obvious that it all stops here. Fleeing westward by train is no longer an option and people are much too tired and desperate to walk …

By coincidence, Elsbeth strands in the oldest city in Thuringia: Arnstadt. A city where Johann Sebastian Bach once lived and where the inhabitants had lived through more than thirteen centuries of history, including executions of rebellious elements. These executions took place by hanging on the gallows or by beheading, while witches and heretics were usually burned at the stake. There was also a huge city fire. At first sight, a perfectly normal pattern for medieval life in such an old, medium-sized city. By the mid-twentieth century, however, humanity clearly hasn't learned too much from history. Things don't seem to look any better today at all. Almost everything here lies in ruins and even now there are many fatalities to mourn. Only the means of killing people have become much more sophisticated today due to advances in science than during the Middle Ages. However, the irresistible need to exterminate each other has remained …

Elsbeth Zimmermann does not realize at this very moment that Arnstadt will be her (provisional) final destination. Tired to death and with despair in her eyes, she gets off the blocked train that night. Until then, she has behaved sturdily, although she has been close to total despair on several occasions. However, each time she looks into the eyes of her little Joachim, she takes new courage and sees herself strengthened repeatedly in her will to survive. But now it really becomes too much for her and she gradually shows signs of resignation. She raises her eyes to heaven in despair, thinks of her unfortunate husband Fritz and asks herself:

"Mensch, wohin kan Ich nur nog gehen?" ("Man, where can I still go now?")

In the streets of Arnstadt, as now in almost all other cities located between the Rhine and the Weichsel (Vistula), we see mostly women with children and people of the older generation clearing the rubble in search of deceased victims and missing family members. Meanwhile, thousands of people are still dying of total distress. In days, or for some even in weeks, they have not been able to find any food anywhere. And still there is the threat that they will perish in the conflagrations that are looming everywhere.

"My God, will we ever be safe anywhere then?"

says Elsbeth to herself while muttering as she also beholds this terrible havoc in Arnstadt. On a mental level, she is really on the verge of collapse now and her resignation looks like an open book. Her desperate attitude and that fearful look in her eyes, and especially the crying little Joachim, gets the attention of a certain Frau Kranz, a kindly elderly lady who happens to be passing there late in the evening.

"Bitte, Fraulein, darf ich Ihr hilfen?" ("Madam, can I help you?")

Frau Kranz asks spontaneously. Because she believes that Elsbeth cannot just stand there all night with that toddler on her arm, she offers to follow her to her own house, so that she and Joachim have a place to stay for this one night. The buildings in the whole neighborhood where this friendly Kranz family lives, are quite severely damaged. Large cracks appear menacingly here and there in the structures. But they will have at least a roof over their heads. And they don't need anything else. While she arrives at the Kranz house, Elsbeth quickly reads a small, damaged plate nearby on the streetcorner: *Obere Weiße* it says ... Fortunately, the Kranz house is still somewhat habitable, and that is all one can ask for at this very moment.

The only thing that counts in these days of deep misery, is to make it to the next morning alive and well.

Like Elsbeth, the Kranz family no longer has any reason to look happy. One descendant of Frau Kranz has, with certainty, already been killed in this war and another family member was reported missing some time ago. The comfort and warmth these generous people convey to Elsbeth Zimmermann and Joachim is mutual. That elderly couple from Arnstadt immediately finds some self-solace in the presence and spontaneous, innocent laughter of that little nine-month-old toddler Joachim. And what is also particularly important on a moral level: mother Elsbeth Zimmermann can finally vent her hurt feelings here with these people. While little Joachim sleeps in his new bed with these good people for the first time that night, she tells these strange but very hospitable people her moving story. She tells them -stuttering and sniveling- that a few months after their marriage, her husband had been killed on the Russian front. She tells of the stories that circulated about the frequent -even systematic- rape of every German creature of the female sex between roughly 12 and 75 years of age. She also recounts her recent flight from Tilsit in harsh winter conditions. The cursing by the older people and the incessant weeping and wailing of the hungry children, those many thousands of dead horses she had seen, and which were immediately eaten on the spot, all those people killed by the freezing cold, the total chaos and upheaval, the scary, grim attitude that people adopt in the face of sudden death ...

The Kranz family, who take care of her and her baby, will become especially important to Elsbeth and her little Joachim. Four years they will eventually live under their roof. Joachim will eventually even see Frau Kranz as his own grandmother. At the end of 1990, a year after the fall of the Berlin Wall, Joachim will visit her over there. After a performance in Vienna, Austria, on the occasion of his *Rise & Shine* tour of Europe, he briefly crosses the old East German border incognito ... in the other direction than he had done 42 years earlier. We'll get back to that ...

As of the second week of April, the war seems to be drawing to a close. April 12, 1945 is actually a special day, and this for several reasons. To begin with, it is the day that American president Roosevelt dies. This good pacifist, who would have preferred to keep the US out of the war but was cowardly confronted with a fait accompli by the "Divine" Empire of Japan on December 7, 1941, is no more. It had been apparent to him for some time, that his health was awfully bad. And it is also on this very day that Arnstadt and most of Thuringia and Saxony are occupied by American ground troops. "Finally!" the

American GIs think and many Germans are thinking just the same along with them. Until then, they had been mostly afraid of falling into Russian hands or being rounded up and executed by their own extremely fanatical Nazis. For Joachim, who turns exactly one year old today on April 12, the arrival of the Americans brings a unique birthday gift. Those American soldiers generously hand out chocolate and cookies. However, those cookies are not called "concrete cookies" for nothing, and they are rock hard to bite into. The smallest children without any teeth can suck them like rusk.

Still on April 12, 1945, American soldiers also liberate the Buchenwald extermination camp. They are stunned when they discover what terrible, degrading conditions have taken place in those so-called "labor camps". The stories that had been circulating everywhere and had also come to the attention of the American soldiers, seemed to them at first greatly exaggerated. Surely such a thing could not be true! But the horrible reality even surpasses every hypothetical imagination people may have had earlier. The American soldiers therefore forced inhabitants of the area to visit the camp in order to see with their own eyes what their superiors had done to some innocent prisoners; just because they weren't born or raised by "Nazi standards". Both generals Patton and Eisenhower were sick to their stomachs and declared that this was by far the blackest day of their lives. General Eisenhower comments on seeing the horrific scenes at Buchenwald:

"In seeing these horrific images, we realize more than ever before why we are fighting here. Nazism must be exterminated to the core by all possible means, and we will not lay down our weapons until this is done!"

Several SS camp guards are put against the wall without a fuss and immediately shot mercilessly by American G.I.'s.

"Wir haben es nicht gewust!" ("We knew nothing about it!")

As many surprised looking German citizens from the surrounding villages claim. During the past years, however, those German citizens from the vicinity of the camp had regularly held all kinds of fun parties, had enjoyed swimming in the nearby lakes and had -as far as they could- still made the best of life. As if there were no problem at all. Meanwhile, a few hundred meters away, German camp guards and their fanatical collaborators were massacring their poor and helpless fellow men. By the thousands, their totally emaciated, lifeless bodies were burned and thrown into mass graves. Granted that they themselves may not have been able to do much against it, but that they hadn't known about it at all? ...

Elsbeth sees how the American soldiers arrive in Arnstadt and she feels very much relieved. So, she has fortunately been able to stay ahead of those much-feared Russians and she and her one-year-old son have survived so far. Despite all the misery she had endured, she seems safe, just like all those other Germans who had tried to move westwards as far as possible. All the efforts and the well considered choice they made to fall into American or British instead of into Russian hands, have paid off. She wonders how the future will look for them. But as long as there is life, there is hope and that's the most important thing at the moment. They will live in that zone occupied by the American Army Forces. The Russians are a bit further away. BUT! ...

... BUT indeed, because there is a vicious poisonous snake crawling under the uprooted grass in that bombed-out German state of Thuringia. Much of the zone occupied by the Americans is suddenly being evacuated by them and Soviet soldiers are taking over the area. An agreement between world leaders will completely change the future of many Germans from one moment to the next ... and for so many of them for the rest of their lives ... including ... the people in Arnstadt. Yep!

Heimatvertriebenen and Aftermath of May 8, 1945

"The devil's curse brought the whole world to it's knees."

From 1941 to August 15, 1945, Americans, British and Russians had been allies in the fight against the Nazis and the fascists. It had clearly not been a warm-hearted alliance, but one out of necessity to stop the diabolical triple alliance of Germany, Italy and Japan. But, with their ideologies so diametrically opposed, is further close cooperation between the Soviet Union and the Western world even possible in the future? Frictions between East and West are indeed increasing after May 8, 1945, with

Cecilienhof in Potsdam, where between July 17 and August 2, 1945, Germany was officially divided into four occupation zones. (Photograph by the author)

Soviet politics beginning to show more aggressive traits in the process. But first, Stalin will now order a large-scale "redistribution" of the inhabitants over all those zones that will come under Soviet control. A repeat of history with all those unreliable Germans, Ukrainians and other problem populations? No way! But what will we do with those Germans who stayed behind in East Prussia? Let's deport them! From now on Germans belong in their own homeland and those who don't want to, we'll move to Siberia if necessary ...

Millions of German Heimatvertriebenen *will become victims of Stalin's "purification" actions ... or is this rather a good thing for some individuals in the end? ...*

June 1945. In Europe, the Second World War finally ended a few weeks ago. Except for neutral countries like Sweden and Switzerland, Europe is largely in ruins. Sweden, in fact, was only *officially* neutral, because there was a lot of Nazi sympathy ... and a huge steel export from Sweden to Germany to support Hitler's war machine.

Not only the buildings are in ruins. Also, the overall complex situation at political and human level has yet to be completely unraveled, and living circumstances are extremely unstable almost anywhere. In the confusion that ensues after the last bullets have been shot and the guns finally stopped firing, the entire world once again becomes entangled in all kinds of uncertainties and squabbles. Everywhere, there are power shifts or political and personal settlements about to happen. Former Nazi collaborators are being executed or given (life-) long prison sentences in all European countries where the Nazis had ruled. Many politicians find the time right now to proclaim other tendencies and they feel called upon to make a bid for power.

They have been exceedingly difficult years, in which the main goal for all citizens was only to survive. Not only in Germany of course, because almost the whole world has to lick its wounds and recover from the suffering they have endured. No matter where, everyone has his own issues at the moment. But in the victorious countries, the survivors can now, finally, all return home. At least, if that home is still there, because the destruction is enormous in many countries, and many thousands of people literally have to rebuild everything. For the Germans, however, very uncertain times are ahead, but there is no one in the world who is bothered by their fate. Besides, aren't those Germans themselves the cause of all the misery the world is now facing? And those Germans had not cared too much either about the fate of the many millions of other people who had to flee elsewhere in the world, some time ago.

As far as (defeated) Germany is concerned, altogether some fourteen to fifteen million citizens had fled in the direction of homeland Germany from late January 1945 onwards. Among them, Germans from East Prussia and many Poles and Czechs with a German ethnic background from Pomerania, Silesia, Sudetenland and elsewhere. A total of two million of those refugees would not survive the war. They perished in the ice-cold winters, from total deprivation, hunger, disease, in the murderous bombing, were executed for treason by their own SS or simply murdered by aroused Russian soldiers or -for some reason- revenge-seeking fellow citizens. Even after May 8, 1945, the situation for the surviving German fugitives remains very unclear for a long time. Many were also more than a thousand kilometers away from their own *Heimat*. The dire refugee situation should in essence be clarified for these German displaced persons, and additional international agreements would have to be concluded.

Meanwhile, millions of surviving refugees are crammed together among the rubble in Germany itself. In some places, especially in the larger cities, the number of refugees at the time of the ceasefire is as high as 25% of the total local population.

The reason for this is probably also due to the fact that the *local* population had also been decimated by the terrible bombing and that many men had died as soldiers or *Volkssturmers*. Some refugees were in the Western Zone after May 8, where Americans, British and French were in (provisional) control. Overall, these people consider themselves among the lucky ones.

In Western Germany, citizens had, indeed, not really been afraid of the invasion by American and British soldiers, as we already saw in the previous chapter. Especially Germans who had been war-weary for some time, had been secretly hoping that they would be spared from further misery once they fell into western hands. The Americans, by the way, were quite generous in handing out chocolate and cigarettes to the starving German people everywhere they passed.

However, the situation is completely different for those in the zone now occupied by the Russians. In the east of Germany, therefore, they are all the more insecure. Where is *their* future? Can they stay here in these refugee camps, or do they have to go back home? Or do they have to go elsewhere? Are they really trapped forever in that gigantic, yet so unpredictable Soviet empire?

While awaiting final decisions regarding Germany's political future, every German -refugee and native-born alike- is trying to make a provisional way through the total chaos. There's no time to think about things for too long and to sit by the sidelines. There may not be a clear perspective in the political arena yet, but with complete certainty, what is absolutely needed in the first place … is food. Where their new hearth will be, has become somewhat of an afterthought for most people at this point and most of them are already satisfied that they survived that cursed war. Of course, all of them -without exception- are missing some family members and that, in itself, could be a reason to go back to the region they initially came from. They want to find those people again. But are those missing persons themselves still there and, moreover, are they still alive? Perhaps then all the effort of going so far back is simply useless?

Therefore, some tricky decisions have to be made. So folks, listen up for a moment: has your house been flattened, have you been crippled, has your father or son died in battle as a soldier, has your mother, sister or daughter been raped by enemy soldiers, has your brother been convicted for desertion, have you lost relatives during the war, or are you somewhere with your very malnourished or sick children far away from home? Well folks, you have shed enough tears now! Get over it, roll up your sleeves and get to work! Wherever you are, from now on you only have to look forward and build a new future for yourselves! Start planting crops in the fields and in places where the soil has not been irreparably ruined by debris, so that soon it will be possible to harvest again. Life goes on and everyone is expected to make a new start, no matter how deep the misery you are going through! Although, regardless of the previously established agreements with the other allied countries, it looks like the Russians will do their own thing anyway in the zone they occupy. They have the tacit approval of the US, by the way ...

In 1943, an earlier agreement in Tehran between the US, the Soviet Union and Great Britain had already made one thing very clear: US President Roosevelt was willing to make far-reaching concessions to Stalin in order to keep the Soviet Union on his side in the fight against Nazi Germany. Control of *the whole* Eastern Europe zone would therefore be left to the Soviet Union after the allied victory, at least as far as the US government was concerned. British Prime Minister Winston Churchill's proposal to open a second front in the Balkans early in 1943, confronted an immediate (and expected) protest from Stalin ... and from Roosevelt. Nevertheless Stalin could use *all* the help he could get, even if this help is started so close to home, he absolutely wanted **NO** interference from Western countries in a zone so close to the Soviet Union. So, for this reason, Stalin saw no point in Churchill's proposal. Churchill feared that this concession to Stalin was too far-reaching and saw that his intended grip on Eastern Europe could *never* be corrected.

Roosevelt, however, saw no merit in this for the time being. In time, this meant that Stalin had the green light to impose his will on the entire zone. The only thing that was not yet known, was where exactly the East-West border and the control zones would come.

In Yalta (on the Soviet peninsula of Crimea), the three leaders Stalin, Churchill and Roosevelt had a new meeting early February of this year, 1945, in which they concluded a revised agreement on the occupation of Germany by the Allies after their victory. Russia also announced that it would join the fight against Japan, which was, of course, additional good news for the US. Moreover, in Yalta the proposed principles about who would occupy which zone, were already a bit more concrete. The French would also be allowed to occupy part of Germany. But first, we had to wait and see how far each army would be able to advance individually on German territory. That was not stated there directly in these words, but that was clearly going through the minds of each of these three leaders. In this regard, the intention of each army was to push through as far as possible on German soil, and to claim those zones for themselves at least for the time being. It was a matter of being able to put some better trump cards on the table at later negotiations. So, Americans, British and French of the (free) French army advanced as far as possible from the West and Russians from the East. On the Upper Elbe near Torgau in Saxony, Americans and Russians finally met on April 25. The Americans already occupied most of Thuringia and a large part of Saxony. The Americans had progressed further than the Russians had secretly hoped.

But Stalin immediately claimed Thuringia and Saxony for himself after the Americans and British hinted that they, too, wanted to occupy part of Berlin. The Americans are again immediately inclined to give in, and they withdraw, to the great surprise and displeasure of the many Germans there who thought the Russians would no longer bother them.

To settle the very last details about all this, an ultimate last meeting is planned by the Allied leaders. In the Cecilienhof, in that very fashionable small town of Potsdam, behind the Wannsee near Berlin and constructed according to the Dutch model, the British, American and Russian leaders will put their heads together once more. This in order to determine the last political details for the defeated Germany and their citizens once and for all. That meeting is scheduled for July 17 and will last about two weeks. France is not invited and is very displeased about this. Incidentally, the composition of the three leaders has been greatly altered by circumstances. In the meantime, US President Franklin Roosevelt has passed away and is replaced by Harry Truman, while Winston Churchill has been voted out of Downing Street 10 and replaced by Clement Attlee. But Truman also gives in to this additional demand of Stalin, so that the Americans hand over Thuringia and Saxony entirely (and permanently). In exchange, the French, British and Americans accentuate their claim to a part of the capital Berlin, which consequently must also be divided into four zones. Stalin agrees, but emphasizes that he is making a very generous concession. Berlin, after all, is an integral part of the Russian occupation zone and this city is surely the symbol of both the rise of the Third Reich and their total defeat. That German capital was overrun and captured by the Russians *alone*, and they also found Hitler's burned body and examined it for authenticity. According to the Soviet pathologists, Hitler's burned body was indeed found there with 100% certainty just next to the entrance of his bunker. Deciding whether or not it was the *Führer* himself, his teeth were compared with his dentist's file, and this brought complete certainty, still only according to the Russian report ...

With the partition of Berlin, a western (read capitalist) antenna also comes into that part of Germany, where Stalin wants to position his own system of communism at all costs. It is unofficially agreed that the western and eastern zones will be governed as much as possible as one entity, and that there will not be any difference between the treatment of inhabitants in the eastern and western parts of that new Germany.

However, that would be impracticable when you have to deal with two ideologies so far apart. Each party gives the impression of making some concessions, but in the end, it is clear that no one is really satisfied.

So, to give Stalin his way, the Americans leave the whole part of Thuringia and Saxony where they were still present, unannounced, and the Russians immediately take their place. This is a huge disappointment for all those Germans who had first thought that, despite the uncertainty about the future, they were in *Western* hands. Indeed, no one had seen this scenario coming. As a result, millions of Germans in that Russian zone will never be able to see their families on the other side of the new East-West border again, but of course they cannot know that yet at the moment.

After May 8, the general Russian stance toward German citizens is also somewhat unclear to many people. The people living under their rule also do not know at first what exactly to expect, but they certainly do not expect great glory. Even after the end of hostilities, they still fear -rightly so- new deportations, executions and rapes. Some Germans do see their chance to secretly flee from the Russian zone to the freer West. The border is not yet hermetically sealed everywhere, and the greatest fear of the Russians at that time is not (yet) that too many people will flee their region. What they do fear the most, is that some Nazi war criminals will slip across and escape to the West so they can escape the punishment the Russians have in mind for them. They also want to put highly skilled German scientists under their "protection." So, the new Iron Curtain is not yet completely closed, but it is strongly guarded nevertheless …

Elsbeth Zimmermann and her hostess, Frau Kranz, watch with dismay how the American soldiers make room for Russian soldiers in Arnstadt. She again becomes afraid for the future. She fears that all the efforts made have been in vain. The fear of millions of people in the entire area comes true, indeed. Soviet party leader Stalin was not to be trusted before and he proves once again that this mistrust is well founded.

The Soviets had already been busy for some time (since 1937 to be more precise) redistributing entire populations *within their own* Soviet Union. It is very clear that, even long before the war, hundreds of thousands of their own compatriots had been deported for the most idiotic reasons to the Gulags* to exhaust themselves in the general interest of the Soviet Union. Often no decisive reasons at all were needed to send someone there. Just a vague suspicion that someone wasn't sufficiently Stalinist was enough to banish the whole family. And if Stalin applied this principle widely even to his own compatriots, why should the Germans be spared?

So, he simply continues the deportation program in his control zone. He and no one else decides where people will live in the future.

Soviet labor camp of "general use and interest", often located in Siberia.

As for the Germans who are spread out over Eastern Europe, they must all live in the actual homeland Germany itself and that includes all inhabitants of that far away East Prussia as well. Because from now on ... that is no longer a German state but has become an integral part of the Soviet Union. The last Germans who -no matter what- had decided to remain in East Prussia, will therefore soon be expelled from that region forever. It's against their will, but there is no mercy. Is anyone among those residents not satisfied with that? Well, no problem: there *is* an alternative. There are even two and you can choose: work yourself to death in a Siberian labor camp? Or would you rather be buried in the nearest cemetery with a bullet in your head? You just name it ...

During the war years, Stalin's large-scale redistribution plans were necessarily shelved. However, from "V" Day, being May 8, 1945 (May 9 according to Soviet archives), he restarts the deportations. In the new Soviet zone, besides the Germans in East Prussia, several population groups are now sent simultaneously from East to West and from North to South or vice versa. So, many are again subjected to Stalin's "geopolitical" views. Among them, thousands of Ukrainians, Uzbeks and Georgians, who *were* already part of the Soviet Union before. But none of them should be allowed to cause internal upheaval again.

Stalin says he now has a particularly good reason for doing all this. Many of those people -especially Ukrainians- had indeed not so long ago smoothly collaborated with Nazi Germany. To prevent such a thing from happening again, there is only one reliable remedy: to ruthlessly suppress those who had not been eliminated during the last war or, if necessary, to bluntly silence them for good. Stalin would no longer tolerate situations in which rebellious Ukrainians or others are all called upon to turn away from the Soviet Union -if necessary, by force- and to opt fully for resistance and secession, in which the geographical heredity of the Crimean Peninsula is continually questioned.

Stalin was already deporting Ukrainians in 1939, because in his opinion they already had been completely unreliable before the war.

It became a vicious circle. Indeed, in 1941, in response to Stalin's prejudice, more Ukrainians chose the outstretched hand of the Nazis to turn further away from Stalin and the Soviet Union. Therefore, many Ukrainians voluntarily joined the SS troops that fought on the German side against Stalin's Russia with full conviction. A Belgian guy, who in the process had absolutely nothing to do with it in the first place, would even take on an important pioneering role a bit later. Albert Haesebroeckx, a Belgian war veteran of the regular Belgian troops (he was no volunteer for the SS!) was taken prisoner by the German army on the Lys in Belgium in May 1940. Albert escaped from a prisoner of war camp in Germany in 1943. He couldn't return home, but he ended up in Ukraine, where he spontaneously joined the UON (Ukrainian Nationalist Organization). As a fierce anti-communist, he will constantly send militant anti-Soviet messages into the air via a local radio station called "Aphrodite", located somewhere in a basement. All this to strongly encourage Ukrainians to continue resisting the Russians. In between all the propaganda messages, Albert Haesebroeckx also played western songs from the French, German, English and even Dutch repertoire in the area between Odessa and Kiev, to allow the people there to soak up some more European "culture".

However, for those Ukrainian nationalists, things didn't turn out at the end as hoped. Hitler eventually lost the war and afterwards, it is Stalin's turn to tighten the chains on the Ukrainians once again.

In October 1947, as a punishment for their defection, another 80,000 Western Ukrainians were deported to Siberia (= the so-called "ZAPAD deportations"). Many Crimean Tartars underwent the same fate. And, of course, it does not stop there. Uzbeks, Kazakhs and quite a few White Russians are not given the benefit of the doubt and share fully in the blows ...

Most East Germans, including a certain war widow Elsbeth Zimmermann who now lives in Arnstadt, have understood it all very well. She herself is irrevocably trapped in the Russian Zone and she is not allowed to ever return to her old home. She fully realizes that this beautiful and beloved East Prussia will only be allowed to live on in her fondest memories. Just as she will miss her husband Fritz for the rest of her life, she will certainly miss that once so peaceful region. But she realizes, like so many others, that she must go on ... and that she's lucky to be alive ...

With the Russians in her neighborhood or not, Elsbeth Zimmermann continues to search for her way in life and she soon finds work in her new home in Arnstadt. She is secured by the spontaneous help of the Kranz family, and they have promised her she can stay with them as long as she wants. Also, the other people in the completely destroyed Thuringia try to gradually get on with their lives again after May 8, 1945 ...

So, is Stalin's "distribution program" of people in his immense occupation zone almost completed by now? Not yet! All Germans have to live in the homeland as we saw, but... all foreigners must leave. And he won't forget the individual cases either. Among those, we have some foreign soldiers who were captured by the German Army during the war, and all foreign civilian workers in the Germans industries. So, we leave that generous Kranz family (including Joachim and Elsbeth) alone for a moment and go to Jena; about 35 miles to the East. In Jena, we get to know Herr Albert Melzer, a successful businessperson. The reason we mention him will become very clear in a moment ...

Albert Melzer had been the regular supplier of fuel and coal to many customers in Greater Jena. Although the city of Jena is in ruins just like the other cities in the region, Herr Melzer wants to revive his business in the triangle region between Jena, Erfurt and Arnstadt. He asks if he can count on his old customers to deliver again after summer. Besides the negotiations about restarting his business, he also complains a lot to anyone he meets about the fact that his daughter Annelore must leave Germany immediately at the orders of the Russians. The modified "civilian status" that Stalin has in mind for *every* German in his control area suddenly applies to her as well and essentially to all native Germans who do live in the actual homeland ... but are married to a foreigner ...

Albert Melzer's daughter Annelore is a handsome young woman of twenty-two years old. On May 7, 1945, one day before Armistice Day, she married Belgian war prisoner Albert De Beukeleer. Albert was requisitioned via a *Werbestelle* in German-occupied Belgium in 1942 and put to compulsory work in Carl Zeiss' optical factory in Jena. Now that the war is over, he is actually free. But he must leave German territory on Russian orders at once, or he risks being sent on to the Gulags as well. Annelore has to leave Germany too, although she can choose a (bizarre) alternative: she can stay, but she must then divorce her brand-new husband Albert again. If she does not, she *and* Albert must also leave German territory for good. Annelore does not have to think about it, and she spontaneously follows her heart. That heart, by the way, had already been put to the test for long enough. For was this Annelore really predestined to marry this foreign worker of Belgian origin whom she hardly knew? No, of course not! It didn't look that way a few years ago and if it had been up to her family, it certainly wouldn't have happened now either. Marrying an ordinary Belgian who speaks a sort of *Niederdeutsch**? Such a person is by definition considered by Germans of the well-to-do bourgeoisie not good enough to be allowed to marry a German girl from the moneyed middle classes.

Annelore is indeed of rather good "stock". Her family owns, or rather *owned,* a beautiful and huge housing and apartment complex in the prestigious Damenviertel in the center of that beautiful city of Jena.

On the same location as they managed a huge fuel and coal business, they also operated a driving school for truck drivers before the war. But now, their entire business complex is completely destroyed. Of all those healthy businesses, like everything else in Germany: nothing remains today.

The Melzer family had experienced the rise of Nazism in the 1930s very consciously. Annelore herself had been a member of the *Hitlerjugend* for many years. "*Deutschland* über *alles*" was therefore music to the Melzer family's ears at the time and everyone looked up to their great leader Adolf Hitler with an enormous admiration. That charismatic figure had succeeded in completely restoring German self-respect. That he had diabolical and pernicious ambitions that went far beyond merely restoring German pride, was not yet immediately apparent to the mil-

---

* *German dialect, spoken in some old Germanic regions.*

lions of people in Germany in the 1930s who worshipped him so passionately and unconditionally. Annelore's little brother had even been allowed to shake hands with the great leader in the deep brown uniform when the *Führer* drove through their region in his beautiful Mercedes 540K Cabriolet. Everyone in the family was extremely delighted and from that moment on, everybody looked up to little Gerhard Melzer with an enormous admiration, even great reverence.

"Little Gerhard is our family hero. Our great Führer *kissed him on both cheeks and caressed his hand."*

Therefore, when war broke out on September 1, 1939, this Melzer family from Jena was immediately behind the German (expansion) plans. That it required fighting, was unavoidable. The fighting would not last too long, by the way. Hitler had promised that and his word was a powerful synonym for will, law and truth.

So, the Melzer family did some incredibly good business before the war as a wealthy company in fuels and as the operator of the driving school. As long as the war was going favorably for Germany, all the misery of bombing, deprivation and sorrow was still far away for them. Until the day when terribly sad news arrived there too ...

Jena, Thuringia in 1935. Thirteen-year-old Annelore Melzer with her little brother Gerhard at the entrance to their large housing complex. The sign points to the driving school that the Melzer family operated.

Little Gerhard died in the summer of 2021 at the age of 87. While authoring this book, I suddenly received that sad news from his hometown of Jena.
Gerhard Melzer was an interesting source of information for this part of the story.

At the beginning of the war, Annelore had become engaged to Peter Heinz, a German fighter pilot. So, in essence, she would be marrying that boy. Even the gold rings had already been designed and the jeweler had engraved both their names "Annelore/Peter Heinz" in those rings forever and ever. It was just a matter of waiting for Peter Heinz to take a short leave of absence to perform the ceremony. Just as Elsbeth Zimmermann and Fritz Krauledat had done, Annelore Melzer would marry Peter Heinz during a brief leave of absence of this young, handsome, and extremely proud fighter pilot of the Luftwaffe.

But just as Fritz Krauledat would never return home, Annelore's fiancé Peter Heinz also failed to come home. On a mission in enemy Russian territory, he had been shot out of the sky with his Messerschmidt B-109 and had been reported missing ever since.

Annelore's world collapsed and for the next few months she could not be comforted. She could no longer sleep since she had received the miserable news at home. Her pillow was soaked with tears every night because of the painful loss of her beloved Peter Heinz. Her beautiful dream suddenly became a nightmare. So, life is full of surprises. Not only for her, of course, because all of Germany has now been led straight to the road of perdition by it's opportunistic Nazi leaders. The whole beautiful country lies in ruins and there is an enormous famine and an acute housing shortage. Many hundreds of thousands of young German girls mourn the loss of their loved ones in the horrific fighting.

No one knows what to do next. In the winter and early spring of 1945, everything in Thuringia is also in ruins, and so Annelore is now also one of those many who have lost a husband or a fiancé. In order to make a living, she even had to have a job at the local Carl Zeiss optical factory in the city of Jena. From their earlier beautiful dream with the promising prospect of a world-dominating Third Reich, the Germans were brutally awakened, and now people in Germany, too, suddenly found themselves in the bleak reality. Everyone had to roll up their sleeves. Even those people from the well-to-do bourgeoisie who had seen their thriving businesses of yesteryear lost. Work in the factory or starve. There was no alternative, for no one ...

Carl Zeiss Jena was still running at full speed in the early spring of 1945 to keep the German war industry going. Albert De Beukeleer, the deported Belgian worker, simply did what was expected of him, no more and no less. He would like to return home as soon as possible and he hopes the Germans will give up soon, so the war can come to an end. One day, however, Albert meets the beautiful Annelore Melzer on the factory floor and "returning home" suddenly becomes less important to him. He feels enormously attracted to her. It starts with an ordinary wink to each other and a joke that Albert makes to her ... in Dutch. That joke is only half understood by Annelore, but in the end that is the funniest part of the whole situation, because it makes her laugh.

It is the body language that is clearly the most important detail at that moment. Albert is no longer so eager to return home after that wink, quite the contrary ...

But ... foreign workers who get on well with local girls? The Germans in general and Annelore's family in particular do not support this at all. A Belgian prisoner deployed as a forced laborer who dares to approach a German girl just like that? A Belgian farmer's son taking it up with a young German girl from the upper middle class? This is totally unheard of! You can't expect people who, in 1942, considered themselves superior to everyone else on earth, to have any sympathy for them.

Annelore, however, is also attracted to the tall, slender, sympathetic and also rather handsome Albert. At first glance, he does not seem likely to become the great love for her, but her feelings are certainly partly related to that gentle veil of warm sympathy that Albert reflects on her. She wants to feel reassured in these uncertain times after the grievous loss of her Peter Heinz. She needs gentle support and some additional cheering up, and she clearly shows this to Albert. Yet, she actually feels a little uncomfortable because of this. Not because she is dealing with someone of foreign origin who is about seven years older than she is, but because of the guilt she feels whenever she thinks of Peter Heinz. But every time she sees this tall Albert in the factory, she suddenly feels better. That funny stranger, with his seductive blue eyes. That handsome and clearly very honest Belgian man, who could make her laugh again for the first time in a long time. Her deep sorrow slowly fades away ...

When the region of Thuringia shares in the blows of heavy bombing in the spring of 1945, Albert and Annelore spontaneously exchange regular smiles. Each other's company helps them both to stay afloat in these days of fire, misery and death. But on March 17, 1945, American B17 bombers suddenly appear over the Carl Zeiss factories. Albert is not on duty at the time and is resting on his bedpost in the prison camp on the hill, just outside town. Down below, things threaten to end badly for the people in the city center and the workers still at the factory ...

When Albert sees that the factory is under full bombardment, he cringes. He suspects that Annelore must still be at work at that moment, and he wants to get to her out as soon as possible. He doesn't hesitate for a moment and wants to storm down the hill. If Annelore is lucky enough to be alive, it will be a race against time anyway. Many people lie under the rubble and some parts of the irreparably damaged infrastructure are in danger of collapsing. But the exit from the camp where he has been staying, is blocked by some petulant guards who fear that the enlisted will want to take advantage of this opportunity to escape. Albert's yelling at the guards doesn't help and he rams himself right through the exit by beating up one of the guards and knocking down the other. He risks getting a bullet in the back, but he doesn't even care at that point. He *must* and he *will* find Annelore, even if it costs him his life. He runs like hell and, without thinking enters the factory site which has been bombed into rubble. This is not so difficult, because there isn't even an entrance anymore. He constantly calls and shouts Annelore's name and after a few minutes of searching, he finds her unconscious among the rubble. Fortunately, she quickly regains consciousness, but she is completely groggy, and her trachea is full of concrete dust, so she almost coughs her lungs out. But unlike many others for whom any help arrives too late, she is virtually unharmed apart from some serious bruises and a bloodied temple. When she sees Albert, she bursts into tears and with her last remaining strength, she wraps both her arms around him. She is determined never to let go of him.

As part of the smoldering concrete threatens to collapse, Albert carries her outside as quickly as possible and immediately notifies her family. They are grateful to him, but despite his recent heroic act of saving her, they still resist the engagement that follows a few days later. Albert De Beukeleer and Annelore Melzer marry without the blessing of Annelore's parents. But now they are faced with the problem of forced deportation. On the orders of the Russians, Albert and Annelore leave Jena together and search for a future in Belgium. On June 1 they arrive with the "beast train" at Antwerp Central Station.

Except for a worn-out burlap sack containing some basic necessities like underwear, they have nothing. Despite today's beautiful weather, both their futures look pretty bleak. Despite the beautiful spring day, the yellow ribbon Annelore wears in her dark blonde hair, is indeed about the only ornament that brings a little color in this drab period. What strikes her when she comes out at Koningin Astridplein, is that Antwerp and the rest of Belgium, just like Thuringia in her homeland, are also in ruins. That, in turn, is the result of the *German* terror. At the beginning of the war, it was their bombing of the Belgian, Dutch, French and British armies and towards the end it was their V1 and V2 rockets that had caused death and destruction here. Only then, Annelore starts to realize what kind of misery her own compatriots have caused elsewhere …

Annelore Melzer is certainly not the only German citizen to be forced to leave Germany and move (whether to Belgium or not). But she is apparently the first person who has to leave Germany because she is married to *a Belgian prisoner of war*. Later, she will be allowed to visit her family in East Germany from time to time. However, on each visit she is shadowed the whole time by the Eastern Bloc security services. She is not allowed to take photographs and her personal suitcase is always searched thoroughly "*for any weapons and secret documents that may have been smuggled in.*" The car in which she travels is turned inside out every time she enters or leaves East Germany.

Counter-visits by East-German relatives in the other direction, without filling out an endless series of totally absurd forms, are only possible after the fall of the Berlin Wall in 1989. Those who do it anyway during the Cold War, know that their relatives back home are held as collateral by the regime, until they have returned from that place of damnation the West is considered to be. Those who have dared to visit the West, by the way, can forget any promotion at work or in their profession for the rest of their lives.

Albert's and Annelore's expulsion from Germany on Stalin's orders is, of course, only a ridiculously small detail in the whole rearrangement of populations under Soviet rule. The word *Heimatvertriebenen* will eventually affect many millions of Europeans living behind the Iron Curtain. Stalin and the Soviet Union now have complete control over the entire eastern part of Europe and, in addition, the large-scale redistribution plan in his zone is gradually being completed. All "foreign" and unwanted persons are banished from the Soviet empire.

In the meantime, the Russian secret service KGB also immediately starts looking for a way to get its hands on the atomic secrets, which for now are exclusively in the hands of the Americans. For the time being, they are not looking for a direct (military) confrontation with the free western world, but they do want a strong back-up to enforce their communist positions in all the countries they have occupied since the spring of 1945: Poland, Hungary, Romania, Bulgaria, Czechoslovakia, Yugoslavia and the previously absorbed Balkan states. Disagreements between East and West continually increase, and when the German Federal Republic (West Germany) introduced the "Deutschmark" as a means of payment in West Berlin a few years later, against Stalin's wishes, the Soviet Union promptly sealed off the enclave of West Berlin from the outside world in 1948. According to the Soviet Union, introducing the "Deutschmark" in West Berlin was not in accordance with the agreements of Yalta. An air bridge from the West must be put in place to supply the free people living in West Berlin with food and fuel. A further consequence is the establishment of the North Atlantic Treaty Organization (NATO) in 1949 by the western countries. A few years later, the Russian response came with the conclusion of the Warsaw Pact that was to serve as an Eastern European counterweight to that aggressive North Atlantic (terror) threat ...

The Americans, thanks to their generous Marshall aid plan, have a foothold in Western Europe and see themselves assured of the democratic (read capitalist) system there.

The continent of Europe is now irrevocably divided into a large capitalist part on the one hand and a large communist part on the other. Germany, both their recent common enemy, was also neatly divided between the two camps, which until recently had been allies in the struggle. Neither camp, however, is simply satisfied by this new situation. A new mutual threat is emerging that will continue to escalate, and sometimes the security arrangements are really at risk. Indeed, on some occasions, East and West have come remarkably close to confronting each other head-on.

The people living in a zone within five kilometers of the East German border are driven out once again. Houses, railroad infrastructure and even the bridges are being demolished to create a buffer zone to get a better view of all possible candidate refugees and -according to the Soviet slogans- *"of a possible western invasion."* The East-West border is being increasingly fortified. A very wide strip of several kilometers along the side of the East German border becomes a *Sperrzone* and is completely surrounded by double rows of barbed wire and palisades with machine guns.

The break between East and West becomes formal. The Iron Curtain is stretched tight. The Cold War has begun ...

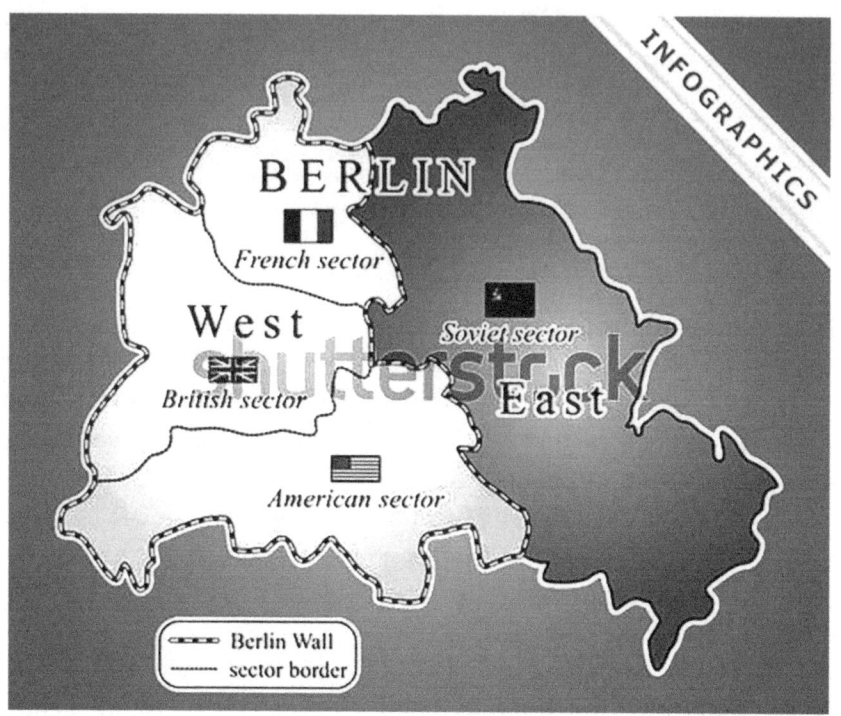

The four sectors of the city of Berlin. The western section (lightly colored and surrounded by white-black squares in the picture) is enclosed and completely surrounded by a 3.5-meter-high double wall from 1961 on. The entire border line between East and West Germany is also hermetically sealed until 1989.

Soviet cartoon from 1958 illustrating their own vision on NATO. Nazi leaders are first imprisoned, then, after fraternizing with the British, they once again take the reins, this time no longer in a Nazi, but in a NATO uniform.

Through a Hole in the Barbed Wire

"The truck came by and put us in the back and left us where the railroad track crossed the line."

1949. Living for four long years under Russian rule has not yet been a Godsend for anyone in the eastern part of Germany. After all, the zone occupied by Russia is strongly held in check, and Stalin does not loosen his iron-clad stranglehold for a moment. Just as the French wanted to make the Germans pay as heavily as possible after the end of the First World War, the Russians are now doing exactly the same to "their" part of Germany. In fact, the Soviet Union will put its communist stamp all over the territory they occupy after the war: Poland, Czechoslovakia, Romania, Bulgaria, Hungary and of course, therefore, that eastern part of Germany, renamed "Deutsche Demokratische Republik" (GDR)* in 1949. This new East German state was to become a faithful vassal state of the Soviet Union, where freedom was severely restricted, not to say that there was no freedom at all. Border crossings will be increasingly difficult, and everyone will be expected to stay where they are ... forever.

The question, however, is whether everyone will just do that ...

Eisenach, Thuringia, East Germany, 1949
On hill reaching 1300 feet, the great medieval castle of Wartburg silently watches over the entire area. Pastor Martin Luther had once taken refuge in that gigantic mastodon during the severe religious troubles and persecutions of the "heretics" in Europe. But now, from down here, you can't see that stately, robust watchdog standing there at the top of the hill. After all, visibility is far too limited tonight. Thick wisps of mist are winding their way everywhere through the

---
* *It had NOTHING democratic.*

valleys in the gently rolling landscape along the southern foothills of the Hartz plateau and the dark Hainich forests. In the desolate area that has formed the border between East and West Germany for the past four years, visibility is currently reduced to almost zero due to the numerous low and chilly fog banks all around. Everywhere, it is eerily quiet, and this strange, scary soundlessness is only drowned out from time to time by the dull sounds of a few barking dogs.

It is almost midnight. A rattling, over-aged truck has left the main road just before the town of Eisenach and has very deliberately chosen an alternative route. In the old days of Germany that main road connected the town of Arnstadt (Thuringia) with Kassel (in the neighboring state of Hessen) some 70 kilometers on. But that main road is strictly guarded today.

Because of the totally soured relations between communism in the Eastern Bloc on the one hand and capitalism in the West on the other, the passage just beyond the town of Eisenach has been completely closed off today. Moreover, the entire border is guarded by East German soldiers with machine guns. After all, Kassel is now in *West* Germany. Although that town is only a stone's throw away, it has literally become a completely different world, to which none of the East German civilians are allowed to travel anymore.

On the giant front grille of the heavily roaring vehicle, the brand emblem: *"Opel Blitz"* is clearly displayed. With its 3,600 C³ and 75 hp engine, this truck now uses a secondary road for a short time. In doing so, the truck is forced to plow occasionally right through the poorly traveled dirt roads along the fields and move as close as possible to the forest edges. However, with its mechanical and permanent "all-wheel drive" propulsion system, this is no problem for this strong truck. This ramshackle old car, which now bounces along the difficult roads, belonged to the German *Wehrmacht* during the last years of the war. Back then, German soldiers and all kinds of military equipment were transported on the back of the truck. Although the truck has now been demilitarized, those old, original war lights are still mounted on the solid steel fenders at the front and rear. The heavy growling Opel engine in the front has clearly had its best days, but it is still reliable enough to keep on doing its job for a while. Despite the dense darkness and the low-hanging fog, this truck is deliberately driving around *without* any lights at this very moment …

There is an underlying reason this old car is driving along small paths through the misty darkness. The driver and his companion hope to remain unnoticed by the frequently carried out patrols of the many East German border guards. To dampen the noise of the engine a bit, the driver has also deliberately engaged one gear higher than is actually appropriate, so that the engine speed drops a bit. It makes the truck stutter a bit and this gives the rear occupants the impression that the driver could actually use some additional driving instruction.

But it does reduce the engine noise. Being quiet and totally unnoticed is clearly the main message and it is even a matter of life and death in this case …

Next to the driver in the cabin is another man. Both these men are active during the day as full-time railroad workers and they do maintenance work on all possible railroad infrastructure in this whole area. And they still have a lot of work to do. Toward the end of the war, the entire German railroad network had been totally shot to pieces by British and American bombers. Twisted remnants of steel rails still stick up in all directions in many places to this day. New tracks have already been laid in a new bed, but many clearing operations are still underway. And the railroad itself in this part of Germany will probably also have its terminus in this small town of Eisenach in the future, just before the new border between East and West Germany. A through connection to Kassel (and beyond) seems out of the question since the drawing of a formal border between East and West Germany. Neither by road nor by rail people will be able to travel from East to West anymore.

However, the two railroad workers sitting at the front of the truck are not only active as railroad workers. By night they are part of an underground network that tries to smuggle refugees from East to West. Because they now know this border region like the back of their hands, they try to make their meager salary go up a notch by guiding people at night who want to flee to West Germany. Through a tangle of all kinds of intermediaries, candidate refugees in the deepest secrecy finally end up with them. Because of their sound knowledge of the terrain, the railroad workers can easily ask for a fee for their guiding work, and the fleeing people are eagerly willing to pay it. Some even spend their last *Pfennig* to be able to afford a respectable guide. That new East German *Mark der Deutschen Notenbank* recently created by the new communist regime, by the way, has almost no value compared to the old *Deutsche Reichsmark*. So, what does it all really matter whether we have money left over or not ...

These "border guides" in their spare time know that by their actions they are putting their own lives and the lives of the candidate refugees at risk, yet together they decided to take on this life-threatening challenge. For a little more food on the table for themselves, wife and children, some people take enormous risks. But they are always incredibly careful. These men of the underground movement and the refugee candidates only speak when it is absolutely necessary. Everything is done through sign language if possible. Of course, optimal caution is necessary, because it is possible that not everyone ... is a candidate refugee. Nothing is done in too formal a way, because there is a great risk that some spies are active who can expose traces of such illegal networks resulting in the arrest of the collaborators*. But effective communication fortunately does not need many words. Exactly as it was pointed out, the driver and his guide have just picked up all these people who are now sitting in the back of the truck at various places along the way, without saying a single word. All this with only one purpose: to put them, after payment, in complete silence over this new border of shame. Just like their two guides, however, each of the people seated in the back of the truck know just as well that this whole undertaking is fraught with mortal danger. All along the artificial border between East and West there are concrete posts with double rows of barbed wire attached to them. Large beams of light mounted on tall wooden towers constantly trace the border line.

That border had not already been hermetically sealed everywhere in 1949, and fortune seekers wriggled through the barbed wire with some regularity. Obstacles, even if they consist of high concrete walls and barbed wire, will never definitively stop fanatically persevering candidate refugees. However, machine guns loaded with war ammunition will, of course!

Armed patrols of East German border guards can emerge from the misty background anywhere at any time. They patrol incessantly, while those large beams of light continually shine through the misty strands across the entire border area. When someone is caught attempting to flee, no mercy is to be expected either. The border gendarmes of East Germany are unequivocally briefed in this regard: all those who want to flee to the West are allowed by the communist regime to be shot immediately on the spot, without any warning and without any excuse. *Schiesbefell*** is what this is called. The border guards on the East German side already experienced it as part of their regular day's work, to remove from the barbed wire at dawn some bullet-riddled and bloody bodies of a few unfortunate people. They

---

Apparently, during the "Cold War" between 1949 and 1989, for every fifteen East German citizens, at least one person was active as a spy for the SED Communist Party.
**A formal shooting order on refugees did not come until 1952, but even in the preceding years most refugees were shot without question.*

also have to watch their own backs, because they have undermined the entire border strip themselves. Often the border guards also find the remains of dead deer and wild boar that have walked over a landmine. But very often there are also the lifeless bodies of people who did not make it to the West. Men, women, children ... no one is spared. Those who manage to slip through the barbed wire, however, should not be too quick to assume that they have already made it. Bullets fired from East German territory do, of course, easily cross the border and are still deadly over a long distance in *West* Germany. Many refugees who have overcome the double row of barbed wire and have already crossed the border, are often still fatally hit in the back at a moment when, in their uplifting euphoria, they already promptly begin to cheer. A little too soon they think they have reached the promised free land. On the western side of the border, too, bodies are often removed of unfortunate people who had managed to escape, but were still shot in the back ...

1946. A border patrol conducted by an East German army force does not leave much to the imagination. (Bundesarchiv - Wikimedia Commons)

Elsbeth Zimmermann had fled Tilsit just over four years ago, in January 1945, just in time for the Russians. Now she no longer flees from murderous Soviet soldiers and from the war, but from a rigid and deadly regime. In the meantime, she has become a sturdy young woman in her thirties who knows that life isn't fair. On this bleak and chilly night, she and fourteen others are sitting in the back of the rattling truck. Tonight, she is one of the new candidate refugees too. She is very tense, and you can read the fear in her eyes. Despite the fact that she has had to endure a lot of human suffering in recent years and has had to deal with severe setbacks on a personal level, she has managed to pull through so far quite well.

She has also come out of this difficult period much stronger as a person. A few years ago, she was completely on her own and she also had a son with awfully bad eyes to take care of. So, she was forced to deal with the unpleasant situation, but also to look further ahead for better opportunities for herself and little Joachim. But now, at this very decisive moment, she is afraid, very, very much afraid! She is trembling and shivering all over her body. It is indeed freezing outside because of that icy fog, but those cold shivers are more the result of the feverish and highly unbearable tension that currently reigns in the back of the truck. Elsbeth is well aware of the dangerous situation she is in all of her own accord. Not that she is so much afraid for herself, because she could have been killed several times during the past war years, but especially for her five-year-old son who will have to flee together with her. And that little one will soon literally have to run for his life. And he will have to do that alone. She constantly wonders:

*"Will my little Joachim make it? Will he understand what is being whispered in his ears? What will he do when perhaps a strong beam of light suddenly shines into those hypersensitive eyes of his? And suppose he **does** make it through, but I **don't**? Who will take care of him then?"*

Elsbeth looks around and her soft, yet clearly worried gaze crosses that of her younger sister Ida, who is also in the back of the truck and will flee with them. Elsbeth suddenly needs a little support in these tense moments. With pleading eyes, but also confidently, she looks straight at her sister. Ida knows exactly what Elsbeth means by this, and she nods her head, smiling gently. *"It's OK, it'll be all right!"* seems to be what Ida means. Elsbeth feels reassured by Ida's nodding. After all, Ida had promised to always take care of Joachim if anything happened to Elsbeth.

She' s completely confident again now and is convincing herself this is all in the interest of her son ...

Obere Weiße in Arnstadt. Joachim and his friend Gerd in their Tiroler Hose, *just before Elsbeth and Joachim's flight through the barbed wire from East to West.*

On her way to the scary crossing at the East-West border, Elsbeth tries to suppress her fear by thinking of totally different things. In her mind she sees the long horror movie of the turbulent last years flashing by once again ...

Lost and deserted she arrived with her nine-month-old son totally bewildered in Arnstadt in the early spring of 1945. Fortunately, she was taken care of there and she is eternally grateful to the Kranz family for this. She was also lucky enough to end up in the American zone ... for a brief time, however, because the Russians took over from the Americans there in the end. Life under the tight communist regime had not been easy either. But they had a roof over their heads, and they had food, just enough basic necessities to live or survive. That was their guarantee and even though life under Russian occupation was awfully hard, it was much better than the uncertain situation during the war years themselves. But as Germans they were constantly watched by the Russians. People constantly had the feeling that they were walking on eggshells everywhere and were followed in all their doings ...

Elsbeth Zimmermann's thoughts go back for a moment to that generous Kranz family. They themselves had lost everything during the war and yet they still found the space to give her and Joachim shelter. Those good people had really been guardian angels for the two of them there in Arnstadt for about four years. She and Joachim had to say goodbye to them just now in a very emotionally charged moment. Many tears were shed when Fraulein Kranz received a heartfelt hug from five-year-old Joachim. Possibly that farewell is for good. The generous Frau Kranz realized during that emotional moment that she would probably never see the boy again. After the earlier loss of one of her relatives during the war, she again felt that something special was being snatched from her life here. But she did realize that the choice made here was primarily for the future prospects of the little boy ...

Elsbeth's thoughts go back even further in these difficult moments. Even further than to that extremely dangerous period of the spring in 1945. She realizes how peaceful life had once been in the rural surroundings of Tilsit, East Prussia, long before the bloody and all-destroying war broke out.

Despite the fact that this region had been the center of all kinds of war scenes several times in the past, and that it had become a real ethnic mix, it was all in all a beautiful, peaceful place on Mother Earth privileged by God. Green pastures with lots of healthy grazing cattle all over the Baltic countryside and farmhouses scattered all over the picturesque landscape. There were large fields completely covered by sunflowers, and thousands of beautiful tuberous plants stood in the gardens nicely bordered with wooden posts. The Baltic Sea was teeming with jumping whales, and the many amber brown stones washed up on the sandy beaches were the best evidence of this. It looked like a fairytale land, and you constantly had the impression that you were walking through a medieval painting in East Prussia, where time had stood still ... until that G.D. World War broke out and the murderous gunpowder came to tickle people's nostrils there too. Again, the people there felt plenty of fear, because they knew that Adolf Hitler's ambitions would not be limited to the occupation of Poland, just to open a corridor through Danzig to the ancient German cities like Königsbergen, Tilsit and Memel. Elsbeth had also personally witnessed in the spring of 1941 that in the region where she lived, entire German armies with highly motivated *Wehrmacht* and fanatical SS soldiers advanced during Operation Barbarossa to the Soviet Union to fight their ideological opponent: communism. To typical German marching music such as *Oh, Du schöner Westerwald, Ob's stürmt oder schneit* and *Drei Lilien* they moved forward with motivation under the cover of their heavy *Pantzers*. The Russians would be defeated before the winter and the fighters were absolutely sure of that…

Four years later, however, a completely different scenario was unfolding. Head over heels, she had just managed to flee from the Russians, who in turn went to attack in January 1945. Oh My God! Life can be so indescribably hard and unjust. Throughout history, her maternal ancestors had also been able to confirm this. After all, she herself was of French-Austrian Huguenot origin and her ancestors had also fled beautiful France many generations ago.

At least ... the few of them who could still flee back then. Perils of religion and all kinds of struggles, ranging from far-reaching intolerance via pure hatred to the irresistible urge to murder as many dissidents as possible, had made many French fanatical and Puritan Christian believers take up arms. They would gladly silence all those excessive "heretics" once and for all. Bartholomew's Night is therefore in the history of the Huguenots a painfully memorable day. All Huguenots were massively persecuted, chased out of their homes and bluntly murdered in the streets for months from that very night on, while no authority wanted to intervene, and no form of justice could prevent it. Many Huguenots, in their fear, jumped into the rivers, hoping to escape that way, but there too they were pursued by cowardly murderers "in the name of God". Operating from small boats, they held the Huguenots, who were begging for help, under water until they drowned, or they mercilessly hacked at them with all possible weapons such as knives, swords and whatever they could lay their hands on. The Seine, the Rhône, and the Saône in France colored red with their blood. For a long time after the events, the corpses floated by the hundreds in the filthy river water. The Zimmermann family had been hunted all the way to the very hospitable and gentle East Prussia. Generation after generation, this horrible story made it into the family lore and each time it was passed on to the growing offspring that they should always remember this. They would remember that cursed day of Saint Bartholomew every year. Silently anyway, for the sake of safety ...

Elsbeth met a certain Fritz Krauledaitis in Tilsit, who in turn had come from Lithuania to this same worry-free East Prussian enclave. They married in the summer of 1943 and during a brief period of leave from her husband, Elsbeth became pregnant. It all looked so promising, until the country was destroyed by heavy artillery and the green, fertile meadows of that part of the Baltic plain were bulldozed by heavy tanks and hot-tempered, vengeful Russian soldiers ... Where has that time gone and what will the future bring us? And is there any future at all, or are we about to come up against murderous machine gun fire?

... An abrupt swerve of the plodding truck suddenly wakes Elsbeth brutally from her horrible daydream. Through the misty haze, she hears the sharp steam whistle of a heavy locomotive in the distance. That train is standing over there on the other side of the barbed wire, evidently ready to steam off in the direction of Kassel. She realizes that now is really not the time to bring up all those things from the past. She would do well to focus more on what is about to happen now. Furthermore, like everyone else, she hopes that she won't have to sit in this truck for too long. The cold in the back of the truck is becoming unbearable and little Joachim also has a cold, which irritates the other refugees immensely. Everyone is again asked to remain quiet. Elsbeth's son Joachim continues to do nothing but cough and that is starting to get on the nerves of the guide.

Little five-year-old Joachim sits a bit huddled up next to his mom in the trunk. He is carrying a small backpack with some insignificant things in it. There are some ordinary, everyday things in it like socks and some underwear. But in that small backpack, there is also a tiny little box and in that box is a valuable object with an extremely high emotional value: the golden ring* of his father Fritz. That ring is meant for him and Elsbeth deliberately puts it in his backpack in case something goes wrong with *her* during the crossing. It is the only tangible object that Joachim has of his father, apart from a few somewhat already yellowed photographs.

Given his tender age, Joachim doesn't really realize what's going on. So, he still just sees this extremely uncomfortable trip with that bumpy truck as an exciting game. *"We are going on a very special ride late tonight,"* his mother had told him this afternoon. She hadn't told him more, because she was afraid, he would tell on. He himself, by the way, does not fully realize why this bizarre "game" has to happen in complete darkness, while they sit in the truck freezing from the cold ...

For him, there is also another, much deeper reason why he cannot really consciously experience this bizarre adventure with that truck. The little boy experiences this whole adventure almost purely by ear.

---

* At 77, John Kay is still wearing that golden ring.

Indeed, he has terribly bad eyes. His vision is so limited that he can hardly distinguish things, even at a small distance. On top of that, the little fellow cannot tolerate any light and is always somewhat relieved when the sun disappears behind the horizon at night.

All kinds of eye problems were diagnosed not long after his birth, when he sat in his little baby carriage screaming at everyone and everything, every time even a pale ray of sunshine shone into his eyes for a brief moment. The diagnosis of the pediatrician in Erfurt was ultimately harsh:

"Frau Zimmermann, es tut Mir Leit, but your little son is suffering from a very severe form of Achromatopsia."

What a terrible diagnosis! It is determined that he is essentially 100% color blind, and, in addition, little Joachim is very short-sighted and hypersensitive to all sunlight or artificial light. The serious eye condition from which he has apparently been suffering since birth, understandably brings with it a great deal of practical inconvenience. He sees things on this globe only in a variety of shades of gray. Furthermore, the range of his visual acuity is set at only 10 to 20 percent of what an average person with normal eyes can see. According to the standards of the health service, this even classifies him as being "legally" blind. In practice fortunately, he is not, but the ophthalmologist in Erfurt assumes -and fears- that in time he may well become completely blind if his diet is not drastically improved.

While explaining Joachim's problem, the ophthalmologist in Erfurt made it clear to Elsbeth that there was really only one possibility for Joachim to improve his condition. Does she really want better medical care for her little son? Well, then she could only do one thing: flee with him "to the other side."

He did not utter those words, for such a thing was dangerous because of the many shady characters sent out by the East German regime as snitches everywhere. So, he only gave a wink, while drawing a large semicircle through the air with his right index finger. What he meant exactly was quite simple:

"Best you can do, is to make your way from THIS Germany into THAT OTHER and better Germany!"

Elsbeth largely blames herself for her son's vision problem. The stress of war, losing her husband, a lack of proper and sufficient nutrition before and during pregnancy. To alleviate the problem with his hypersensitive eyes, the ophthalmologist advises Elsbeth to have Joachim wear dark glasses during the day. Therefore, those heavy glasses are always on his nose on doctor's orders. Now that it is completely dark outside, he has put the glasses in his backpack with his father's ring, together with a few other items.

Joachim's future and his state of health are the main reasons why Elsbeth makes this risky crossing. Her own sister Inge already lives in West Germany, and it turns out that there are some very good ophthalmologists practicing in the region there. Moreover, it seems that in that free Germany there is also more opportunity for a much more varied diet. Apparently, they don't eat herring twice a day with turnips, heavily seasoned with *Kummel* to give it all some flavor, like the people there in Arnstadt. Possibly, a better-balanced diet will eventually benefit his myopia ...

They are getting closer to the East-West border now. The guide can already clearly see the barbed wire fences and halts the truck at a sufficient distance. To go any further would be too dangerous because the East-German *Grenzpolizei* are patrolling all the time.

The location where they will soon attempt the transition, fortunately seems deserted.

The border guide once again orders everyone to be completely quiet and just when he is repeating this for the umpteenth time, Joachim suddenly starts coughing again. The people become acrimonious, for they are afraid that this will betray them. Suddenly they hear the dry barking of automatic machine gun fire somewhere nearby. It seems as they are not the only ones venturing out this evening. The guide tells them that another group of people, consisting mainly of men, a little further on will also attempt to cross. That might be their luck, because it will possibly cause confusion among the border guards. Their own group of fifteen people, mostly consisting of women and children, will try a more difficult yet seemingly slightly safer route. With their hearts pounding, Elsbeth and Joachim arrive at the barbed wire, and both are urged to hurry immediately. Doubts, however, take hold of several candidate refugees. In front of them there is nothing but a gaping darkness and no point of reference to focus on. Moreover, the machine gun fire nearby makes a huge impression on them. But the guide is formal! No more time to think about it now!

"Going back is not an option now, dammit!!! Get down and crawl!!!"

As the guide holds up the barbed wire, Joachim spontaneously throws himself on the damp chilly ground to crawl under it. Says the guide to five-year-old Joachim:

"This is no game, boy! If you really want to get to the other side, then you run like hell! And keep your head down as deep as you can, because if the border guards see you, they will shoot you down."*

Beams of light once again scour the entire area. Elsbeth is still afraid that a sudden strong burst of light in Joachim's eyes could cause the little boy to panic. He is urged to move forward more quickly.

Joachim obeys and crawls flat on his belly under the barbed wire that is being pulled up grimly by the guide. He coughs again, which once again exasperates the others. He keeps his head down, but the backpack is too high. It gets caught in the barbed wire. The grim-faced guide, with trembling hands, immediately intervenes. Joachim wriggles further under the barbed wire and slips through:

"Nur verswinden! Sofort!!!" ("Now, get the hell out of here!!!")

Joachim has resolved to run as fast as he can with his short little legs.

---

* *From the song* Renegade, *Steppenwolf Album* Seven.

He doesn't look back, but he knows he is safe because he hears the encouragement of his mother Elsbeth and Aunt Ida who are following him closely. Again, they hear machine gun fire in the immediate vicinity. They run with all their might ... 5 meters ... 10 meters ... It is pitch dark and still there is that fear of being hit in the back ... 15 meters ... 20 meters ... The foggy, freezing air hurts Joachim's throat and lungs.

They are all out of breath, but they must keep running. It's all or nothing now! They can still get a volley of deadly bullets in the back. They have to give it all for another twenty-five meters until they reach a small slope. There they can take shelter for a while and catch their breath first. Completely drowsy, emotional and tired, all three of them fall down behind the raised grass verge. A few more persons immediately follow in their tracks. Again, machine guns are barking in the immediate vicinity. Still, it is best to stay behind this slope for a while! They have to recover from the exertion, the stress and the fears expressed.

"We are through. God how is it possible? We made it!"

A few more gunshots sound, but now a little further away from where they are sitting.

However, when they want to move on after a few minutes, they make a grim observation.* They see that of those fifteen people of their party, only six have made it up here. What happened to the others? Did they end up elsewhere or were they all shot? The darkness and the fear of being caught prevent them from looking around.

Once they have caught their breath the little group moves. They made it, but there is certainly no euphoric joy. Their group is more than halved and they are quite sure that some others have paid with their lives for their attempt to escape. They say a quick prayer for

---

* *In an interview with John Kay in a hotel in Mechelen for Belgian magazine HUMO on 23 May 1969, John stated that of the fifteen persons who fled, nine had been shot. However, I have not been able to have this statement confirmed by any source.*

those who stay behind. It could just as easily have been one of them. On the one hand, they are grateful for having made it. On the other hand, they are extremely sad about what possibly happened to the others. The remaining refugees, including Ida, Elsbeth and Joachim, can board a steam train that will take them to a relief camp a little further down the road. Once there, they are given a jug of warm milk and assigned a place to sleep for one night. Motivated volunteers immediately take care of them, and it is clearly noticeable that they are very passionate about helping the new refugees as best as possible. Immediately, the necessary registration documents are drawn up, so that they can instantly consider themselves *West* German citizens. Elsbeth even receives a small amount of money in *Deutschmark*. The solidarity among the people, refugees and supporters is indeed remarkably high. Probably, this is because they are acutely aware of the situation they are coming from. The first step has been taken, but it is of course not the intention to stay very long in that refugee camp. Elsbeth immediately wants to search for relatives who live somewhere in the wide area around Hannover. In addition, she has to look for work and therefore she moves on immediately.

She brings her little son Joachim for a few days to a small town called Westkirchen, where her sister Inge already lives. Aunt Inge will kindly pamper Joachim for a few days, while Elsbeth will take care of all the necessary administrative formalities. Moreover, she must also first find a place to live with Joachim. Elsbeth has promised Joachim that it will only be for a few days, but of course the little boy is not entirely comfortable with that.

Inge is truly kind to Joachim, but nevertheless Joachim has the feeling of a toddler going to kindergarten for the first time and seeing his mommy leave. He is very crestfallen and thinks that he will not see her again.

Because she is well trained as a tailor-seamstress, Elsbeth easily finds work in the garment industry in Hannover. The re-emerging economy in West Germany also quietly increases the demand for slightly better and more expensive "fashion" clothing for women. Elsbeth

Lightly armed East German patrol on foot. (Bundesarchiv/Wikimedia Commons)

finds her calling and immediately sets to work full of enthusiasm. She finds a place to stay in Kronenstrasse, in a building that had been partly vacated because of damage to the roof caused by the bombings a few years ago. From her bedroom, she can even see some swaying trees through a small hole in the wall. But it turns out to be safe and so for her this is quite suitable. Once she has arranged all that, she returns to Westkirchen to pick up her son Joachim and together they move into that small flat on the third floor in Kronenstrasse. Compared to the situation some time ago, this looks like paradise. Repairing the hole in the roof can wait …

Joachim, who since his birth about five years ago had never seen his mother even a single step away from his side, is immensely relieved when he is reunited with her. She had only been away for a few days, but to him that seemed like eternity. Elsbeth had used her *Deutschmark* to buy him some nice presents to amuse himself in his unknown environment: a big hunk of modeling clay, a drawing book, some pencils and a series of coloring crayons. Although he is almost completely color blind, Joachim is delighted. All those different "gray tinted" colors are really genuinely nice. Joachim amuses himself all the time with his fun toys. He colors the drawn figures beautifully. Sometimes he stops for a moment. Then he puts the colors aside and starts to vocally express his enormous happiness to his mother repeatedly. Then he begins to turn a few rounds of joy at the kitchen table, while constantly singing a homemade tune:

"Ich habe meine Mutti zurück ... Ich habe meine liebe Mutti zurück!"
("I have my mother back ... I have my dear mother back!")

In which, while hopping each time, he makes two steps on one leg and then two on the other. After each "run" through the living space he sits back at the table, out of breath, and diligently continues to scribble in his notebook. Elsbeth smiles at him when she sees how happy he is. She feels happy at the sight of Joachim's spontaneous expressions of child happiness ...

On Christmas Eve of that tipping year 1949, Joachim's mother Elsbeth can finally enjoy a well-deserved moment of rest. What she has achieved by then has literally cost blood, sweat and tears. But they are firmly convinced that it will all be worthwhile.

Here, together with her son, she can build a really full life. Elsbeth herself is incredibly grateful to the Lord for this, but on the other hand she misses her deceased husband more than ever, whom she would have liked to have at her side. She prays very often, and every evening when she is alone in her bed, she still thinks of Fritz. Her handkerchief lies all wet on her night table every morning. But the end of the year 1949 is a milestone in their existence. Elsbeth and Joachim experience a unique Christmas.

For Elsbeth this is also a real, warm-hearted Christmas; one as described by the message from God. Happiness and peace reign in this small place. Joachim is also happy to have his mother with him again and with all his nice toys. Elsbeth Zimmermann can experience her first peaceful Christmas since 1938, exactly eleven years ago today, when all the commotion began in East Prussia and peace was hard to find ...

Elsbeth and Joachim

*35/37 Kronenstrasse Hannover. The arrow points to Elsbeth's apartment.
(Photo Thorsten Möser)*

Between the Ruins in Hannover

"When I was in Hannover, I listened to the American Forces Network, and I heard among others Bill Haley and Little Richard. While I became a big Rock & Roll fan, I dreamed I could one day be in America, learning how to speak English and playing this kind of music. It was nothing but a fantasy ..."

For East German citizens, after 1949, it becomes totally impossible to flee to the West to build a new life. Elsbeth Zimmermann and Joachim Krauledat were able to flee just in time. The border became increasingly protected and from 1952 everything was hermetically sealed off. Double rows of barbed wire line the entire border and more wooden towers with floodlights and machine guns are built. According to the new East German authorities, that border is being fortified to deny Western terrorists access to their zone. Also in Berlin, the barricades between the Western zone and the Russian zone are being reinforced. The Berlin blockade drives the chilly hostilities between East and West to the highest possible level. Espionage activities increase and there is constant harassment from both sides. Americans are no longer seen as occupation forces in West Germany, but as protection. They are doing their best to familiarize those West Germans with their lifestyle ...

By the end of the 1940s, Germany still had that heavy moral legacy to carry because of what Nazism had done to the entire world and to all humanity. The main culprits for the cataclysm in Europe were called to account in Nuremberg in 1945 and most of the leading figures with a heavy criminal war record were executed. At least those who were still alive at the time and had not committed suicide or to the extent that they had not run away. Many would indeed smuggle themselves out of the country with a false identity, often stolen from a deceased compatriot, to get asylum somewhere in Spain or Latin America or to go into hiding for good.

Meanwhile in 1949, Elsbeth and Joachim secured a 460 square feet spacious place in the center of Hannover, on the Leine River. The city lies in the middle of a region where agriculture is thriving thanks to its vast, fertile fields. Even if they managed to cross over from East to West just in time, Elsbeth understands very well that she, her sister Ida, and little son Joachim were extremely lucky the night they escaped. And even though in West Germany the inhabitants today consider themselves lucky to live under a freer regime, the aftereffects of the war are still making themselves felt there too.

By the spring of 1945, Hannover, like most other cities in Germany, had taken in a great many refugees. But because those refugees could not (or were not allowed to) return home, they had helped to clean up the rubble and remove the bodies of the many victims. Yet people everywhere are gradually becoming aware that they must get on with their lives. There is no point in mourning forever about things that, by definition, are all perishable eventually anyway. The slogan "Roll up your sleeves, get back to work and build something up" seems to be catching on in Germany, shot and bombed to pieces.

Hannover, like almost all other German cities, suffered enormously towards the end of the war. By the end of December 1944, in fact, that city was also explicitly targeted by American and British heavy bombers.

The reason for this is not so well known by the public today, but in and around the entire railway network of Hannover, there were thousands of barrels of synthetically prepared gasoline ready to support the Ardennes offensive of Adolf Hitler's armored forces in Belgium and Luxembourg. (In the USA better known as "the Battle of the Bulge"). This fuel was truly indispensable for the advancing German Tiger IV tanks that had to make their way through the Ardennes snow, to recapture the port of Antwerp as quickly as possible. Everything was already neatly loaded onto the train wagons and was ready to leave in the direction of the Belgian region of Malmédy and Bastogne. The Allies, however, had gotten wind of this planned German supply and immediately put in a devastating air fleet. The entire area around Hannover was as good as wiped out. Hitler's offensive was spontaneously halted in Belgium on the Hotton/La Gleize/Houffalize line in mid-January 1945, and the main cause of the German fiasco in January 1945 was ... an acute lack of fuel for the heavy German armor ...

Germans are by definition certainly very energetic people, and despite all the setbacks and that heavy moral legacy they had to carry with them, they never stay idle for a long time. The country literally and figuratively crawls out from under the rubble and miraculously begins an unprecedented reconstruction. After a few years, the financial and economic recovery across Western Europe reaches cruising speed. Of course, people partly owe this recovery to themselves and to their own efforts, but also to the successful Marshall Plan which, from 1949 on, enables Europe to gradually rebuild everything thanks to generous support in American dollars. American investments quickly put the economy back on track and stock markets recover. The open market economy in the West and the hard work, are paying off. Steel and automobile industries are booming and German state symbols with trademarks such as the automobile manufacturers Mercedes-Benz and Volkswagen and the chemical giant Bayer are soon in an incredibly positive upward spiral.

All of Eastern Europe, on the other hand, now falls under the sphere of influence of the Soviet Union. This planned economy, which arises from the basic principle of communism, is at odds with western principles.
    The system of planned economy is -by nature- "rational" and leaves no room for deeper development in which the principle of supply and demand would drive up profits ... and a deeper desire of working harder. Competition on the production lines or tradable market shares, are taboo. Such a thing is always called "capitalism" and that is precisely what communism is against. This communist system is

-in its totality- in a sense quite generous to the population in general. Meaning that this regime will protect all inhabitants behind the Iron Curtain from famine, and a roof over their heads will be guaranteed for everybody. Health care is also widely accessible to everyone, but sometimes the material facilities to support health care are insufficient. The regime's ambitions do not extend much further. Everywhere long rows of tiny apartments rise from the ground, and in the bigger cities the apartment buildings are separated by extremely wide boulevards. Along these broad avenues, on May 1 each year, Labor Day, the Communist regime displays the huge and powerful arsenal of Eastern Bloc weapons. But while behind that Iron Curtain there are major investments in war material, the food shelves in the stores for basic products other than bread or potatoes, are more often empty than stacked. People in Eastern Europe soon get used to it. People with a healthy motivation to work, will also quickly realize that this planned economy offers no prospects for real progress, a further development of the lifestyle and a wider spreading prosperity. By definition, the communist system does not really lend itself to *Germans*, for they are traditionally regarded as hard workers who want to move forward. (No matter what that -extremely cowardly- butchering *Rote Armée Fraction* socialism fanatically dared to declare later in the 1970s.) In that sense, Germans had all worked their asses off up until right before the war, but a little later they had just as grandiosely erred in the promises of their *Führer*.

And now they are experiencing something they are not used to as Germans. Motivated workers in East Germany see the same (meager) amount appear on their paychecks every month as the people who are barely able or willing to lift a finger. Working overtime or putting in vigorous efforts to get ahead in life, does not help the average man in the street one little bit.

However, there is sometimes an outlet for people with talents in sports. They get the chance to build a better life through sport, but later on it will turn out that the athletes have been puppets of the regime during the entire East German GDR period. They are systematically given necessary stimulating "potions and pills" to deliver top performances at world's highest level. Women in sport are administered male hormones on a grand scale in order to boost their performance, which means that they do indeed perform, but that they grow a male beard, and their monthly periods stay away for good. But they win medals at the world championships or the Olympic Games and are the ideal showcase for their own regime. Moreover, the people in the GDR and the other communist countries eventually find out that the top members of their own communist party, who want to convey the philosophy of communism to all citizens by all possible means, are all too happy to make an exception *for themselves* to their own austerity rules. All this in order to give themselves an ample advantage on a material level. Even though in Eastern Europe, too, the rubble is being cleared away to make way for long rows of flats, this "calculated progress," as was to be expected, eventually shoots itself in the foot in the late 1980s in all European countries lead by communists.

So, in Western Europe, the economy bubbles up all over from 1949 on, and people once again see the future as bright. The other side of the coin, however, is that the West Germans are becoming increasingly alienated from their former fellow compatriots: the East Germans. Almost every German experiences that the deep sense of solidarity which existed at the beginning between East and West, continues to diminish over the years.

Where families are no longer scattered along both sides of the border, the sense of belonging indeed fades.

Eventually, some even consider those "other" Germans strangers, notwithstanding that they speak the same language and often have the same ancestry, traditions and customs ...

But after 1949 there is professional activity in all of Germany, both East and West. Factories are operating at full capacity and agriculture is looking for new ways to increase harvests. But again, much more than in the East (where streets in some places, except for the big cities, are getting ever more gray), new houses and skyscrapers are springing up everywhere in the West. Major renovations of existing buildings that are still salvageable, continue uninterrupted ...

Also, in Kronenstrasse in Hannover, work is in full swing today. The necessary maintenance work is (finally) being done on the apartment building at number 35/37, in which Joachim and his mother now have been living for a few years. The gaping hole at the top of the facade is being closed and the structure of the entire building is being thoroughly renovated. Seeing the trees sway through that hole will soon be a thing of the past. In the garden behind the flats where they live, also some smaller outbuildings are erected. These will serve as garages or as extra storage space for gardening equipment or other tools.

According to Elsbeth Zimmermann, there is a very friendly and gentle man among all those casual laborers doing the necessary repair work there in Kronenstrasse. That man, Gerhard Kyczinski is his name, stayed in a Russian prisoner of war camp for more than five years during the war. He was not released until several years *after* the war. His life experience and time in the camps under extremely difficult conditions taught him that he should thank heaven for every day that follows his release from that camp. Elsbeth is somewhat curious about the exciting stories that this kind and helpful Mr Kyczinski has to tell.

Subconsciously, she increasingly feels the need to listen to him more and over and over again. She certainly does that because she likes to hear him talk about his experiences. But another reason is that she wants to get more of a feeling *for* and connection *with* her husband Fritz's time during the war. She listens attentively to Gerhard's experiences and as a result of his spontaneous expression of warm sympathy towards her, Elsbeth feels herself slowly reviving. Instinctively, she feels more like a "woman" again and she no longer sees herself exclusively as "Joachim's mother". For many years, she had not had these deeply feminine feelings and *if* she had them, even for just a moment, she had -consciously or unconsciously- flagrantly ignored or hidden them. Somehow, she feels guilty because she longs for some affection again, but she is firmly convinced that the spirit of her deceased husband Fritz understands her completely and that he even supports her fully in this. After all, she is far too young to remain alone. Besides, Mr Kyczinski is a very gentle, charming man and he is the first and only person who has been able to make her laugh again since that cursed day in the spring of 1944, when she received the disruptive news of her husband's death.

In 1950, Elsbeth marries again, and she becomes Mrs Zimmermann-Kyczinski. Joachim, now six years old, gets a stepfather. This helpful and nice Herr Gerhard Kyczinski promises Joachim, right away, that he will never try to replace his real father, Fritz Krauledat. Even though Joachim has never seen or known his own father. A promise that Mr Kyczinski will also keep*.

Joachim is now going through elementary school in Hannover. The educational system in West Germany in those years is certainly not yet running under optimal conditions. Due to the chronic lack of a solid infrastructure everywhere, education is given in "shifts" in most places. Sometimes an early shift until a little after noon, followed by a shift that lasts well into the early evening. Forty to forty-five students in one class is more the norm rather than the exception. Joachim does not like to go to school, however.

His grades are very disappointing in all subjects, much to his mother's annoyance and concern. She fears for his future if he does not improve. There are a few different reasons for his poor grades at school. It is not so much lack of intelligence, knowledge or insight, which is somewhat of a relief for his mother. It is more that he cannot focus too well on the things written on the blackboard, because he cannot properly read them as a consequence of his bad eyes. The teachers therefore put him at the very front of the first row, but that doesn't change the situation at all. At the slightest reflection of light on the blackboard, his vision becomes almost nil. Moreover, he hardly dares to ask the teacher to clarify things, because other fellow pupils think Joachim is acting terribly ridiculous. He is therefore not taken seriously by his classmates and peers. Therefore, he is often the center of other children's teasing. Because of the overcrowded classes and the large numbers of students, the teachers do not always notice this

---

* *Joachim has been very grateful to him for that throughout his life.*

immediately. Children can be hard on each other, and they often make fun of someone's physical imperfections. Joachim does indeed have some of these physical imperfections and the severe bullying at school he suffers becomes almost a daily occurrence. His fellow pupils do not see the real need for those peculiar little glasses with the thick, round and dark lenses. Wearing glasses, that's as far as it goes, but this? They are completely unable to understand how light-sensitive his eyes are. The fact that the teacher always lets him sit in the first row, causes even more annoyance with his classmates, who think he is being given preferential treatment. He is not only teased about his bad eyes, but also about the fact that he has no father and that he never knew him either. Moreover, he is laughed at because his mother Elsbeth is forced to pick him up personally every day after school. Overall, there are few favorable stimuli to boost his school results.

Joachim is always happy on Sundays, because there is no school. Then the boys can have fun in the dilapidated houses on the outskirts of Hannover. No one worries about the children playing there among the otherwise very unstable ruins.

All around the city center there are remnants of bombed-out houses and old apartment buildings, the rubble of which has still not been cleared. It is downright dangerous to be there or to play there, but the clearing services that have yet to remove the debris, clearly do not consider this an absolute priority. Large concrete chunks are sometimes breaking loose from the damaged buildings. In some basements there are even still crates full of grenades that were used by the elderly *Volkssturmers* to eliminate American and British tanks. There are some signs hanging near the ruins that say *Gefahr, nicht eintreten*. But those signs work like a red rag on a bull with the children, because that danger is an additional challenge for the boys. Playing hide and seek between all those dangerously overhanging ruins is therefore by definition a lot of fun. But Joachim is invariably the bad guy in this game, because his poor eyesight means he can hardly ever find anyone hiding among the ruins. Sometimes, someone gives him a sudden push in the back and then he often does not even know who gave him that push. But he gradually learns to get rid of it and when he can remember with certainty someone who has somewhat assaulted him, he somehow takes revenge for the moral and physical damage suffered. He always finds a rusty nail among the rubble so he can use it to secretly puncture someone's bicycle tires.

From the walls of the dilapidated houses, the boys sometimes cut loose the water pipes. Turns out that they sometimes have a layer of copper in them. Nearby lives an iron and scrap dealer who pays them with a smile a few *Pfennig* for each meter of copper pipe they bring to him. Besides playing war and hide-and-seek between the houses that have been ruined, there is also plenty of soccer in the open spaces between the houses. Goals are marked on brick or concrete walls with a piece of chalk. West Germany becomes *Fussbal Weltmeister* in 1954 and the boys also experience this intensely. The West Germans beat soccer favorite Hungary, with great celebrities like Kocsis, Kubala and Puskás, in the final by three to two and that final is played over and over again between the ruins. Joachim, however, is not taken very seriously when he plays soccer.

Fortunately, he is still allowed by the others to play soccer with them, because his bad eyes allow them … to dribble past him very easily. To them, it seems as if Joachim is not even there, and their ironic laughter is present all the time. After each match there are also a few penalty kicks. Everyone gets a turn and Joachim gets to kick his eleven-meter shot as well. One day, when it is his turn to take a penalty kick, some of the boys start grinning in advance. An insidious villain has replaced the ball with a white block of concrete. It will be fun, tough that visually impaired Joachim can't see the difference The boys are already sniggering when Joachim makes his run in all ignorance …

He kicks as hard as he can. But instead of shouting *TOR* (goal) out loud, he screams out in pain one second later, much to the delight of the others. Limping on one leg and moaning in pain, he stumbles home with a bloody and swollen foot and torn toenails. Sobbing profusely from the pain and furious at the narrow-minded cowardice of his friends, he complains to his mother.

For Elsbeth it has been enough. She removes Joachim immediately from the local school with all those cowardly bastards and she lets him go to the somewhat elitist Waldorf Institute. Even though there is a rather long waiting period to get admitted to that school and it is quite expensive, Elsbeth manages to get Joachim registered very soon. Fortunately, they understand his situation and want to support him in his further education.

The *Waldorfschule* will be a true revelation for the boy. The way of teaching is totally different there. Instead of imposing a total package of learning material on a whole class, each person's individual talents are explored. The system can be compared to the (Belgian) Freinet Systems.

The Waldorf School also places great emphasis on understanding and patience. It is not surprising that this school had been closed earlier during the Nazi regime, precisely because far-reaching mutual tolerance was preached by them. Under the Nazis there was indeed only one rule and that was based on maximizing the distinction between the races. The emphasis was more on the maximum diabolizing of other races and cultures, with the corresponding philosophy in which the physically weak were discarded with rather than helped. In total contradiction with the philosophy the Waldorf School wants to display ...

Joachim finally fully blossoms there. His introverted traits -an automatic consequence of his insecurity- gradually ebb away and the boy grows more self-confident. Moreover, he is no longer "wanted," and the bullying eventually vanishes. He finally starts liking going to school and the results are impressive. He also likes the fact that he doesn't have to focus exclusively on the theoretical subject matter, but that he also gets ample opportunity to show off his practical talents. Boys and girls sit together, and it is assumed that boys also do typical girl things, like knitting a scarf or sewing on buttons. Girls are also allowed to do all kinds of fun crafts; something that by definition is almost exclusively done by boys. He sees that he is respected by his peers and that that respect is mutual. So, he learns from an early age to be broad-minded and tolerant towards others; something that will stay with him for the rest of his life. So, Joachim becomes friends with a very resourceful and handy schoolmate. A boy who is highly creative and who manages to turn just about anything he lays his hands on -in a manner of speaking- into pure gold.

One day, with the help of a small cigar box, a few decimeters of copper wire and a few lamps, that clever boy is able to resourcefully design a "long-wave" radio set. He removed the tiny speakers from an old army headset he had received from an American soldier, and, to everyone's surprise, he was suddenly able to receive a range of radio stations via a self-developed turning knob that he mounted on the wooden box. So, the children can listen to some music and all the publicity messages. They can also listen extensively to the American news bulletins. Despite his lack of English, Joachim learns some English expressions. That way, he is already getting a vague initiation into American politics in general and from the age of twelve, politics will play an important background role in his life.

Now there is also time to soak up some culture. One evening Elsbeth takes her son Joachim to the local theater. Not to attend a play, but to watch and especially *listen* to a Russian Cossack choir on tour. The bizarre attire in which these men perform, coupled with the passion and total abandon with which the choir conveys the music to the audience, leaves a deep impression on Joachim. He becomes completely overwhelmed by the whole event. Even though none of the people present understands a word of Russian, they are all so moved by the intensity of the whole event that everyone in the room reacts very emotionally. Elsbeth does not see it, but behind the thick dark glasses of Joachim the tears well up out of pure emotion. Emotions that will pave their way through his personality and that will continue to characterize him throughout his whole life. The same emotions that he could not control when, on March 29, 1968, he received that phone call in San Francisco that his daughter Shawn was born; the same emotions when, almost 40 years later, he saw the fall of the Berlin Wall and the exuberance of all those celebrating; the same emotions when, much later, he wrote the beautiful song *For The Women In My Life* for his solo blues album *Heretics & Privateers* (in the year 2000). Every time, tears roll down his cheeks and there is absolutely nothing he can do to change it. John Kay, the "slender" wolf all over. Indeed, that strong, howling wolf sometimes wears woolen socks ...

The day Joachim turns ten, his friend loans him this homemade radio as a birthday present. He lies in bed that night with this musical cigar box, when mother Elsbeth comes to have a look at him. She suspects that he is asleep, because it is completely quiet in the room. However, Joachim is just listening to some music playing through the primitive headphones. He has picked up an interesting station and is listening intently to Radio Luxembourg. Exactly on his tenth birthday -April 12, 1954- he hears for the first time the song that initially serves as a model for all the Rock & Roll music that follows from then on: *Rock Around The Clock* by Bill Haley. For him, this is a real revelation compared to all those typical German charm songs that his mother loved so much. Rudi Schüricke is indeed still immensely popular throughout Germany, but for him it could sound a bit less polished. Some time later he hears a still young Elvis Presley singing "That's all right, mama" and he is totally crazy about that music. But one day he hears something unique! It even seems like something otherworldly to him. It's something that completely blows him away and that will change his life completely from then on. In the summer of 1955 Little Richard sings his world-famous hit *Tutti Frutti* ... That unimaginably chaotic and noisy intro with "Bwoapbabeloebabel-ab-emboee", first makes him think that someone is falling down the stairs, but Little Richard apparently uses this as a surrogate for a vocally imitated drum intro that he has in mind and mimics with the mouth. Joachim is puzzled here, because he doesn't understand one iota of the lyrics. A bit later, his interest in Little Richard's music only grows when he also hears him loudly singing *Long Tall Sally* through the radio. He doesn't know what it all means, but one thing is certain: now that he has heard this, he wants to make music like this himself one day. After attending the performance of the Russian Cossack Choir, he had already caught the virus and the urge to be on stage himself. But now that he's hearing this uplifting music here, he is really convinced of what he wants to do someday. Joachim dreams:

"My God! If only one day I could leave Germany and go to America. Then I could learn English and play and sing this kind of music."

The years go by. Joachim sees that the Allied "occupiers" everywhere are trying extremely hard to make the (West) Germans feel good, so that they do not see them as occupiers but rather as protectors. American and British culture houses are being opened in West Germany for the larger public. There are also television screens everywhere, and Germans get to know better the British and American way of life this way. People are, however, witnessing that the political disputes with the Iron Curtain are increasing and that the alienation of their former compatriots behind the Iron Curtain is growing in proportion. They also increasingly realize that the British and Americans are there to protect them from a possible Russian invasion. But despite the political power play, daily life goes on as usual. Stepfather Kyczinski, handy with all kinds of chores and creations, sees that Joachim has been caught by the music bug and makes his own guitar for him by hand, constructed from plywood slices. Whenever he has some spare time, Joachim sits on the bottom step of the stairwell in the apartment building where he lives, loudly imitating Little Richard and singing all sorts of words that are both wrong and incomprehensible. Mathias Greffrath, a boy who lives in the same apartment building on the first floor, often comes and sits next to Joachim on that bottom step and looks at Joachim with admiration the whole time. Mathias is only one year younger than Joachim and he looks up in awe at him during this special private audience ...

At night in Hannover, youthful teenager Joachim often lies in his bed dreaming he is standing on a stage with a guitar in his hand and a microphone in front of him. At the time, it is nothing more than a distant and elusive fantasy. But didn't Walt Disney once say, *"If you can dream something, you can actually live it!"* And surely Walt Disney is not just anybody, for he has proved this to be true more than anyone else. Wait for it ...

Hannover, June 1958, just after Joachim Fritz Krauledat left for Canada. Steadily, the very last ruins of the Second World War where Joachim had played as a child are being cleared in the city and new construction is expanding. (Photo Bundesarchiv)

Part 2
The New World

Under the Leaf of the Maple Tree

March 1958. In contrast to East Germany, West Germany is a country where people have many more opportunities to be themselves. The free Western world offers many perspectives, and the heavy moral legacy of the Second World War is also fading into the background there more quickly to make way for an even broader forgiveness. People with sufficient energy and a healthy ambitious spirit can develop themselves to the fullest. The Marshall Plan enabled Western Europe to rise from the ruins and boost the economy in the process. Yet there were West Germans who assumed that while building a new life elsewhere might involve some risks, the rewards were all the greater if they succeeded.

The Kyczinski-Zimmermann family has relatives living in Canada. In their correspondence, they regularly hinted that there were many more opportunities there ...

Hannover, April 1958.

Herr Gerhard Kyczinski is an exceptional Mr Fixit and Elsbeth Zimmermann is a well-educated and experienced tailor. So, they both know how to get things done and are quite happy in Hannover. There is already a world of difference between the situation of Elsbeth and Joachim today and the bleak situation of some years ago in Arnstadt, in that other Germany. Despite all the future opportunities they have here, they are influenced by some optimistic sounding letters from distant relatives who had previously emigrated to Canada. It seems there are so many more opportunities over there for people with a well-motivated mindset. Increasingly, the conversations in the Kyczinski-Zimmermann household revolve around the question of whether they, too, might do this. After some hesitation and weighing up all the possible pros and cons, they finally take a very radical decision. They decide to follow the example of family members and cross the Atlantic and build a completely new life on the other side. For the time being, they cannot go to the United States of America, because they can only get a work permit there and not yet a permanent residence permit. Canada, however, is more spontaneously willing to admit German migrants permanently. There is apparently more faith in people *in general*, because they realize that their own country Canada was actually built by all kinds of people of foreign origin and by the work ethic of each individual. And that they are therefore better off with motivated people of "foreign" origin than with some of their "own" people who just sit on their lazy backs. To want to achieve something in life, origin is secondary to the conviction to do well. Initially coming from France, the Netherlands, Great Britain, Belgium, Germany, Ireland, Poland, etc., immigrants have built Canada into the thriving country it is today. Mr Kyczinski can apparently get a job in Toronto in a company as a bricklayer and general handyman. Elsbeth can also find work there quite easily thanks to her experience in the garment industry.

For Joachim, this move means that for the second time in his still young life he has to leave his friends behind permanently. Of course, he remembers nothing about the move as a baby from Tilsit, East

Prussia to Arnstadt. A few years later, as a five-year-old he had to say goodbye to his kindergarten friends there and now, after playing in the ruins in Hannover for almost nine years, he has to do it again. Riding bikes with them, playing soccer and romping around among the rubble, all that is now definitely over. He says goodbye* forever to Mathias, his friend who lives on the first floor of the same apartment building in Kronenstrasse. Mathias, a year younger than Joachim himself and the boy who had always admired him so much for his impersonations in front of the mirror downstairs in the stairwell, will miss him very much. A feeling which is guaranteed to be mutual, by the way. But Joachim does not have to say goodbye to some other opportunistic and egocentric elements, on the contrary: he will not miss them at all ...

A few weeks before Joachim turns fourteen, the whole family is at the airport in Hannover for a final crossing of the Atlantic Ocean. The flight itself is also quite an experience. They have never sat in an airplane before and now they are going to cross the Atlantic. An extremely luxurious plane, and according to John "equipped with four propeller engines," will take them across in about ten hours. That could at that time -at least according to the author- only have been a Douglas DC-6. A Boeing 707 perhaps? That plane was already equipped with reaction engines, and no propellers ...

Upon landing in Toronto, Joachim asks himself the question:

"So, this is Canada. And where do we go from here?"

He knows that a totally new life is dawning for him and that he will have to get it on track himself. His parents already have their own professional pursuits and cannot invest all their time in him.

They too must move forward if they are to prove themselves in their unfamiliar environment. So, it will not be easy for Joachim and his visual handicap will certainly not make things less complicated for him.

---

* *Mathias will visit Joachim much later in John Kay's beautiful mansion in Franklin.*

Amazed and extremely curious, he looks around him in the ultra-modern metropolis of Toronto. Surely it is unimaginable, all those new and formal high-rise buildings and those beautiful parks everywhere. And unlike Hannover and so many other places in Germany, there are no ruins to be found anywhere here. Toronto is apparently a city of no less than 1,500,000* inhabitants. Surely, that's huge! And he consoles himself with the fact that Toronto is largely made up of immigrants. If they have all succeeded, I, Joachim Fritz Krauledat from that modest German town of Hannover, West Germany, will soon also be able to ...

Joachim in Toronto

Joachim realizes that he has already removed one of the major obstacles standing in the way of his quiet (well, quiet?) ambitions: he is now indeed on the other; the *good* side of the Ocean. When he was lying in his bed in Hannover secretly listening to the American military radio stations and Radio Luxembourg with that primitive, homemade receiver, he knew that he would be able to realize his ambitions much more smoothly in the United States. Although he now lives in Canada, the nearest border to the US is only about 65 miles away. Literally, the distance is very small, but figuratively there is still a long way to go before he will be able to realize the rest of his dreams. This is already a first step in the right direction. The rest will come ...

But Joachim is not at all happy in his new surroundings in the beginning. Despite the fact that he has exchanged his slightly introverted character traits of the past for the personality of a somewhat more self-confident young man after his stay at the Waldorf School, he again has to contend with a lot of practical inconveniences.

---

* *Estimated number of inhabitants in 1959.*

To begin with: he is immediately confronted with the same problem as before in the elementary school in Hannover. He is allowed to sit in the front of the class because of his poor eyesight, but here too, even sitting on the first row, he cannot read what is written on the blackboard.

Moreover, his knowledge of English is still totally inadequate to understand and to make the necessary progress in his studies. There is one essential difference however compared to Hannover: the behavior of his fellow students is completely different. He fortunately notices that in his new home, he is not bullied as much as before. Apparently by definition, the average Canadian citizen and student is quite broad-minded. He is even helped by most of his peers, but that help alone obviously does not solve his problem. It is imperative that he strengthen his knowledge of English in the short term and that his level of study is raised. Joachim is therefore urged to first take classes at the Deer Elementary School. These are special classes established by the government for the visually impaired, but not totally blind students. Those special classes are taught in Canada under the aegis of the CNIB*. In a regular class, he would have difficulties overcoming his problems of poor vision and language. However, thanks to the help of this institute, his problem with nearsightedness is largely redirected, because the learning material is not only put on the board, but also on paper and is handed out individually to each student. No more illegible scribbling on a board that he can never decipher even from two meters away. Each individual in the class and each person's specific visual problem is taken into account.

In the meantime, music continues to be his greatest interest. His spectrum has expanded enormously in that respect, because in Toronto he can receive many more radio stations than he ever thought possible. Especially from the neighboring American state of New York -barely 100 kilometers away- he is led into the whole wide universe of all kinds of music genres.

---

* Canadian National Institute for the Blind.

As a big rock & roll fan, he was introduced to music completely unknown to him until then: folk music, rhythm & blues, gospel and even liturgical and Gregorian genres. Moreover, in terms of popularity, folk music is steadily gaining ground.

Joachim is also surprised by the enormous flood of words that the English-language radio presenters and disc jockeys use in their broadcasts. He had never heard anything like that before and at times he is almost blown away by the loudspeaker in the radio station. All those spontaneous cascades of all kinds of information and strung together expressions of enthusiasm, even just to announce one song or another. It's miraculous. It opens up a whole new world for him. He also notes that especially in blues and folk music, there are opportunities for someone, able to play a few simple chords, to accompany oneself on the guitar quite easily. He therefore decides to focus on this genre for the time being. But unfortunately, he doesn't have a musical instrument! The guitar that his stepfather had made for him in Hannover, had not made the trip to Canada because it was "too bulky" in his luggage. So that guitar is still the problem. He talks to his mother about it, and she does listen to him. Elsbeth realizes that this whole new situation is not easy for him, and she decides to give him what he asks for, on the condition that he actually does something with it and of course if it is affordable … and if *he* contributes some of his own savings too.

That same summer of 1958, Joachim and his mother Elsbeth enter the gigantic Simpsons-Sears department store. In one of the windows they see the ideal guitar for beginning musicians. Not too expensive and nothing special in itself, but for the moment he only needs the essentials: six strings on a wooden sound box, with a plectrum control knob at the very top for each string. The price tag hangs on it and is clearly legible. Elsbeth whispers to him:

"Nur 55 dollars! Das ist machbar. Was sagst du, Joachim?"
("Only $55. That is possible. What do you say, Joachim?")

Joachim's shy smile is the answer to his mother's -somewhat unnecessary- question and about ten minutes later an overjoyed Joachim walks out with a real guitar in his hands. He even got a few plectrums for free. He doesn't mind the guitar being non-electric for the time being. First, let's learn how to play a little. He reads aloud the brand logo on the top of the wood next to the string tuner and mutters between his teeth *"K.A.Y."*... He doesn't realize at that very moment, that those three ordinary letters from the alphabet will soon and for the rest of his life play a leading role. It's not just about the guitar anymore, but about those three ordinary letters.

Every minute of spare time, Joachim is playing his six-string instrument. A bit later and thanks to schoolmate Stan King, who is just as keen a music lover as he is, he comes in the possession of a score by folk singer Hank Williams. First, he had to master the solfège a little better and then he could start. He reads the first chords of the song *You Win Again** which he tries to imitate on his new instrument. He learns to pluck four to five chords in a row quite easily. But when he tries to synchronize his guitar playing with the singing of the lyrics, he realizes that this is not as easy as he thought it was. Clearly, there is still a lot of work to be done ...

One day, Joachim receives the generous support of Lady Fortune. As is often the case in life, it is important to have a little luck at the right moment. Charles Goodyear similarly invented rubber by chance once after an outburst of rage, throwing all his chemical elements on the stove out of desperation, and the rubber suddenly emerged naturally after vulcanization. Alexander Fleming also discovered penicillin in 1928 in this way by accident, when he saw that fungi were growing on bacteria and in the process noticed that those fungi were actually destroying those bacteria. Our Joachim is also helped by chance here.

Not that Andrew Wollensak was as great an inventor as Fleming or Goodyear, per se. However, the type of deluxe tape recorder his firm had designed, is not only in use in Canada in wealthier private circles but is also quite widely used in libraries and in schools. Especially in schools for pupils with some learning difficulties due to physical imperfections, such as, among others ... poor eyesight. In order to

---

* *His own version of that song appears in 1972 on his first solo LP* Forgotten Songs & Unsung Heroes.

improve his knowledge of English and specially to improve his pronunciation, the school had offered him a special set of lessons on tape. The CNIB lent him a Wollensak tape recorder. But the big secret is not so much in the tape recorder itself or the curriculum, but rather in that one single blank tape which he also received. On that tape he can record his own pronunciation of English, rewind it, and improve himself. However, he feels that he can also use this "high-tech medium" for something else. Joachim will benefit greatly from it and with it -partly willingly and partly unwillingly- he will be able to combine the useful with the pleasant. After all, he does something with it that will give his life a rather revolutionary turn. He starts secretly recording all kinds of songs that are played on the radio. In the library/discotheque in the neighborhood he can also borrow records -for free- and he starts recording those as well. However, the recordings are never of a decent quality. In those days, recordings with a tape recorder are not done via a direct connection to the device, but by means of a microphone that is placed at the best possible distance in front of the radio. You always have to try that out first. If the microphone was too close to the speakers, you were guaranteed a sound distortion and if it was too far away, the recorded sound was barely audible. In addition, you were always forced to produce no unforeseen noises, because these were of course also recorded and could be heard when the tape was played back ...

One day, he dared to sing a few sentences in English through the microphone and record them simultaneously on that one empty tape. Curious about the result, he rewound the tape a little later and listened with beating heart to his own very first recording. But the quality of the recording is truly deplorable. He is even shocked by the enormously poor results of what he has just recorded:

*"This is absolutely terrible!!! I can't be **that** bad, can I? ... "*

Will he put his musical ambitions on hold right away? No, he won't! His goals are not thwarted by this temporary sobering up. On the contrary: he is focusing even more on a musical future; so much so that his studies are beginning to suffer as a result ...

Wollensak tape recorder, Joachim Krauledat's secret weapon.

Joachim Krauledat continues to find his way in this totally new, spacious world. His voice is not yet the revelation he hoped for on the tape recorder, but his guitar playing is already at an acceptable level after a year or two of practice. He decides to go a step further by signing up for a small public audience that takes place in a radio studio near the US border. He takes the Greyhound shuttle bus and heads to the Niagara Falls neighborhood for a mini performance. There he sings one song by the Everly Brothers and one by Hank Williams. Right away, his debut performance in front of an audience is made and it tastes like more. The combination of feeling weak in the knees accompanied by fierce palpitations and clammy hands, so classic for the nervous novice standing in front of an audience, are quickly replaced by an extra-adrenaline rush at the next opportunity. He senses that this is really becoming his thing. In his dreams, he sees himself on a big stage soon ...

Just like Father Time, Joachim's adjustment period in Canada goes by very quickly. While his peers usually go out in groups to play sports on the weekends, Joachim realizes that he will have to limit himself in all possible areas, including sports, because of his bad eyesight. Tennis and other individual sports also require exceptionally good eyes, and well-equipped fitness centers for playing individual indoor sports as we know them today, do not yet exist at that time. His physical education teacher at school then encourages him to come and do some individual strength training with weights in the local gym of the school. Such things must surely be possible, because in doing so, his bad eyes are not really a handicap. The gym teacher at school is also doing what he can to help Joachim as much as possible in his difficult period of adjustment. However, this man will also be very important for Joachim at a completely different level. Because he constantly has trouble pronouncing Joachim's name correctly, he looks for an easier way to communicate with him and especially ... to address him. Indeed, every time he tries to pronounce "Joachim Fritz Krauledat," he chokes on the enormous number of syllables. The intonation of so many difficult vowels and consonants in succession is always an insurmountable obstacle. That has to change, he thinks. Such a difficult name is indeed totally unpronounceable for someone with an "Anglo" accent. That way, Joachim's baptismal name is repeatedly reduced to a caricature of himself, until the day the good man in question finds a solution himself. He suddenly decides to just replace Joachim's first name with the quite simple "John". This saves energy and embarrassment and the automatically erupting jeers of all the pupils present. And because Elsbeth Kyczinski-Zimmermann is also addressed as "Mrs K" all the time there in Toronto (because that strange name Kyczinski is just as unpronounceable as that other strange name Krauledat) he also uses only the "K" as the initial of Joachim's last name. So, John "K" it will be. That "K" sounds phonetically like "Kay" in the alphabet and immediately the name John Kay is born ...

The reference to his "Kay guitar" as if his name were derived from that is purely coincidental ...

John continues his studies in high school, he feels good and his level of education gradually improves. He obviously wants to finish his secondary studies, but the focus on music remains much greater than the ambitions to get really good grades at school. He also visits music clubs in the Toronto area more frequently and puts on some modest performances in the wider area of that city. Just him, his guitar and an ordinary harmonica held in place with a special aluminum mini frame around his neck. In this way he can play the guitar, while at the same time using only his lips to play the harmonica. He doesn't need anything more than that, and besides, he has a very good friend in the meantime: Klaus. In this period, he also gets to know the true Delta blues icon Son House and he also sees the unique blues legend Bo Didley perform a couple of times.

After two years of separate lessons in the special Sight Saving Classes, he returns to the Humberside Collegiate. Meanwhile, his mother and stepfather are increasingly playing with the idea of moving from Canada to the US. They would now be able to get the required permanent US residency permit. Apparently, Mr Kyczinski could start an import business there. So, at about the end of 1963, they leave for the not-too-distant town of Buffalo, just across the border. However, Joachim prefers to stay in Toronto for a while; at least until after he has finished his secondary education. A bit later, Joachim gets his high school diploma. In the end, his school years turned out to be quite successful, despite his difficult start and his strong focus, which was much more on music than on his textbooks. Sure, he lost a year, but considering all the inconveniences he had to suffer, that was not so bad.

Further study is out of the question for now. But with his very weak eyes, future opportunities in all sectors are limited anyway. His color blindness, hypersensitivity to light and nearsightedness are the reason why he realizes that he will never be able to drive a motorcycle or a car.

"Das macht nichts! Ich werde Musiker! For the rest, we'll find a solution ... "

After finishing his high school studies, his good friend Klaus finds that the time has come to seek new horizons for a while. He wants to explore the West Coast on the other side of the US. Klaus, meanwhile, has bought a nice sports car. And John Kay? He gets to come along. *"California, here we come!"*

Front of the Humberside Collegiate in Toronto

California Horizon Blue(s) and Sparrow

At home in Toronto the Kyczinski-Zimmermann family have not at all forgotten their own healthy ambitions in the '60s. They have been thinking about moving to the United States for a while now. At first, in 1958, they were not allowed to do so, but after a few years of arduous work in Canada, the cards are in their favor this time. Buffalo, in upstate New York and just across the border from Canada, will soon be their new home. Mr Kyczinski can start an import business in the nearby state of New York and Elsbeth can work in the clothing industry, just like she did earlier. While John (Joachim) is spending his last months at high school in Toronto, they are gradually getting everything ready for their move to the USA.

John, after finishing his studies, will not be moving to Buffalo for the time being. But because they have often talked and dreamed about the remote West Coast of Southern California, Joachim wants to see the other side of that immense America first after finishing high school. And that trip will be worthwhile. Driving all the way across the United States from East to West along legendary Route 66 is an adventure in itself. He cannot drive himself because of his bad eyes, but his good friend Klaus can. Klaus, by the way, has a very special sports car: a Triumph TR3 (a). Just after graduating from school, John and Klaus set off for the American West Coast. They have a 4,000-kilometer trip ahead of them. Especially for a young man of about twenty years old, sitting in the passenger seat of a purebred, spartan, British sports car, it will be a real adventure. But it is only after that unique adventure on the West Coast that his life will change dramatically. Where? When he gets back to ... Yorkville, Toronto ... We'll quickly find out how! ...

A British sports car like Joachim's friend Klaus had. This is not Klaus' car. This one is owned by the author of this book ...

Would Klaus and John have known in the 1960s that the name "Triumph" -already then- stood for a symbol of tradition? No, I'm not talking about that brand of luxury women's underwear here. After all, it is also a very prestigious sounding and well-known brand name for vehicles, both two and four wheelers. Its emblem first symbolized something we catalog under "typically authentic British" motorcycles since 1897. From 1902, the factory also produced typically British cars. However, the company was not founded by a Briton, but as has been the case so many times: by an energetic German. Also, much later -from 1994- the rights to the brand passed into the hands of the German BMW, which, unlike the world-renowned, popular "Mini", has had no concrete plans with it. Now the group, like that other British giant brand MG motors, is in Chinese hands.

Due to the emerging difficulties in the British car industry at the end of the 1960s, the Coventry plant finally ceased to exist in the late seventies. Cut-throat competition from Japan regarding reliability, price and the overall quality of the finished product that rolled off the production line, killed the British car industry completely in the end ...

But the true enthusiasts of that famous, idiosyncratic brand stayed true to real British traditions, often even against better judgment. Many car enthusiasts have driven Triumphs over the years and many still do today. They value nostalgia and British tradition more than having a car you can get into every morning, and which starts and runs without a hitch. With a British car something technically is always going wrong, not to mention the extreme susceptibility to rust. But Triumph certainly has its charms, and along with its sporting appearance, you also have to allow for the bad things. And that appearance is a pure one, connected directly with its rich automotive history. In 1953 the Triumph TR2, with registration number M 575, broke the world record for "pure speed" on a long stretch of newly built road in Jabbeke, Belgium, for cars with a cylinder capacity of up to two liters.

After his studies at the Toronto high school, John Kay sits down in the bright red artificial leather passenger seat (with white trim along the edges) of his friend Klaus' navy-blue Triumph TR3. It may not be the authentic TR2 world-record holder but its successor on the production line: the TR3 (a). John will feel after a few miles that this car is indeed a "tool" for sporty driving pleasure on the one side and for pure spartan driving devoid of any luxury on the other side. Fast, agile and a bit of a challenge to drive, but almost without any comfort and every unevenness in the road surface is felt in the knuckles and the bones. On Route 66, by the way, many stretches of road are still poorly finished or not finished at all in the mid-1960s, or in a pitiful state. On top of that, the canvas cover doesn't close the car properly and during a heavy rainfall you are guaranteed to get soaking wet on the inside. The heating of the car is also totally inadequate, but of course you don't expect winter conditions in summer on Route 66. There's only dust, dust … and more dust. Goggles and a face mask are definitely recommended. John's dark glasses are now more of an asset than a handicap. But with the canvas hood open or closed: the engine noise is deafening and that in particular becomes very irritating in the long run.

If you take that route all the way from Chicago to Santa Monica-Los Angeles, you can be somewhat relieved if you arrive at your destination in one piece and not completely wrecked … but you are still facing a return trip …

Dust and a lack of any comfort in the car or not: Klaus and Joachim are having a few fantastic weeks during their trip to the other side of the US.

John Kay (right) with his friend Klaus and their famous Triumph TR3 (a) on their way from Buffalo to Santa Barbara, California. He had no idea at that moment he would return to the West Coast a lot sooner than he expected ...

They forget all about their worries and the stress of school exams. They enjoy themselves immensely and discover the vast beauty of nature all along that amazing Route 66 in America. When they finally arrive at the Pacific Ocean, they are completely flabbergasted by what they see over there. As John Kay will explain almost 60 years later in Arnstadt (see chapter Arnstadt 2022), he and Klaus had lots of fun and were pleasantly surprised by the unbelievable beauty at the Pacific coastline. But they are also surprised in some way by life in general in the West of the United States. The people they meet there seem to be totally different and more friendly and relaxed than elsewhere.

After touring around for a while and having a lot of fun, they both decide to return. John will go to the city of Buffalo, where Gerhard and Elsbeth Kyczinski-Zimmermann have settled well in the meantime.

This short trip to the West Coast was certainly a welcome break and it was also very relaxing after all those school efforts. John also learned a lot during his holidays on the American West Coast. He gets the impression that the whole region radiates the American way of life so much more. To reach and to see that Pacific Ocean for the very first time in his life and meeting all those friendly people, convinced John already at *that* moment, that this certainly wouldn't be his last visit there. So, he keeps in mind that his farewell to the West Coast is only temporary, at least as far as *he* is concerned. He doesn't know *why* precisely he thinks so, but he certainly feels that way. And such feelings don't often deceive him. He will be proved right, by the way, as we will see in a moment ...

There isn't much time, however, to enjoy and rest after both those 2,500-mile trips. In Buffalo, he has to find a job. As a 20/21-year-old young man, the things of life are not just handed to you and if you want some food on the table, you have to do something for it. Making a living from music may be your ultimate dream, but until you walk into the spotlights and earn your living with music alone, you are forced to take on other activities. It is certainly not the intention to end up in the gutter, with or without a guitar.

Back in Buffalo, John has quite some difficulties finding a respectable job. His bad eyes always bother him in one way or another. He also discovers that Canada is more empathetic than the US towards people with bad eyesight or other disabilities. He starts working in a candle factory, but that is really nothing for him in the long term. In the meantime, he dedicates himself totally to music again. He focuses on all possible genres and Appalachian blues is something new again. He also starts his own band: John Kay and the Congressmen, but that pilot project is not long-lived. Actually, it is not set up with professional purposes in mind, it is more a way of just "jamming" together. John is having an enjoyable time and keeps on searching for some better way of making money. He also keeps on working on the more difficult guitar work, while simultaneously accompanying himself on the harmonica and he perfects his general musical skills. The genre he performs most of the time, lends itself perfectly to this. He is also increasingly influenced by the work of folk singer Woody Guthrie and especially by blues man Son House, whom he has seen at work recently. He sees protest singer Phill Ochs performing at the Newport Festival in the summer of 1964. McKinley Morganfield (Muddy Waters) is also on stage there during that weekend and that performance will stay with John for more than 50 years. He will always refer to this special man when singing *Hootchie Cootchie Man* live. He also learns to play the mouth harp in that period, an instrument he will use much later in several songs and which accentuates the specific sound he has in mind for himself. Those screeching mouth-organ and penetrating mouth-harp sounds, together with the extremely specific but so recognizable and really beautiful organ keyboard playing of John Raymond Goadsby, Jerry's unique drum roll and John's grainy rough sounding voice, will later give the Steppenwolf sound that distinctive touch: unique in the yet very universal world of music ...

John also receives some unpleasant news during this period. Although he is still a German and not a Canadian or an American citizen, he is contacted for military service in the US army. The fear grows that eventually he will be drafted into the army. The Vietnam War rages ever more fiercely and the US, in the name of President Johnson, wants to respect the commitment they made to the regime of non-communist South Vietnam. In the mid-1960s, protests against the war were not so widespread and thousands of young men, barely nineteen sometimes, had to fulfill their military obligations in a remote location in South-East Asia. Most of them, of course, against their will. Later on, especially after the summer of 1967, many people from all kinds of hippie and other pacifist movements who don't see the point in doing any military service anyway, will leave the US. Not in a million years would they consider fighting in the jungles of South-East Asia or anywhere else. With the generous financial support of home in many cases and -first of all- well equipped with all kinds of "love and peace" gadgets ... and certainly amply in possession of the necessary "stuff" as well, whole groups of hippies move to the Spanish island of Ibiza in the Mediterranean. Others, on the other hand, will dutifully complete their military service far from home and they will return to the US ... some between four boards.

Fifty-eight thousand names of American soldiers killed in Vietnam are engraved on a black granite wall in Washington D.C.

Joachim, however, will never have to complete military service nor will he have to do any kind of alternative community service. His thoroughly bad eyes are to his advantage this time. If you can't distinguish colors and have a vision of only 10% to 20% of a normal pattern of vision, it is certainly not appropriate to enlist, let alone *handle* weapons. Of course, this is a relief on the one hand, but on the other hand John will start to turn away increasingly from the military apparatus as a whole and especially from the unscrupulous politicians who abuse this powerful military apparatus for the wrong reasons.

His personal views on the Pentagon and "Uncle Sam" in general will even become one of the most striking features of his later writings. We'll get back to that later ...

After staying in Buffalo for not even a year, the Kyczinski-Zimmermann family comes up with yet another surprise*. They have decided to leave the East Coast behind for good and to move to California, to the region where John returned from not so long ago and about which he had told them such wonderful things. So, their stay in the city of Buffalo has been very short-lived. All their belongings were loaded into a Chevy Van and the Kyczinski-Zimmermann family is heading for the West Coast. John acts as their guide along the immensely long roads he discovered himself not so long ago with the Triumph.

We can now -already- consider John Kay a man of the world. He adjusts smoothly to new situations each time. His hunch that he would end up on the West Coast, was quickly realized. Arriving back in California, John continues to find his way among the various music genres. He now shuttles between all kinds of clubs, bars and coffee houses to promote his own musical skills. Rock clubs Trouba-

---

* *After their retirement, Elsbeth and Gerhard will return to ... Germany. They will move to Aachen, close to the Belgian and Dutch borders. John and Jutta will visit them there regularly.*

dour and New Balladeer on Santa Monica Boulevard are a very welcome new workplace for him. He plays at all kinds of venues where budding artists can display their talents. Not only musicians who can play a few chords can come and demonstrate their skills, but also comedians who are able to make people laughing, are welcome there. John regularly performs there as an acoustic blues singer, of course accompanying himself on guitar and harmonica. At the Troubadour, by the way, he is not only active as a musician, because earning a living with music alone is not an option for him at the moment. He is also involved in the daily management of the establishment.

He helps on the work floor, such as showing the guests to their seats, serving drinks, clearing the tables and all the normal, everyday things that are needed in such establishments. He may also be called upon as an extra help in the kitchen to wash glasses, dishes and plates and to do the correspondence. For the time being it is not really his dream job, but he considers himself quite lucky, nevertheless. He earns some extra money left and right and he can focus on his main preoccupation: music. And he has seen several good musicians passing by the clubs in the meantime. He is glad that he can learn something from all these people. For the first time in his life, he sees blues and country singer Hoyt Axton perform in the Troubadour and he sings a song that will later also become extremely important to John: *The Pusher*. A song in the authentic blues style with lyrics that are strongly directed against drug use and even more against the people who make (a lot of) money from it. John absorbs this message very well and will also include this song by Hoyt Axton in his later overall repertoire. Their excellent cover of *The Pusher* will, together with *Born To Be Wild*, form the intro of the important cult film *Easy Rider* by director Dennis Hopper. From then until more than 50 years later, these two songs are among the greatest successes of John Kay and his Steppenwolf in their live performances. At the Troubadour, John also comes into contact with Morgan Cavett, who will later on also play a very important role in his music career and who will also write several songs for him and his band.

Notification of performances in the New Balladeer, where John performs regularly.

During the time Joachim is experiencing his debut years in music, the overall music trend throughout the US is quietly shifting. Popular music from the British Isles is increasingly influencing existing popular trends. Among others, Pat Boone, Elvis Presley, Little Richard and Fats Domino are still immensely popular in the US, but they are gradually being outstripped by the new trend of typically glitzy, British boy groups such as the Beatles and the Rolling Stones. These up-and-coming British musicians, with hip hairstyles, make the boys wildly enthusiastic and the girls' hearts beat faster.

So, that typical British pop becomes also the most popular music style -far away from England- on *this* side of the Atlantic Ocean too, and will dominate the charts from now on. The blues/rock and folk genres also underwent changes and even the remote American *West* Coast does not escape from these British influences. This, of course, has a direct effect on performances in coffee houses and smaller clubs, where the number of people attending the genre of music that John loves so much, is beginning to decline. Apparently, everyone is suddenly going crazy about that typical British pop and that doesn't fit into John's plans. So, it's time to change plans! John feels that the time has come to change his strategy if he wants to take a step forward. He literally needs to think a little more broadly. From 1965 onwards he therefore begins to expand his target area and he travels across the United States with his guitar and harmonica in his hand. On tour, he also visits his former home in Canada, and he ends up back in … Toronto. Back to the early base. Let's keep the notion in mind, that this time Toronto will *really* become important to him, and for a few different reasons.

Back in Toronto, Canada, he is somewhat surprised to find out that socially, culturally and musically a lot has changed since he left the place a while ago. Everyone -here too- seems to be completely under the spell of the Beatles, the Rolling Stones and that typical British pop music.

Fortunately, he finds an easier way to get in touch with those people who pull the strings in the music world behind the scenes.

He also meets other musicians who will gradually flourish. Some of them will soon even make a big name for themselves. Gordon Lightfoot sings *In The Early Mornin' Rain* in one of the coffee houses and a little later in Toronto John also meets Neil Young, who will soon play with the Mynah Birds. John's introduction to Neil Young is somewhat peculiar, as we shall see in a few moments …

In Toronto, John also sees the band Jack London & The Sparrow perform in club Chez Monique. Lead singer of this group, Jack London (aka David Marden), is a very talented singer from London, GB. Jack chooses in the fall of 1965 after the earlier release (in April) of the eponymous album *Jack London and the Sparrow* to have a career on his own. Despite the broadly British-sounding contribution, that album doesn't really seem to take off in terms of popularity. The song *Hard Times With The Law* is released as a single, but by then Jack has already left the group. The band will soon see several changes of members. Nicolas Kassbaum, also a German migrant from Plöhn near Hamburg, switches from the Mynah Byrds to Sparrow. John Goadsby, a somewhat eccentric organist who has received a very broad musical education and who, if necessary, can easily play all kinds of tunes on a classical church organ, also joins Sparrow. In itself it all seems to be about trivial details, but in reality, these simple mutations are important events in the further life of John Kay and that too for a number of different reasons …

For despite that welcome infusion of fresh air by the recruitment of new members, Sparrow, after the departure of Jack London, suddenly finds itself without a lead singer. The band members then put their heads together and ask themselves what to do next. So far, they are mainly focused on music that is very close to British pop, because they think that this genre of music would make it easier for them to get into the spotlights. They even engaged British lead singer Jack London a while ago with that in mind. But the guys in the band actually want to go in a different direction. Sometimes it really gets to them when, while playing some gigs, they are asked to play the most popular hits from the mainstream charts. And in fact, they would like to have a broader input of their own. When they see John Kay working a few times solo, with his acoustic guitar and harmonica, they decide to make him an offer. They would like to engage him as the new lead vocalist for their already greatly altered lineup of Sparrow. Through his striking and rough bluesy voice and the addition of the nasal sounds of the mouth harp and harmonica, they can focus on something else and try out a totally different trend. It's a tough gamble, to say the least, and they realize that. Maybe it will all end in a fiasco. But they've been stagnant for a while now anyway and ... he who doesn't dare, doesn't win. When the guys from Sparrow contact John:

"What? Me? Becoming a singer in a band? Well ... yes, I'd like that!"

says John when he is asked to join Sparrow as their new lead singer. He is invited to join the others to practice in the McCrohan family's garage, where Sparrow holds routine rehearsals. Dennis and Jerry McCrohan may have changed their name into Edmonton (sounds more English?) their father owns a reputable business and the name on the house bell at the family home is and always will be McCrohan. John is pleasantly surprised at the sight of that beautiful, large house with that huge room set aside just for them and equipped with all the necessary comforts. Apparently, Father McCrohan is getting along very well in life. John gets to know the others and he also gets to know Sparrow's new organist. When that new organist John Raymond Goadsby and John Kay meet, it ends in a funny moment. Two men called "John" by their first name in a group of only five people. This will soon cause confusion. John Kay therefore spontaneously conjures something out of his imagination. It goes like this:

"Hi, John!" ... "Oh, hello, John!"

"John, is it all right for you if I call you Goldy from now on?"

"That's fine with me! You can call me Goldy or whatever you want ..."

John Raymond Goadsby becomes Goldy Goadsby, but according to his own words, this does not fit together. He decides to call himself "Goldy McJohn" (apparently, McJohn is his mother's name). Under that name he will be immortalized in the music world.

In no time, John Kay is settled in and after a few weeks, he is officially appointed as the front man of Sparrow. Thus John Kay and the Sparrow is born, though their name simply remains Sparrow ...

Full entertainment in the shed. Here is a New Year's Eve performance on January 3, 1966 in club Chez Monique in Yorkville, Toronto, where The Sparrow provides the entertainment. John Kay, for once without his dark glasses, is on the far right of the photo with acoustic guitar. We also easily recognize the man with the fringe of beard: Dennis Edmonton aka Mars Bonfire. (Photo Madison Sale - Courtesy of York University digital library, Toronto Telegram collection, Fund F0433. ASC00612.)

John really does feel good about all this. He's also happy to have washed up in Toronto again. He knows the area and also a lot of people from his school years. Moreover, he can also speak his native language quietly to one of the other members. After all, Nicolas Kassbaum is also German. The other members of the band ask themselves what they are talking about sometimes. Not that the German language sounds very strange to them, because German is spoken a lot in Canada. The country has indeed many immigrants of Austrian or German origin … John feels at home again in Toronto. What Hannover was to him in Germany, Yorkville Village is now to him in the New World. But Toronto suddenly becomes much more important to him than he had ever thought possible before, and for yet another reason. Suddenly an incredibly special woman enters his life …

After one of his performances in Toronto with Sparrow at the end of October 1965, Nicolas Kassbaum takes an already overjoyed John Kay aside for a moment and proposes to go together for a drink in a nearby club. John's beginner's luck gets an extra boost from Lady Fortune, because then something happens that will drastically change his life. Also, partly thanks to Nicolas, that blond boy from the village of Plöhn in the German state called Schleswig-Holstein. On the way to the place where Nick and his girlfriend have an appointment, the conversation continues in German.

"Joachim, my girlfriend will be there as well. But she is not coming alone. She is in the company of another girl who has seen you perform a few times at Chez Monique, and she seems to like you very much. Her name is Jutta, and she is also German. Jutta is from Hamburg."

When they arrive at the club, the two girls are already chatting at a table. Nick and John greet them and without making it too obvious, John casts a cautious glance at that pretty, young dark blond lady sitting there next to Nick's girlfriend. Instantly, he feels his heart racing much faster. *"My God, what a pretty girl!"* he thinks …

They start chatting and laughing spontaneously. A bit later though, Nick and his girlfriend leave the club rather unexpectedly. It is obvious that this is a set-up to bring John and Jutta together and leave them alone. Thanks to Nicolas, they get to talk together and they seem to connect with each other instantly.

John tells Jutta -again in their native language German- about his flight as a baby from East Prussia to Arnstadt and about his later stay in Hannover before emigrating to Canada. He talks about his tough time at school, his bad eyes and that he wears his dark glasses often on doctor's orders. He also tells her about his playing in the ruins and about his best childhood friend Mathias Greffrath, whom he had to leave behind in Hannover in April 1958 and for whom tears welled up in his eyes when he left there for good.

Jutta, in turn, tells John about the great German port city of Hamburg on the Elbe, of which she has some good, but unfortunately also some bad memories from her youth. She tells him that there too -just like in Hannover where Joachim lived- during the final phase of the Second World War everything was in ruins. Just like John had lost *his* father during the war, she also had lost her father. It also turns out that she is a Beatles fan and that is another element they have in common. Jutta even knew the Beatles personally in Hamburg, and she saw them perform regularly in the Indra Hall and also in the Kaiser Keller when all the band members lived in the building just next door. This was all in their early days, long before the Beatles had scored one single hit. Back then, there were even five of them and no Ringo Starr behind the drums yet. By the way, despite all the effort these Liverpool boys put in there, they didn't enjoy much success during that period of the early '60s. The rewards were totally disproportionate to all the energy they put into it. But they kept on trying and eventually, their efforts paid off. From their *Love Me Do* in 1962, everything suddenly accelerated for the boys, and they moved back to their beloved spot on the Mercy River in Liverpool, UK. However, just before the Beatles scored their first success on the international scene, Jutta decided to leave Hamburg for good and she moved to Canada ...

She was barely eighteen when she took that big step to work on the other side of the Atlantic to build up her own life. An inconvenient situation at home made her decide to leave Germany, and preferably go as far away as possible. Because she loved music and everything around it immensely, she was determined to get a job somewhere in Canada in the music business. She ended up in Yorkville, Toronto and became a waitress in basement halls and clubs for budding musicians. She couldn't have been closer to the music.

The pleasant conversation between John and Jutta continues for a while, but Jutta suddenly interrupts the conversation. It is getting late, and apparently, she has to get up early tomorrow morning.

"You know, Joachim, I have to go now. But I would like to talk further tomorrow? What do you think, "Meine liebe Junge?"

whispers Jutta in John's ears, adding a friendly wink. Jutta leaves and John is left somewhat orphaned. Suddenly, he even feels completely empty. But he promptly gets down to business and decides to follow her. He absolutely doesn't want to miss the boat. At about 10 p.m. that evening, Jutta Maue walks along the streets of Yorkville, Toronto homeward to her residence on Lowter Avenue. Ten meters behind, she is followed by a very convinced young man, who has just spontaneously fallen head over heels in love with her. He certainly can't stay too far behind. It's dark outside and he has to keep all his attention on it. *"You never know I might lose her,"* he thinks. Jutta and John talk further in Jutta's apartment and they find each other in all passion that night. They will never, ever let go of each other from that day onward ...

One or two days later, John has to tell his (former) girlfriend that there is someone else in his life now. He wants to quickly pick up a few personal things at his (ex)-girlfriend's place. On the way to her, he is thinking about how to tell her this in the least hurtful way possible. That will be difficult and obviously no fun. When he rings her doorbell, however, he is surprised to find that his girlfriend ... also has found someone else.

Apparently, she wants to give shelter to another musician who has washed up in Toronto. When John sees this young man:

"Hi, I'm John Kay and I'm here to pick up some stuff of mine."

"Hi, I'm Neil Young and I'm playing here with the Mynah Birds from now on. But I don't have a place to stay, so this lovely lady invited me to move in with her. By the way, she hadn't told me she already had a boyfriend."

No hard feelings! John's love problem is immediately off the table, as it is automatically solved by someone else's "housing problem" ...

John and Jutta's intense meeting that evening in Yorkville, Toronto, are the beginning of a lifelong commitment. But first, Jutta will get this derogatory comment from her circle of friends:

"What the hell are you doing, Jutta? Come on girl! You can do a lot better than that! What future do you have, with a man of limited talents who is also practically blind?"

Nevertheless, completely convinced of what they were doing, they will get married a bit later (on February 24th 1967) and they remain a couple to this day. So, in 2023 they are married for 56 years. Their diamond wedding anniversary is not far away. They have a daughter, Shawn, born on March 29, 1968; just before that strikingly hot and extremely wild summer of *Born To Be Wild* arrived. The summer that turned everything upside down for both Jutta and John and also for many other people from their entourage and elsewhere in the world. We'll get to that later ...

Jutta will soon notice that having a relationship with a professional musician is a serious challenge for a standard pattern of a happy couple. Nevertheless, she will devote all her energy to the success of John's career, and she will later, after 1980, also become involved in the management of his band.

From then on, and for the rest of his professional career, John will be more often on the road than at home. Bringing up Shawn is therefore mainly Jutta's task. It happens once that little Shawn doesn't even recognize her own father when he comes home after yet another long

A very pretty Jutta Maue in 1965, at the time she first meets John. Twenty-one-year-old she is at the time ... (From Jutta's private collection)

tour. But on those few days that John is home, the moments he spends with his daughter Shawn, are very intense. However, even in the later years of his lengthy career, he is on tour so often that sometimes he can only be home with his family around Christmas.

The music absorbs John's time almost completely which was also the case in the very early days when Jutta and he had just met in Toronto; even long before Shawn joined them. But the music genre they play, needs some more room for expansion, and because the gifts in the form of fat paid contracts are not just thrown into their laps, Sparrow decides in 1966 to leave Toronto. They move to the city of New York in the US, an important bastion of the music industry. Performing in clubs and venues is fun, but they would also like to do some studio work and, most importantly, finally sign a solid record deal.

They get a good reference from Canada, and they sign a trial contract with the Columbia label. Commissioned by their producer, they will record a whole series of demos in New York, assuming that there are some songs that may have success on the charts*. But in New York the coin also has a less shiny flipside. The prestigious club The Arthur, where they can work almost full time thanks to their manager, is more a place for the rich and well-to-do. Unfortunately, this also has a few disadvantages for them, because the boys are crammed into a sort of straitjacket; almost literally. Suddenly they have to be "uniformly" attuned in terms of clothing and on top of that, the manager of the club orders them to always wear a tie. In order to be successful and to get the audience on board, they all have to look a bit like the (then) Beatles, both in terms of physical appearance … and with regard to the music they have to perform on stage. So, a white shirt and a tie in a tight suit it is!

The boys don't like it and it is also hard work in The Arthur. Moreover, during the day, they like to continue to work on their own arrangements. There is no sign of any success in the charts as yet. Songs like *Tomorrow's Ship* are only a modest and local success. This softer pop style is indeed still too much related to that corny music genre they think they should finally give up for something completely different.

Dennis McCrohan -aka Edmonton-, their lead guitarist and alongside John also the main songwriter so far, will soon draw his conclusions as a result. *Good Morning Little Schoolgirl*, a cover of Sonny Boy Williamson's 1937 blues version, is already doing a little better and is more in line with what they are really aiming for.

They continue in vain and a little later they release *Twisted*, a song

---

* *Those demos were released in their entirety on one album in the summer of 1969 under the title* John Kay and The Sparrow.

written by John Kay himself. But for the time being Sparrow does not have any success. The band subsequently decides in the fall of 1966 to leave New York. They increasingly get the impression that they are just wasting their time there. They worked extremely hard for a year, but their stay in The Big Apple did not bring them any further. Quite unexpectedly, they get the wind in their sails, but that opportunity is on the West Coast. At that very moment Sparrow receives an offer to give some performances in the Whisky a Go Go club in faraway Los Angeles. To start with, they are allowed to be the support act for the Sir Douglas Quintet, a band that had already proved itself a bit more and is therefore the main attraction on the bill. John still remembers the freethinking mentality on the West Coast during his trip there some time ago. According to him, there are now indeed more opportunities on the American West Coast. He especially remembers the kind generosity of the people in metropolitan cities like Los Angeles and San Francisco. He thinks that people there are now probably much more open to the progressive and blues-related music genres. After all, there is yet another metamorphosis going on in the music world in California. The all-changing pattern of life under the motto of "Love and Peace" that will soon lead to the "Summer of Love" in 1967 is already beginning to emerge on the horizon. The band members think they are doing the right thing in jumping on that progressive bandwagon full of positive energy. John is able to convince Nick, Jerry, Dennis and Goldy to take this big step. The group rents a small transport truck, stuffs it full of equipment and personal items, and the five of them trek along the road to the other side of the United States in search of a new life ... and finally some more success.

A few days later, the boys are housed along Santa Monica Boulevard, and they are able to have a great time there for a while. Along with groups such as The Doors, Johnny Rivers, The Byrds, Iron Butterfly and even the Dutch Golden Earrings, (earrings with an "s" at that time!), Sparrow becomes a welcome guest in Los Angeles. But as suddenly as it had started for them, it also suddenly goes downhill in LA and in the hip entertainment district. Not just for them, but for all the budding talents and even the established names who perform there. A couple of rioters -under the influence or not- cause too much mayhem in the nightlife district and almost all clubs are closed down by police order until things calm down again. Sparrow and many other groups become technically unemployed instantly as a result. It is really not easy for them, and the despondency gradually gains ground ...

But a small light will emerge on the horizon just about 600 kilometers further to the North. The boys are now also getting offers from San Francisco and once again, the moving van is at the door to haul all their things. *"Actually, we'd better get a loyalty card from some moving company."* Jerry jokes. At The Matrix in San Francisco they get a regular spot. In the middle of April, they are scheduled to play six times and they can also perform in some other clubs located in San Francisco, Santa Cruz and Oakland. But the distances they have to travel each time are quite large and it has its repercussions on their physical condition. Fatigue is very noticeable and that ultimately affects their mood. But what is even worse, is that the deeper frustrations strike proportionally. They realize that they use up a lot of energy and that all that effort is out of proportion to the financial gain. And the record contracts they are so vehemently coveting, are not forthcoming.

On May 14, 1967, they perform once again at The Matrix in San Francisco and a large part of their performance there is recorded on tape. Those recordings -of inferior quality by the way- will two years later be the subject of a so-called live album called *Early Steppenwolf.*

Those recordings had nothing to do with Steppenwolf at all, but were actually still recorded integrally as (John Kay & The) Sparrow. They were made without their knowledge. In addition to some of the better-known songs from their repertoire, they also perform a twenty-minute improvised psychedelic version of *The Pusher*. It was apparently the very first time they performed this song live and it is, all things well considered, a very unusual rendition of Hoyt Axton's anti-drug song.

The search for (better) contracts continues, but the real breakthrough they all hope for is not yet in sight. Then comes another offer from Los Angeles, where the troubles between the police force and the troublemakers have apparently blown over. Unfortunately, there is suddenly also disagreement among Sparrow's own band members. Because of the previously accumulated stress situations, at that moment the first real group quarrel* starts. John and Jerry want to go back to LA immediately, because they think there are more opportunities and especially because the most famous record giants are located there. Nick, Dennis and Goldy, on the other hand, would rather stay in San Francisco, because of the unprecedented revolutionary change in the lifestyle of the young people. Indeed, they have quite a few fans among those colorful hippies with their long hair full of all kinds of flowers. These people also seem to like anything that makes a little noise, smells a little like marijuana or tastes like LSD or crack. Unfortunately, some of Sparrow's band members are also more and more attracted to these hallucinatory things. Moreover, for some reason Jerry Edmonton gets into a big fight with the manager of the Galaxy Club and they are temporarily no longer welcome there. Conclusions are drawn by each side. The moment Scott McKenzie sings his world hit *If you're going to San Francisco, be sure to wear flowers in your hair* and causes the city and the entire local hippie community to go into a complete delirium, Sparrow ceases to exist, just when the beautiful summer of 1967 arrives.

They fail to get their guitars in tune as it were, though this time that's only meant figuratively. Their recordings at The Matrix were about the last tones they all played together as Sparrow. The song *Goin' Upstairs* (bring down all my clothes) by John Lee Hooker, a song they had often performed themselves, now applies to them as well. The sacred fire of passion has vanished. So far, their unlimited enthusiasm had kept them on cloud nine, but it is all gone now. Their friendship survives (for the moment). However, they are all extremely disappointed in the managers, the music companies and also a bit in themselves ...

---

* *The first of a whole series of group squabbles ...*

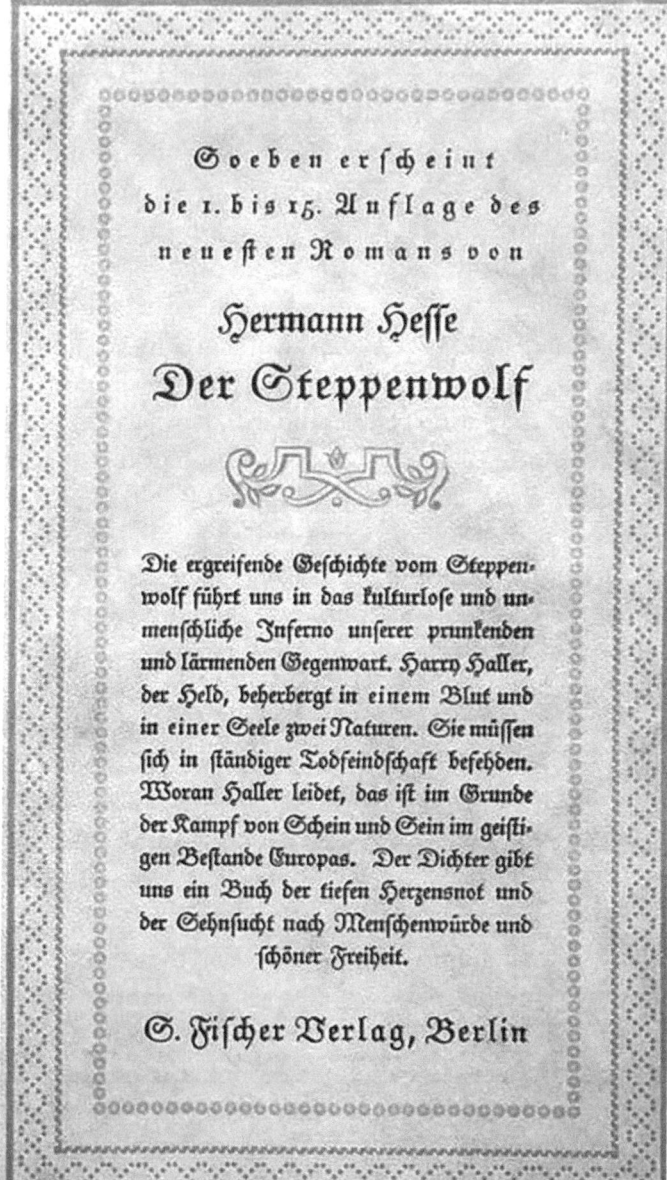

The title of a 1927 book by German author Hermann Hesse becomes the inspiration for the new baptismal name of a legendary rock band in 1967. (Creative Commons H-P Haack CC BY 3.0)

Steppenwolf

"After the Sparrow broke up, Dennis Edmonton changed his name to Mars Bonfire and he went on writing Born To Be Wild. I found that quite ironic in fact. And the reason for that was that this song was very different from all the softer pop songs he had written before. And of course, BTBW became a big, big hit for Steppenwolf ..."

The summer of 1967. Fountain Avenue 7408, Los Angeles. Sparrow has made far too little progress musically, and the sense of cohesion between the members has totally faded as a result of the accumulated frustrations. The boys therefore decide to go their separate ways. Nick absolutely wants to stay in the music business and makes contact with some local musicians on the West Coast. There, he meets a certain Larry Byrom from Huntsville, Alabama, and the German Canadian bass player from the disbanded band Sparrow promptly joins the group T.I.M.E., where Larry Byrom plays the guitar. Jerry Edmonton is searching his way, while he flirts (very briefly) with Janis Joplin's band and Goldy does not rush into anything new. And what about Jerry's brother Dennis, that eternally quiet guy ...?

Dennis Edmonton, lead guitarist and key songwriter of -the now split-up- Sparrow, was always a maverick and he proves it once again. He suddenly makes a drastic decision in the summer of 1967, and he categorically quits as a musician. He says it is not that much out of disappointment because of the lack of major contracts, but rather out of personal frustration because he feels that he has reached his own limits as a guitarist. He feels that further progression is no longer possible for him and the realization that he will never become a real

1967. An old Ford Falcon, the basis for the inspiration of a heavy musical tune that still sounds very militant and revolutionary more than 56 years later. (Photograph by the author)

guitar virtuoso, moves him to do so. He decides to take the (guitar) strap off for a while and to focus on other things. He decides to take a completely different approach to things in life. He even changes his name.

Following in the footsteps of Joachim Fritz Krauledat earlier, and Nicolas Kassbaum more recently, he chooses to bury his Christian name Dennis McCrohan (aka Dennis Edmonton) once and for all. He will henceforth go through life as Mars Bonfire. Dennis is indeed cutting himself short for a while as a musician, but under his new pseudonym Mars Bonfire, he will not stop with everything that has to do with the music world ... and thankfully so, as we shall see. After all, in all irony, under this new name and AFTER leaving the band, he will be playing an even greater role than he ever had before as the songwriter and guitarist of Sparrow ...

Dennis Edmonton (Mars Bonfire from now on) goes to a release manager and is promptly engaged as a songwriter. This more nine-to-five job and a more regular lifestyle, will in the future save him from the stress that musicians have when they have to travel back and forth at any cost and have to perform constantly. He wants to slow down across the board and decides to enjoy his free time more every now and then. With the little money he had been able to save, he promptly buys himself a second-hand car: an old Ford Falcon, six cylinders. Immediately after the split up of The Sparrow, Mars goes out in his car as often as possible. He now wants to enjoy the other pleasures of life to the full. He takes nice trips with his car and regularly visits the wider area of Beverly Hills, Malibu, and the Santa Monica Recreation Park. One of his trips has bizarre consequences and the incident ends up going straight into the history books of the music world ...

Throughout the California hinterlands, it's always pretty hot in the summer and the air-conditioning in Mars' car doesn't work. So, to cool down a bit, he winds both windows all the way down. The wind then plays flirtatiously through his hair and this feeling inspires him to quietly hum a few appropriate phrases. He links those to a constructed tune, and he rehearses it on his guitar at home. *"Get your motor running, head out on the highway."*

One fine day, Mars is once again on the road in his Ford Falcon, and the imagined and somewhat revolutionary-sounding tune is now playing uninterruptedly through his head. *"Looking for adventure, in what ever comes our way"* he adds, humming this self-created melody and imitating the improvised guitar play with his mouth. But while he is enjoying the freedom in his car, suddenly a huge thunderstorm breaks over the region. The storm is accompanied by a heavy cloudburst. Within a minute, the whole road looks more like a swimming pool than a highway. The car becomes increasingly difficult to drive. The water beats against the windshield and the windshield wipers can no longer cope with the influx, even at maximum speed, while bright lightning flashes continuously across the sky above his head. The car loses grip on the soaking wet road surface due to aquaplaning. He has to grab the steering wheel firmly with both hands. Meanwhile, there is a continuous loud roar all around and the deafening crackle of thunder close by make him a little anxious. Those rolling thunderclaps curiously form a nice homogeneous whole with the nice humming and purring sound of the smooth six-cylinder combustion engine in the front of his Ford Falcon. The six pistons, despite the heavy weather in the background, continue to quietly growl their revolutionary work of the crankshaft as if nothing is wrong. That engine is clearly much more at ease here than Dennis himself. Then it calms down a bit outside and Dennis -aka Mars- also starts to relax a bit. He immediately adds his newfound inspiration to the simple tune that has been floating through his mind for several days. With *"Heavy metal thunder"* he joins that infernal thunderstorm and the joyful banging of the six cylinders in his Ford Falcon and adds those words to the rest of the makeshift text he already had. Strolling the streets of LA a few days later, he happens to read on the gleaming chrome air filter of a parked Harley Davidson, *"Born to Ride, Ride to Live."* He weaves all this together and eventually comes up with a basic version of *Born To Be Wild.*

He rehearses the tune on the guitar. To his own surprise, it turns out that its fresh style and sound is extremely different from all the softer pop songs he had written and played so far. *"Sounds quite revolutionary",* he thinks. But once he sets out to mold the tune into a more definitive and user-friendly form, he is forced to give it a rest. He gets into trouble with his landlord and with other residents in the building, because the amplifier of his Gibson guitar is always way too loud when he rehearses his new guitar tunes. So, his tune for *Born To Be Wild* is put on hold for the time being along with a few other songs, such as *Faster Than The Speed Of Life* . *Ride with me* comes later… But about this *Born to be Wild*: just wait and see…

While the boys are (too) often "on hold" musically, we wonder how Jutta Maue is doing in the meantime. She still resides in Toronto, and she hasn't seen her boyfriend John for a while during the past turbulent period. When she learns that the boys are not doing too well overall and are still searching for the best way, she decides to spend more time at John's side. Her US immigration papers have now been processed so she can also (finally) visit her future husband, who already lives in California. The regular break in the band's performances will give her and John the opportunity to rekindle the notion "that they actually are engaged." Jutta realizes that John is in a difficult phase and a little moral support from her will do him some good. So, she moves to faraway Los Angeles and they get married almost instantly. Together they rent a fairly cheap flat at number 7408 on Fountain Avenue, above a garage. John is still often on the road, looking for opportunities in the music world. But when Sparrow split up, he is very happy to have Jutta by his side…

By now, we arrive in August 1967. Jutta has found a job in LA as a waitress, while John and his former pal from the New Balladeer of a few years ago, Morgan Cavett, are knocking on the doors of local managers. They want to follow in the footsteps of Mars Bonfire in the music business and find a job as a songwriter or something like that. It's wasted energy for now. No one is apparently waiting for them. But luck is with John, because at the ideal moment Lady Fortune once again extends a hand. A hand? This time it is a lot more than that! He receives a firm push in the back.

At times, the world does indeed seem much smaller than it actually is. Jutta happens to play a particularly key role in this (and actually completely unconsciously at first) …

Jutta had built up a fairly wide circle of friends during the years she lived in Toronto. That was logical because she is social, adventurous and spontaneous. One of her former friends over there, Dorothy Scully, told her early August of that year 1967, that she was also married. She married a certain Gabriel Mekler, a Jewish boy born in Palestine in 1942*. Dorothy now comes to live in Los Angeles as well, and she apparently gets a job in the same establishment where Jutta works. The newlyweds, Dorothy Scully and Gabriel Mekler, move into the apartment next door to John and Jutta's house on Fountain Avenue. Dorothy and Jutta spontaneously fall into each other's arms now that they can see each other again. And that so far from the place where they first met some years ago. They had already planned to meet somewhere to catch up. But when that happens by such a coincidence, makes it all the more fun of course. They both have to laugh because of these incredibly unforeseen circumstances. They sit around for hours talking like old chatterboxes. That's how Jutta finds out that Dorothy's new husband, Gabriel, cannot only play the piano and guitar very well, but he also turns out to be a renowned producer at the record company … Dunhill Records. Jutta pricks up her ears and realizes that this could be an opportunity for her husband. She speaks to John about it that very night. This is an opportunity that he must not let slip, she thinks. A new spark of hope that it might still work out, bubbles up immediately in John's energetic brain and body. If he indeed gets the support of Gabriel the options are open again. After all, has Gabriel Mekler not been the driving force behind the burgeoning success of Three Dog Night, Janis Joplin and Etta James, among others? He and his most energic teammates Richard Podolor and Bill Cooper also gave singer Cher a hand on the road to success. So why couldn't Gabriel help John and his band?

But first, of course, he has to convince Gabriel that Sparrow is still okay, not only musically but also that the band members still get along well. After all, the group recently split up and the contacts have cooled down ever since… Next, John Kay and Gabriel Mekler meet.

In 1942, Israel did not yet exist.

According to Gabriel, the Dunhill Label is constantly looking for new talent and especially for a breath of fresh air in the music world. After the period of a relatively quiet genre of the mid-'60s, with groups like Peter, Paul and Mary (on the East Coast) and The Mamas & The Papas (on the West Coast), among others, the sound can now be a little rougher. John presents the tapes Sparrow have recorded over the past few years to a surprised Gabriel, who says to John:

"Coincidence doesn't exist. It's hard to understand why no one really bothered to listen to you guys before. I think these demos are good and I will talk to my contacts about it. In the meantime, can you call the members of Sparrow back together?"

John, however, is rather annoyed with this, because the breakup with Sparrow seems final. But he has nothing to lose. He contacts Jerry and Goldy, and they are so enthusiastic that they eagerly agree to try again. But not all five are so eager to comply with John's request. Bassist Nick sticks to his guns and wants to stay with T.I.M.E. Guitarist Mars Bonfire has had enough of all the stress he has been under lately. So they cannot count on Mars as a guitarist. Annoying, but they have to move on now. So, the trio John - Jerry - Goldy (the three people who in retrospect would remain the actual core of the band from 1967 to January 1975) had to look for a new guitarist and bass player in the summer of 1967.

They don't have to search very long for a new guitarist, because John actually already has someone in mind himself. He asks Michael Monarch, a seventeen-year-old young man from the neighborhood. This handsome, cheerful and young guy with mahogany brown wavy hair is extremely happy to jump into the gap. He is not a total stranger to the others either, as he had already practiced with Sparrow a few times and even co-hosted one of the performances at the Galaxy club. Although he is quite a bit younger than the other members, his age in itself cannot be an obstacle. He has been playing music since he was seven years old, and he does it all in a less tense and more enthusiastic way than Mars did. Mars always acted more like a statue, standing still when he played the guitar, both in the studio and on stage during live performances. Michael radiates much more energy, and he also dares to take initiative on stage and that may well benefit the overall sound at the right time. And if necessary, the older members of the group will be able to give Michael a little guidance*. Problem now is just the bass player ...

The trio decides to place a simple add in local music magazines and hang out some flyers in Wallichs Music City, LA's main music store: *"Bass player wanted. Report above garage, house number 7408 on Fountain Avenue"*. That's all it says. Now they have to wait for a suitable candidate to come forward ...

Gabriel Mekler also wants another, slightly more evocative name for this new group. All with the intention of being able to start with renewed energy on a completely clean sheet. (John Kay &) Sparrow is definitively relegated to the archives, much to the regret of the boys themselves. They preferred to keep Sparrow as the name of the group. Gabriel, however, has an ideal name for them in mind. He uses the title of the book that is still on the coffee table in his apartment and that he had recently read. The novel *Der Steppewolf* by Hermann Hesse, a modern classic, first published in 1927, the period of the Weimar Republic in Germany. Gabriel Mekler, as a born Jew, wanted to know how things were in Germany before Jew-hater Adolf Hitler and his brown shirts took over and decided to exterminate all Jews. He finds the name appropriate, but he also associates the contents of the book with young men who have doubts about their own personalities.

It could also be a perfect allusion to the behavior and the experiences so far of ... these Sparrow members. The name of the new band itself is altered from *Der Steppewolf* into a more Anglo- sounding "Steppenwolf". In the meantime, the band members practice daily with renewed courage -but for the time being without a bassist- in John's garage at 7408 Fountain Avenue.

---

* John would find out two years later that this was as good as hopeless.

Suddenly, during a rehearsal a few days later, John's garage door is opened very slowly. While the door hinges are still creaking a bit, an eighteen-year-young man -completely unknown to them so far- is standing on the doorstep. He has long wavy, curly hair. On his back, he carries a large bag, in which the contour shapes of a long-stemmed guitar are clearly outlined. Somewhat surprised and not very sure about himself, he first takes a good look around. Then he says blushing and with a little stutter:

"Oh, hello … are you those guys who are searching for a bass player?"

"Sure, and who are you?"

"Well, my name is John Morgan Russell, but they also call me Rushton Moreve. I saw that advertisement."

The young man is asked to "jam" immediately along a bit and to improvise something himself. He spontaneously starts strumming on those four thick strings of his bass guitar, while letting out some incoherent words that are running through his head at that moment. It goes something like this:

"I like this. Oh Yes! I like this job. Oh, Yes, Yes!" …

Apparently, Rushton Moreve is working as a professional electrician. But even though he's singing *"I like my job"*, his job as an electrician is only temporary, because, according to him, he would rather be a pirate if he couldn't earn his living as a musician.

Together with some other incoherent phrases, he passionately plucks on the four thick strings and immediately makes a good impression on the other guys. Goldy, Jerry, John and also Michael: they all agree: Rushton's introduction is very successful. It's even more than that. John likes Rushton's improvised and crazy tune so much, that he promptly puts it on tape and listens to it several times that same evening on his brand-new stereo equipment in his living room, above the garage. He adds a very strange electronical intro to Rushton's amazing base tune and changes *"I like my job"* in *"I like to dream"* and he adds some other simple lyrics. The assembly of Rushton's improvised bass tune, that electronical "sound machine" addition and the simple lyrics John writes down, will finally lead to Steppenwolf's second major world hit *Magic Carpet Ride*, signed Kay/Moreve, a little later (in October 1968).

Rushton commits himself as the fifth member of Steppenwolf. And as for his name: Goldy McJohn laughingly whispers to him that they should just call him Rushton till the end of time, because otherwise there would be too many "Johns" and that their front man John Kay might pull a surprise out of his magic hat for him …

The days are passing by, and the tension is rising by the minute. They rehearse five to six hours a day in John's garage. For a moment, doubt strikes again, but then Goldy suddenly enters John's apartment with a big smile on his face. He stretches out both arms in front of him and puts them enthusiastically on John's shoulders. He looks John very convincingly straight in the eye:

"John, my dear friend! It seems we have a record deal! I just saw Gabriel Mekler and he couldn't wait to tell me. Reb Foster and Bill Utley are our management contacts at Dunhill. A certain Richard Podolor will do the "arrangements". I told him I would give you the good news immediately."

The spell has finally been broken. This is the opportunity of a lifetime.

Full of enthusiasm, the band heads to the studio and under the guidance of producer Gabriel Mekler, a whole series of progressive sounding rock & blues songs are recorded. Thanks to the professional technical assistance by Richard Podolor and Bill Cooper, the final sound results into something really great. Often the songs are recently written by John, but there are also a few covers from other artists which they played before with Sparrow. Completely new arrangements are written for them with different accents. The most important are Don Covay's *Sookie, Sookie*, a song that Jerry, John and Goldy remember from The Arthur club in New York, and Hoyt Axton's *The Pusher*, which John had put forward as a potential song for their first album. McKinley Morganfield's (Muddy Waters) *Hoochie Cootchie Man* is also given its own fresh sound. These three songs, with their new arrangements, are part of Steppenwolf's first studio recordings. Also *A Girl I Knew*, the first song written by John and his pal Morgan Cavett, is recorded. The aim is to produce an album with *only* really good material, because it has to be a real hit from the start. Potential hit singles -A-side and B-side- will be selected from those songs. They are still looking for some suitable songs to add to their recordings and so Jerry gets in touch with his brother Dennis. Can Dennis -who is known as Mars Bonfire- perhaps provide some useful song material? Jerry asks what he might have on offer.

That same evening, Mars Bonfire is on his way to his brother Jerry's apartment. In his hand he carries a recorded tape of his own, wrapped in a small cardboard envelope. On it, there are some songs that he, as a songwriter, has composed himself at home in his apartment. When Mars rings the doorbell of his brother Jerry, no one is home. Mars can tell by the nervous barking of Jerry's dog, which is quite fierce towards Mars. Mars decides to deposit the envelope with the recordings through the small opening in the door. Later on, he calls Jerry on the phone to let him know he dropped off the envelope at his place. But when Jerry comes home a bit later, he doesn't find any envelope. He's afraid that his dog has been having fun with it and that he will find the remains of the recording tapes in tatters somewhere in the kitchen.

The cover has indeed been shredded to pieces by the dog, but fortunately, he finds its contents -the tape- back in the kitchen in good condition ...

When listening to Mars Bonfire's demos, the members of the band frown at first. It turns out that all of Mars' guitar work is recorded without the use of his guitar amplifier. So, their reaction to his "contribution" is pretty lukewarm at first, to say the least. The demo of that totally new *Born To Be Wild* Mars is so eager to show off here, sounds more like a lament of someone dealing with severe depression. *"You call this song Born to be **Wild**. You really mean this, Dennis?"* It sounds more like a ballad and the boys almost fall asleep. Is it possible that our old and good buddy, Dennis aka Mars, has suffered a brain trauma from that thunderstorm up there on the Malibu?

"Yes, of course I recorded that at home without using my amplifier. But what do you want? My neighbors have complained, and my landlord has threatened to evict me from my apartment next time there's too much noise!" Mars defends himself.

Jerry suggests they give it a go anyway, and he asks guitarist Michael if he sees a possibility of turning that demo of his brother into a screeching rocking intro. Seventeen-year-old Michael immediately gives it a violent kick and he turns that whole *Born To Be Wild* ballad from Mars Bonfire completely upside down. Goldy adds his progressive funky-organ sounds in an amazingly clever way and Jerry makes the drums sound like a rumbling tam-tam in the jungle.

With the addition of Rushton's bold baseline and John's grainy, at times aggressive voice, the song ends up sounding very revolutionary. Mars Bonfire, without even knowing it, has laid the groundwork for a true masterpiece. A ride through a heavy thunderstorm can be really useful ... The band members give the song its final shape and they see it as an immediate potential success ...

The first album of Steppenwolf is ready to be released in November 1967. This happens on a Monday. That Monday is not important in itself, but the next day, on Tuesday, the album is already in the top 50 in the US. Within two weeks, the album is in the top 5 in the US. An unprecedented and unexpected success, and all this without one single hit single being released. Apparently, a lot of people in the States were waiting for this to happen. The guys are lucky that a lot of progressive "underground" stations don't play just the advanced contenders for success of that album and that there is no talk of hit singles at all on those stations. No, they play all the songs that appear on that album. Later, John will laughingly explain that it seemed like the guys at the FM stations were a little too often under the "benevolent influence of some medication" so they didn't care too much about what exactly was being played on the radio, as long as it sounded sufficiently progressive. But that remarkable success has to be put to work right now, and a successful hit can provide an exponential effect in sales figures. So, the success should accentuate their predetermined hit singles in the top US billboard lists. The boys promptly put forward *Born To Be Wild* themselves as the best contender for a 45-rpm record success ... But not everyone is easily convinced. Richard Podolor thinks that using *BTBW* as a hit single is too much of a risk. Admittedly, they are certainly looking for a somewhat rougher genre, but this seems a bit over the top as a single. There is some doubt. The record label's CEO proposes a compromise and suggests to send all the recorded songs to his own teenage daughter and her friends. That way, he thinks, he can gauge the reactions among these younger people, for whom these songs are ultimately intended anyway.

His daughter, however, categorically rejects *BTBW* and gives the reason as "too heavy". Again, isn't that really typical when you ask *only girls* about something like that? She indicates the much softer *A Girl I Knew* as the single with the best potential of scoring in the charts. This song was written by the duo Morgan Cavett/John Kay and *A Girl I Knew* becomes Steppenwolf's very first 45-rpm record.

The five band members themselves thought this was *not* the best choice, but they are forced to do what they are asked. However, it soon looks as if the boys will be proved right. The song does not score very well at all and the other side of the single, *The Ostrich*, does contain a clear human and political message, but the song does not seem commercial enough and not suitable to reach the top of the charts.

A second single appears early in January 1968 and that will be their own version of Don Covay's *Sookie Sookie*. The song already sounds a little rougher and is full of rhythm, so it's great for dancing and swinging. There is also more promotion. Nice video clips are recorded with John and Goldy very well dressed. Everything helps for some more publicity. There is clearly improvement compared to the previous single. But also now, the (expected) success does not come. One of the underlying reasons for this may not lie in the selected song itself, but apparently has its roots in very bizarre and totally different things. Racism was still rampant in the US in the late '60s and may have been *one* of the reasons for the lack of a breakthrough with many radio stations. Tensions ran high again between the African Americans and the US government during this specific period. Martin Luther King was pressing more militantly for a normalization of the American way of life, demanding equal status and treatment for African Americans. More people support the protests and there are more and more demonstrations against racism. But a side effect of this is that, initially, many white and tolerant people in the music business also become victim of the situation. Some stations that are operated by people with dark skin color and who normally broadcast a lot of blues and rock music, suddenly stubbornly refuse to carry this music any longer in their own music studios if it is made by *white* blues artists. Blues music, according to them, is -rightly so by the way- the music that was created by the African-American community. They did that in order to express their deep misery during slavery in America, with all the prejudice towards the black community.

Steppenwolf, whose bluesy genre is also partly based on the goodwill of these stations, is somewhat affected by this and *Sookie Sookie,* just like its predecessor, is in danger of being forgotten pretty soon ...

But actually, there is more to it than just a little ill will on the part of some radio stations. What is at odds with the lesser success of their hit singles so far, is that their debut album *Steppenwolf* as a whole, strangely enough, is still doing very well. So, it must be due not only to marketing or a possible boycott, but equally to wrong choices that their singles are not yet scoring very high on the American charts. They put their heads together and the boys of the group instinctively revert to *BTBW*. Meanwhile, the trio Blue Cheer from their neighborhood finished an underground version of Eddy Cochran's *Summertime Blues*, and it sounds very progressive, too. So, Dickie Peterson, Leigh Stevens and Paul Whaley are sticking their necks out by playing such a hard-sounding genre of music! Iron Butterfly is going the same hard way. And they have had some success with it! Even in England, American guitarist Jimi Hendrix puts more and more of those extreme sounding guitar solos in his repertoire. It seems like the ideal moment to finally release *BTBW* as a single ...

The record company gets nervous but finally agrees. However, there are still doubts about using *BTBW* as the A-side of the single. So, the 45-rpm single takes the slightly less progressive sounding *Everybody's Next One* on the B-side, but the record company lets the radio stations decide which side they choose as the A-side and which song they will play more often. The radio stations soon know which sound has the most potential ... and this time, they hit the bull's eye ...

Everything that will follow after that summer of 1968 for Steppenwolf, can actually be filed under the great general heading of international music history. *BTBW* conquers all the charts and not only in the US. Also, in Europe it is at the absolute top for several weeks in all countries. And the band, its management, the record company and ... songwriter Mars Bonfire will do well out of it. Suddenly, all doors are open to much more success.

Mars Bonfire, who in his nightmares could already see himself working for a living somewhere in Detroit's General Motor factories, had struck a gigantic blow and found a major gap in the market. Steppenwolf is considered in music history to be one of the *absolute* pioneers of rough hard rock. *Born To Be Wild* was the actual, real trailblazer in that field.

```
 1  (1)  PEOPLE GOT TO BE FREE
                              Rascals, Atlantic
➤2  (2)  BORN TO BE WILD  Steppenwolf, Dunhill
 3  (4)  LIGHT MY FIRE
                         Jose Feliciano, RCA Victor
 4  (3)  HELLO, I LOVE YOU  Doors, Elektra
 5  (6)  SUNSHINE OF YOUR LOVE
                                    Cream, Atco
 6  (—)  (You Keep Me) HANGIN' ON
                              Vanilla Fudge, Atco
 7  (—)  HARPER VALLEY P.T.A.
                         Jeannie C. Riley, Plantation
 8  (—)  YOU'RE ALL I NEED TO GET BY
               Marvin Gaye and Tammi Terrell, Tamla
 9  (9)  I CAN'T STOP DANCING
                    Archie Bell and the Drells, Atlantic
10 (10)  STAY IN MY CORNER ... Dells, Cadet
```

Page 183 below: The ten bestselling songs of the American top 100 in the early summer of 1968. For weeks BTBW *hovers between nos. 5 and 2. It will unfortunately never reach no. 1.*

Above: Photo for the front cover of the first album by the original Steppenwolf. Only later on this album was called The First. *From left to right Michael Monarch, Rushton Moreve, Jerry Edmonton, John Kay (with tie and without dark glasses) and Goldy McJohn. This cover photo was also used for the cover of the single* Born To Be Wild.

The summer of 1968, somewhere in West Berlin. Steppenwolf is now currently in the spotlight in the US and are a popular guest everywhere. They can be seen live on stage, in all sorts of TV shows and at the better-known music festivals. But now, we let Jerry, Rushton, Goldy, Michael and John enjoy their success for a while, and we go to the other side of the world, far away from the metropolis of Los Angeles and the American West Coast. We go to Europe. In the free zone of West Berlin in Germany, a certain Mathias Greffrath is at work. Since Mathias finished his studies and completed his military service with the German *Bundeswehr*, he has been working here in this city as a journalist at a local newspaper. He is twenty-three years young and full of healthy ambition. He dreams of one day writing his own works. (Later on he will indeed write several books). Besides his professional activities, which he carries out with passion and full conviction, Mathias is an avid music lover. His editor-in-chief has no problem with the radio playing songs all day long at the editorial office. Often these are typical local German hits, such as from Udo Jürgens, Connie Froboess, Roy Black, Heino and Peter Alexander. But occasionally, they also tune in to the popular international stations, where modern British pop music and even American rock songs are also played. Sometimes this and sometimes that. A matter of letting all employees have their way in turn.

One day in the summer of 1968, Mathias hears a very unusual rock song on the radio. This bizarre, rhythmically strong, and screeching song sounds revolutionary to him. And what about that -never heard before- grainy sounding and venomous voice of the singer! He had never heard anything like this in his whole life: "*We were born, born to be wild. We can climb so high, I never want to die ... born to be wild, born to be wild ...*" Followed by rumbling drums and solid guitar playing combined with rock-hard, heavenly organ sounds and a deep bass line. "*What a good song! What could be the name of that mysterious group?*" Asks Mathias. "*Steppenwolf*" they say a little later on the radio, and it turns out to be an American group ...

"*Ach so! Der Steppenwolf, das war auch ein Buch von die Schweizerischer Schriftsteller Hermann Hesse aus Calw, Baden-Württemberg."*
(*"Oh, Steppenwolf, that was a book by the Swiss writer Hermann Hesse from Calw, Baden-Württemberg"*)

Mathias thinks by himself as he unconsciously smiles for a moment. Because of course he remembers this German literary classic from his own student days. That book had even been required study material for him in high school. At that moment he doesn't give it much more thought. The song is often repeated on the radio. German stations include the summer hit *BTBW* on their play lists and in the summer of 1968, it is in the absolute top of the major charts in Europe. Especially throughout Scandinavia and Western Europe, the song is extraordinarily successful. But in West Germany not only the *hit*, but also *the band* that performs the song suddenly gets a lot more attention. "*That's strange*," thinks Mathias. At first, he doesn't understand why that is, but apparently the reason for all the attention the boys are getting in Germany is that the singer of the song is not American or Canadian at all. In fact, the singer turns out to be ... a German. A singer who is originally German and who brings over from America this kind of music and is successful with it. Again, Mathias smiles to himself, because it suddenly reminds him of that somewhat mysterious boy he used to know in Hannover. You know, that visually impaired boy with the dark glasses he had known there during his early childhood. That somewhat introverted friend of his, whom he hadn't seen for ten years and who, at the time, in that small flat in Kronenstrasse in Hannover, also stood in front of the mirror daydreaming about his own musical career in the United States of America. What was that boy's name again? Ah yes, der Joachim Fritz, the son of our kind and friendly neighbor Elsbeth Zimmermann ...

But in the German *Heimat* the fact that the singer is originally German naturally arouses both the sympathy and further curiosity of the many listeners and music lovers. Reports appear in the major German newspapers and the most popular music magazines. The editors of a few monthly magazines have already been able to figure out that this singer of the band Steppenwolf actually turns out to be a former resident of *East* Germany, behind the Iron Curtain. Someone who initially even came from distant East Prussia and whose mother, as a war refugee, had first arrived in Thuringia with him as a baby. Apparently, he had also lived for several years afterwards somewhere in West Germany after having escaped.

Mathias suddenly realizes that there are several similarities between him and this (as yet) mysterious singer. Mathias' own family at the time consisted almost entirely of *Heimatvertriebenen* (war refugees). To begin with, his pregnant mother, because Mathias himself was born in 1945. After their flight from Pomerania in January 1945, his family (with his pregnant mother) had also finally arrived in Hannover. By the way, more than 20% of the inhabitants of the city of Hannover in 1946 were former war refugees who were stranded there. Materially they had nothing left, but a solid sense of solidarity kept them going in the first years after the war. Little by little, the situation improved, thanks to the generous Marshall Plan and the recovering economy ...

Mathias muses a bit more and sees his childhood years in his thoughts. The ruins next to his apartment where they played hide and seek, soccer matches and other fun games and raced around on their bicycles. Then he continues reading the article and he suddenly notices that the singer also lived in Hannover for a while.

"Ah, der Sanger kommt aus Hannover, genau wie Ich."
("So, the singer is from Hannover, just like me")

Mathias feels an ever-increasing tension as he continues to read the article. He feels that he is about to get the confirmation here of what he has already suspected for a while, but he needs complete certainty in order to believe it.

When he reads a bit further that the singer of the group Steppenwolf wears dark glasses all the time on doctor's prescription, that he indeed lived in Hannover until 1958 and goes by the name of ... Joachim Fritz Krauledat ... Mathias is totally flabbergasted, and he almost literally falls off his chair ...

"Der Joachim? Mensch, das ist mein alter Freund aus die Kronenstrasse? That can't be true!"

Mathias' surprise is complete and to be sure he is not dreaming, he has to read the article over again. Well, I'll be damned! If that is true? Of course, he knows this Joachim! And he even knows him very well! Joachim lived in Kronenstrasse 35/37, just like he did. Joachim and his mother Elsbeth lived on the third floor, while he, Mathias, lived on the first floor in that same apartment building. It was with him that, as a child, he had played daily in the ruins close to their apartment building. Together they had imitated Elvis Presley, Little Richard and Pat Boone in front of the mirror hanging downstairs in the hall with a homemade guitar made of glued plywood. Together they had sung in front of the mirror English songs of which neither of them understood a word. Joachim had been his absolute best friend in Hannover, and he had always looked up to him like someone looks up to a big brother. Together they had spent entire vacations romping among the ruins and they had spent time together tinkering with their bikes. Where they rode their bikes, the ground was littered with glass shards and nails lying around everywhere. Fixing flat tires was as good as a daily occurrence. Mathias also knew about Joachim's unfortunate situation at the time in Hannover and how often the boy had been bullied because of those thick, dark glasses. Glasses that he could not do without, because he could not tolerate daylight. He also remembers his swollen foot, when someone had deliberately swapped the ball for a brick during the eleven-meter kick and Joachim, unsuspecting, kicked the brick hard and cried out in pain.

Out of necessity he even had to be sent to a special school, otherwise nothing would come of studying. When Joachim left for Canada for good in March 1958, he left an enormous void in Mathias' weak little heart. But he knew that Joachim would somehow make it in the world. Joachim may have been a loner, but he was an intelligent loner full of healthy energy. A bit of a rebel and with some introverted traits, but very inventive and energetic without his work ethic turning into arrogance. Mathias is really happy for Joachim. He had always hoped to see him again one day.*

"Das gefällt mir! That confounded Joachim. He's managed to make it after all. Unglaublich!"

Both in and outside the US, the first Steppenwolf album now sells like hot cakes. *The Pusher* also appears on single, but it doesn't swing as much and therefore doesn't reach the top of the charts. However, the boys are so full of ambition that they immediately have enough songs ready for the next album. According to their hard-fought contract, they have to produce new studio material about twice a year.

The successor to the successful first album will simply be called *The Second*. Again, Mars Bonfire will contribute with *Faster Than The Speed Of Life* and in its entirety, the album alternates between slightly softer pop (such as *28*) and firmly bluesy songs. But what is also striking is that some of the songs are getting a more political or socio-problematic content. *The Ostrich,* on their first album was their first militant song.

In the second album, that political accent will intensify. In songs like *None Of Your Doing,* the band will already make it clear how they feel about the traumas experienced by some Vietnam veterans on their return to the US after spending time in the jungles of South-East Asia. But especially in the song *Don't Step On The Grass, Sam* they explicitly draw the card of anti-militarism. In that song they expose some weaknesses (including drug use) in the Defense Department, and they will therefore antagonize a large part of mainly conservative Americans, especially Republican supporters. Many of them, after all, still remember the Second World War and the fact that he is of

---

* *Many years later, Mathias would visit John Kay in his mansion near Franklin. His visit pleased him enormously. What struck him was that, despite his age and the rock image John also projected in his spare time with his leather pants and boots, the expression in his eyes had not changed in over 40 years. Mathias also interviewed John one day in Vancouver. That interview was published in the weekend edition of the German magazine* Stern. *Both Danish Wolfpackers Lars Hendrik Christensen and Nicolai Enig (see chapter Arnstadt 2022) happened to meet Mathias Greffrath in Vancouver by complete coincidence…*

German origin and that he is the one to come up with such texts about the US will meet with a great deal of incomprehension. But all this is only the beginning; just wait and see ... We have already mentioned that the intro of their second big hit *Magic Carpet Ride,* which is also from that excellent album *The Second,* originated from some improvisations with a bass guitar and a converter in John's stereo system. The rest of the song is really brilliantly constructed, with a nicely balanced mix of organ and guitar play and other sounds; never heard before until then. Their manager, Gabriel Mekler, will also write a few songs, but he also wants to make his own contribution in the studio for once. As an exception, he plays rhythm guitar on that song. *MCR* reaches the same heights as *BTBW* in the US in the later fall of 1968, and the group is now really at the very top in the US. In Europe, however, outside Scandinavia and Germany, their unusual-sounding songs do not cause any major euphoria. In Belgium (this author's homeland), *MCR* does briefly enter the charts, but the song does not score as well as its predecessor. The song is also barely played on our stations ...

In the meantime, unfortunately, a few blemishes appear in the general behavior of some of the band members. The use of drugs has unfortunately entered the lives of the boys and, moreover, their increasingly egocentric macho behavior does not help the band's cohesion.

Sometimes the combination of drug use and self-centered behavior is the element that has an exponentially negative effect on their performance and even more on their attitude. Both their manager and tour director have their hands full trying to keep the band members more or less in line. Or as Jutta Maue perfectly describes it much later with a smile on her face, *"The more success they had, the more the egos started to play up."* But for the time being, because of their megasuccess, the boys feel untouchable ...

Fall of 1968, The Second album

And other, somewhat unusual, occurrences suddenly cross their path. Rushton Moreve, the most-recent member to join the band and a bassist in permanent employment of Steppenwolf since eighteen months after their advertisement in a music shop, is with them on tour in the US in the fall of 1968. They are somewhere on the East Coast when, just a couple of days before his twentieth birthday, Rushton suddenly presents the band with a very unpleasant surprise. He categorically refuses to fly back with the others to California, where they have contractual obligations to play a few more concerts this year ...

Rushton has been having some very peculiar worries for a while now. Not that he feels out of place in the band, on the contrary, but he clearly has other problems and one of them is a fear of sudden natural disasters …

His wife and he are members of a group of people who have been analyzing seismographic studies for a while now, and they are firmly convinced that there will be a massive earthquake on the American West Coast in the near future. There will be a giant landslide and probably one that has never been seen in our modern era. The pressure on the San Andreas fault has increased so much for several decades that, according to these people, this cannot continue for much longer. The entire coastline of about 2250 kilometers, from San Diego via Los Angeles and San Francisco to Vancouver, would be completely wiped off the face of the earth and disappear into the Pacific Ocean. Indeed, in theory, all such things could happen, and of course you don't have to be a seismologist to realize that. The entire US West Coast is located on a shifting fault line, and the increasing pressure is likely to become too much at a certain time. Once upon a time this occurred with the island of Krakatau in Indonesia which simply exploded and instantly partly disappeared under water. A similar incident also happened in Europe, with the Greek island of Santorini in the Cyclades in the Aegean Sea. After a landslide, the island was suddenly torn in two and within seconds almost half the island disappeared into the depths. A sixty-foot tsunami raced across the Aegean Sea and also caused huge damage to the surrounding islands. Critics will say that this happened more than 3500 years ago, but in the time measurement of our planet, 3500 years is nothing. That an earthquake will occur on the US West Coast is a 100% certainty, according to experts. According to the US Geological Survey, it is only a matter of time. It could happen within ten to twenty years, but just as easily within 200 years or possibly even 2,000 years.

Bass guitarist Rushton Moreve in 1968. Rushton died thirteen years later (in 1981) in a motorcycle accident ... in Sun Valley, Santa Barbara, California. By then he was living on the American West Coast, the region he had wanted to escape at all costs in the fall of 1968.

According to Rushton and his wife, however, this massive landslide in California is more likely to happen *today* than tomorrow. They are completely terrified and decide to leave California as soon as possible to build a new life away from the impending cataclysm. Ideally, Rushton would like to move to Venice, Italy, but it won't come to that. Jumping out of a plane without a parachute, one of his other fantasies, he won't do either. He will eventually have a lethal accident ... in 1981 with a motorcycle ...

So, Rushton quits while on tour, early November 1968. On a Friday during that month he plays with the band, but the day after he doesn't fly with them to their next gig. Consequence for Steppenwolf: from one day to the next, they are without a bassist. Rushton has disappeared just as quickly with his guitar on his back as he had arrived in John's garage at 7408 Fountain Avenue in the summer of 1967. But fortunately, there is a substitute who knows all the tunes. The guys have him fly over right away.

John, Jerry, Goldy and Michael have asked Nick to come back and join Steppenwolf. Nick leaves T.I.M.E. and is in fact incredibly happy to be back with the boys he knows from Toronto and New York. The tensions that had lingered after The Sparrow's split up are sorted out. Nick, in turn, is replaced in T.I.M.E. by George Biondo. We'll be hearing from George soon too, by the way. Full of energy, Nick rejoins the band he left a while ago. The others are happy that the prodigal son is back. Nick is working hard on the new album that is in the pipeline. All the folds seem to have been smoothed out again.

"I've secretly always loved the band and their music. I was extremely happy to jump back on the bandwagon when it passed by. I was extremely happy that they asked me."

A little later, in the spring of 1969, the third Steppenwolf album is released under the name *At Your Birthday Party*. This time, however, the right pilot single is selected. *Rock Me* is released as a satellite track, it was written by John Kay himself not too long ago for the movie *Candy*. *Candy* is a film about an extremely quirky and mysterious girl, featuring actors like Richard Burton, James Coburn, Marlon Brando and, for the occasion, Ringo Starr. *Rock Me* is a surprisingly nice and swinging rock song that once again shoots up the charts. Not only in the US, but also in Europe the song scores quite well and in a lot of "more progressive" pubs here at home the song sounds through the speakers of the jukebox. When the promising song enters the US Billboard charts after only one week at no. 45, it is thought that a real no. 1 in the US is very soon possible. To further promote the single, the boys are invited for several television and radio shows. They are very welcome guests in Hugh Hefner's Playboy shows and Ed Sullivan also regularly invites the boys in his TV shows. The band is gaining in popularity every time. All over the US, young people are apparently going crazy about Steppenwolf.

The next support activity is planned at the headquarters of the AM radio stations. Making a good impression there almost guarantees an even higher top ranking in the charts. But that's where it all goes wrong, unfortunately ...

At the end of the '60s, AM (Amplitude Modulation) stations in the US still take up most of the "airwaves". The much purer FM waves (Frequency Modulation) are indeed much clearer and are also more resistant to possible interference, but they are "too high" and as such cannot reach far enough. In the 1960s, AM was absolutely indispensable for providing radio reception in remote areas of a country as vast as the USA. So that was the main reason for the existence of AM stations. If that multitude of AM stations would play *Rock Me,* the whole country would be able to hear Steppenwolf regularly, even in the remotest corners. *BTBW* and *MCR* were still stranded at no. 2, but *Rock Me* would be guaranteed to reach the coveted first place. But guitarist Michael Monarch probably put a spanner in the works by one of his youthful stupidities …

Michael has been exhibiting behavioral problems for some time during this period. Although he is a cool and cheerful guy, he is sometimes overcome by unpredictable, impulsive acts. No superstitious behavior like Rushton's, but aged 19 Michael is the absolute Benjamin of the band in 1969 and you could possibly attribute some of his impulsive antics to immature behavior. Or is he possibly under the influence of drugs at the time? Anyway, the boys are promptly shown the door by the big boss of the AM stations. In the end, they may be lucky that no police were called in and no complaint for affront to the nation was filed. What happened there?

After conducting the interview, the radio boss asks the boys to wait in the hall. He would like to have another photo shoot with them. The photographers are on their way to the studio, but they are stuck in traffic. The boys are pacing back and forth, and boredom sets in. In a small courtyard in front of the radio studio, just where the five of them then stand, there is a large marble container containing a large American Stars and Stripes flag. While waiting for the photographers, Michael finds no better way than to grab the flag with both his hands and to blow his nose right into the American national symbol. Just at the moment of his distasteful act, the door of the studio is pulled open … by the big boss of AM himself. He has just seen what Michael has done and he refuses to help the boys any further. He says to one of his employees:

"What the hell! Don't they have any respect? Throw them out of here!"

They are promptly kicked out for disrespecting established American values. This "funny"(?) act by Michael Monarch will end up costing themselves and the record company many millions of dollars. *Rock Me* is no longer played on AM stations in the US after this strange incident and instead of becoming an absolute no. 1, the otherwise good sounding song drops out of the charts after a top listing at no. 10. Their manager and producer Gabriel Mekler and Richard Podolor are furious about the loss of so much money ... and all the negative criticism they get. They are furious with Michael, and he is of course to blame. However, to be fair, we immediately add that this could also have happened to any of the others. They are all still young, they make a lot of fun everywhere, they are applauded on and off stage and teenagers go crazy for them, while an uncountable number of young girls throw themselves on the line for them. They appear regularly on TV and the world seems to be at their feet. And for doing all these fun things, they are also very richly compensated. Such a success story can quickly transform a person who is raised according to normal norms and values, into a conceited (and spoiled) person. The music and film world has been full of such stereotypical figures for more than a century, and Steppenwolf is really no longer an exception to that in the spring of 1969. The interaction between stimulants and drugs accentuates this feeling of untouchability ever more strongly, while the indifference to and even aversion of normal customs and decency in society grows further.

This was more or less the case for all the band members by now, but for Michael it was in a way even worse, because he did not fully realize how much effort it had cost John Kay and the three others to finally get where they are at the moment. Michael achieved it out of the blue, and the lack of awareness made him an unguided missile.

At the same time, however, we have to see Michael's behavior in perspective. Is his act really that much worse than the many unbecoming antics that members of other successful groups dared to pull? Like the members of Led Zeppelin, who throw their TV sets through the window of their hotel room just for fun? The Who smashing their musical instruments after each performance? Jimi Hendrix setting fire to his guitar on stage? Joe Cocker who ends up performing more in a state of inebriation than sober? Or some artists who behind the scenes just shamelessly fondle their groupies? Unfortunately, Michael's behavior is becoming more and more unpredictable. He contributed to the third Steppenwolf album *At Your Birthday Party* with all his conviction and energy. Yes, he did! At last, he had been allowed to make a major contribution of his own to the writing of some songs for the new setup. But Michael is visibly disappointed that not more of his work was selected for the new album, and he makes that very clear. He had indeed worked so hard on it and done his utmost to come up with something substantial. *Round and Down* is certainly a genuinely nice song, but that's about the only song of his selected for that album. Out of deep disappointment and to vent his frustrations, Michael is absent from the roll call several times during the following days and weeks after the completion of the album. Moreover, he simply stays away from an important photo session for the promotion of that third album. John thinks he will show up any moment and says: "*He is probably looking for some food at the market.*" But Michael doesn't show up …

To have five people on the front cover of the album, producer Gabriel Mekler, who is also present, has to take Michael's place.

By providing him with dark glasses, a long overcoat and a hat Gabriel is made unrecognizable for the occasion. So the front cover of *At Your Birthday Party* shows indeed five people. But what most people (including yours truly) won't discover until much later is that lead guitarist Michael Monarch himself is missing.

But Steppenwolf has to move forward. The band is under contract and has to perform. To promote themselves a little better, they go on tour in May '69. First a few shows in the US and then to Europe for the first time. From May 10, '69 they first visit Great Britain and then Scandinavia, Belgium, the Netherlands and Germany, to finish on May 30 in Great Britain again. The fact that they are also coming

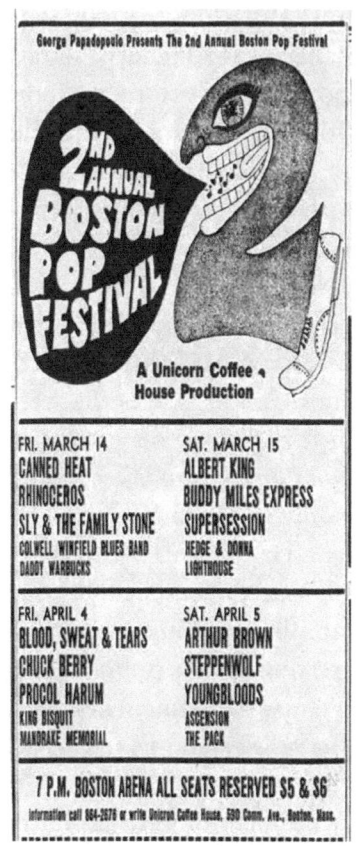

Poster of a festival in the spring of '69

On the way to their very first European tour.

to Belgium is eagerly reported in HUMO and the first reaction of many here is one of disbelief. But it is 100% certain: Steppenwolf is coming to Europe and to Belgium; and apparently to Mechelen as well ... Michael Monarch? Despite his antics from time to time, he's going with them to Europe ...

Mechelen, Belgium, May 23, 1969, 7 p.m.
While a young man of almost fourteen is still at home fretting (see introduction), several hundreds of people have filled the sports hall at Winketkaai in Mechelen that same evening. All the basketball hoops

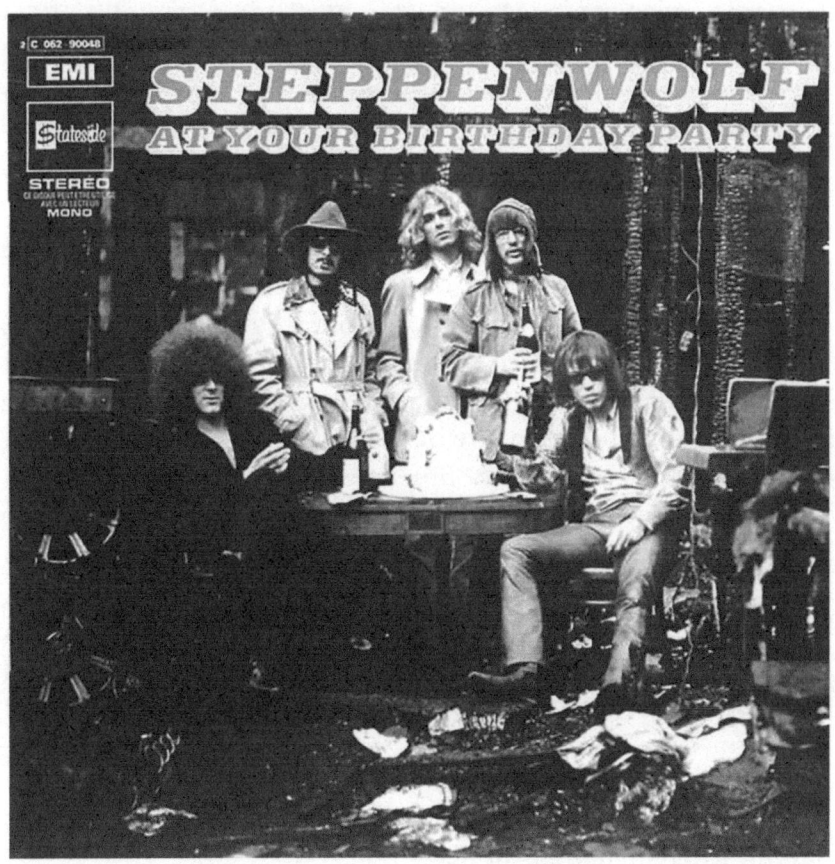

Photo of the third album, showing producer Gabriel Mekler second from left (with hat and long overcoat). Michael Monarch is missing on this photo. This shoot was taken at Canned Heat's burned-out studio in Laurel Canyon near Los Angeles.

were taken down for the occasion, the handball goals were pushed into a corner, the sports floor was covered with thick carpet and a rather primitive wooden stage was set up. That's how it was done in those days. No pleasant outdoor shows with ready-made aluminum tube frames surrounded by gigantic, black pre-stretched canvas as we see today in the events sector. Back then, it was a matter of adapting the existing infrastructure *to* the needs of the moment, *with* the means of the moment. This way, everyone could do their thing at the same venue without working wonders. Practicing sports, throwing a party, putting a group of scouts to bed, or having an occasional orchestra playing music: it was all possible at one and the same venue in a quite uncomplicated way. However, it will soon become clear that the improvisations of that time did not benefit the overall acoustics of the band that happened to be playing.

The quality of the overall sound that night is indeed a complete disaster. And one (un)important detail was clearly forgotten by the organizers in Mechelen ... or perhaps not? They did not cover up the billboard for the Mechelen beer company Lamot. When the event was aired on Flemish television in the program *Tienerklanken* three weeks later -on June 12 to be exact- that sign could regularly be seen above John Kay's head. At that time, any form of publicity on Belgian public television was absolutely taboo, and it was just as strictly enforced as the formal obligation of our newsreaders at the time to wear a tie. So that Lamot sign on TV the whole time is quite a scoop. Nice publicity for that Mechelen beer brand located at the time in Mechelen's Van Beethovenstraat on the river Dijle. That nice and pleasant location opposite the Mechelen Fish Market is still called "the Lamot site" today.

Let's give the organization the benefit of the doubt, whether that sign was displayed on purpose or not ...

Daydream we hear a little later by the drummer/singer of the Belgian group Wallace Collection led by Sylvain Vanolme on that sunny spring evening in the Mechelen sports hall. These guys were the support act waiting for the really big name on the bill. Despite the fact that their song *Daydream* -at least according to the opinion of this author- sounds very sleepy and the extremely annoying French accent of singer Freddy Nieuland does not positively influence the quality of the overall sound, the song was a hit in Belgium at the time. The song belongs to the softer popular music genre that still largely determines the existing trend in Flanders in those years. Indeed, *Daydream* is only a hit in Belgium, because popular music there, in May '69, clearly had not yet undergone that great metamorphosis that people on the West Coast of the United States are already experiencing in full. By the way, the progressive music virus that develops there, will soon spread all over the US via the big meadows of Woodstock. The softer popular music genre from Britain and American bands and singers such as The Beach Boys, The Monkees, Cowsills, The Byrds, Union Gap, The Supremes, The Four Tops, Scott McKenzie, The Mamas & The Papas and so many others is now apparently somewhat out of fashion there. That rather mild, typical mid-sixties sound has given way too much rougher blues and rock with longer and loud guitar solos. Bands such as Blue Cheer, Three Dog Night, Blood Sweat & Tears, Chicago Transit Authority, Jefferson Airplane, The Jimi Hendrix Experience, The Velvet Underground, Janis Joplin and even Eric Clapton's Cream from Britain, which has also plunged into the rougher blues genre (and I apologize for not mentioning so many others here) are now setting the new trend. In the spring of '69, Belgium however is still stuck with that typical British *soft* pop, which also includes bands like The Hollies, Manfred Mann's Earth Band, The Equals, The Small Faces, The Tremeloes and The Who. The Netherlands is musically much more advanced than Flanders (and Belgium as a whole). In the French speaking part of Belgium, it is obviously more the French music which determines what's on the popular hitlists. Also, in Belgium all those corny, typical Flemish or German schmaltz songs are still doing well. The Belgian band New Inspiration from Ghent scores a hit with *I See No Reason Why* and *Nobody*, and the Antwerp/Mechelen Pebbles score with *Get Around* and *Seven Horses In The Sky*. We have here in Belgium also an exceptionally good band, called Jess & James With The J.J. Band. Their story is rather strange and can be compared a little bit to the John Kay story. Jess and James were both Portuguese immigrant workers with no plans whatsoever for a very promising future. They came to Belgium to work in the mines; but as they were extraordinarily talented guitarists and both had a good voice, they started making music on a more professional basis. Influenced by Otis Redding and Wilson Pickett, they scored (to their own great surprise) two big hits in our region before they split up … and returned into anonymity. Of course we still have the eternal Elvis Presley, who made his comeback after spending quite some time in the film studios, and his old fans are immediately drawn to him again. Tom Jones and his label twin brother Engelbert Humperdinck also score high in the Belgian charts ...

So, although the Belgian region of Flanders was absolutely not yet under the spell of the real hard rock sound in the spring of '69, many young people had not just come to Mechelen to see the Belgian group Wallace Collection at work.

No, they came indeed to see the promising Steppenwolf, the real eye-catcher of the evening. But that big, mysterious name on the bill is going to take an awfully long time before appearing on stage. Are those guys coming at all? Maybe it sounded too promising when we read in HUMO that this group would come to Belgium and the Netherlands. After almost an hour of nerve-racking waiting, the liberating message came that the audience had absolutely nothing to worry about and that they only had to do one thing: be (very) patient. With complete certainty, Steppenwolf will indeed be coming to Mechelen tonight. With a big delay, indeed. Maybe even another hour, but they are definitely on their way! The cause of their delay can be explained as follows.

On tour through Europe, they seem to have missed their scheduled flight somewhere in Scandinavia (Copenhagen probably, where they had performed the day before) in the midst of the crowds. The rest of their meticulously planned busy schedule through the rest of Western Europe comes under pressure. This leaves them with the moral obligation to use all possible means to get to their destination, in order to avoid more unwanted claims for damages in places where they were under contract. According to their tour manager at the time, there was only one possible solution: to charter a plane at their own expense to get to Brussels Airport. Because of this "emergency" solution and the total cost of the charter flight, their performance in the sports hall in Mechelen will barely earn them ... 2000 Belgian francs (about ... 60 US dollars!). They even have to pay the road crew with their own money. The performance in Mechelen therefore involves a considerable financial loss for the guys. Among all the other comments, HUMO has the following words of praise for them in their next edition: *"Well done boys, very dutiful! All our respect."*

When they finally arrive, much later than planned, the instruments are quickly unloaded, and the members of the band get ready to give the people what they have been waiting for. The show starts with a lot of energy and *Sookie Sookie* instantly strikes the spark. But the rest of the performance does not go quite as desired. The boys have had a long trip and were obviously already very tired when they arrived in Belgium. The stress of the last few hours has not done any good either. While drummer Jerry and organist Goldy are doing their utmost and John, as always, is pulling the cart, bassist Nick and guitarist Michael are playing pretty much on automatic pilot. Moreover, as mentioned before, the acoustics in the sports hall are terrible and the whole performance is therefore not experienced as a great success by everyone. After the performance, the opinions are therefore strongly divided. Some people think the performance was really great, while others said it was rather bad.

Too many young music fans at the time also assume that all "live" songs sound just the same as the studio song on a 45-rpm record. In those days, by the way, because of the lack of automatically adjustable control equipment and pre-programmed "samples," that was not possible at all. In addition, the corrugated metal roof panels create an annoying reverberation. It's a pity that no other location was chosen for this special event ...

After the performance, HUMO visited the band members in their hotel room in the center of Mechelen. The film crew of Belgian Radio and Television did not dare to go with them, for fear of being immediately turned away.

"What are you saying? Going to their hotel room for an interview? Those guys are having an orgy there right now and they will throw you out before you've said hello. Forget it!"

Alleged orgy or not, it is assumed anyway that the boys are in for a noticeably short night. Tomorrow morning, they already travel on to Holland and then an extensive promotional campaign awaits them in Bremen and Frankfurt in West Germany. Then back to Great Britain to close their first major European tour. So HUMO fears that an exclusive interview as an in-between session is not possible. Yet they try ... and find Steppenwolf's leader John Kay in his hotel room, at ease. He is alone in the room when HUMO's editorial team knocks on the door.

"Bitte, kommen Sie herein!" it sounds in German. (Please come in)

The people from HUMO frown when they hear that John Kay is answering in German. At that moment, none of them has any idea how it is that the singer of the *American* band Steppenwolf speaks *German* so fluently. They are even more surprised when they see that he is wearing ordinary slippers in his hotel room. His normal image is that of a rough hard rocker, with leather pants, motorbike boots and dark glasses.

But now, he surprisingly looks more like a good paterfamilias who wants to take it easy after a hard day's work. In the meantime, John Kay quietly continues eating his dinner. With knife and fork! The boy is clearly well brought up.

"Potato salad is my favorite. This is not a real Strammer Max *as they know it in Germany, but this cold dish with eggs comes close to that."*

The man speaks German! But what the hell is a *Strammer Max*? What does this man have in common with Germany anyway? They don't understand it (yet). But what the men from HUMO notice immediately, is how dimly lit John's hotel room is.

"My eyes are quite bad, and I am enormously sensitive to light. So those dark glasses of mine are not mimicry or decoration as many people might think. Purely doctor's orders! That's why my room is so dimly lit."

John talks about his life in his usual friendly and good-natured way. Although he is only twenty-five at the time, he clearly has a rich life behind him, and he has been very lucky at times. Not everything has gone smoothly. As they ask him what connection he actually has with Germany, he tells them about his birthplace Tilsit, which at the time was in a remote part of Germany (East Prussia) and about the difficult situation somewhat later in East Germany. He also outlines the flight to and his year-long stay in Hannover (although HUMO erroneously writes BREMEN in its article and later publishes it that way). He tells about The Sparrow in Canada and how Steppenwolf evolved from it. The tour of Europe serves to let Europeans get to know them better. He finds it unfortunate that, while their three albums released so far do quite well in Europe, the hit singles do not score as well here as in their native America and Canada. The singles do well in Scandinavia and West Germany, but not yet in the rest of Europe.

He also explains that there are two Germans in the band, two Canadians and only one American and that he himself is still German. Nicolas Kassbaum (Nick St. Nicholas), who had recently replaced Rushton Moreve, is also German, just like him. But Nick is from Hamburg. He tells us that he has no desire to be naturalized, because he has now understood that people everywhere in the world live equally badly and that therefore it makes no difference what nationality is stated on your identity card. He also explains that after *Born To Be Wild* they suddenly landed between two different schools with their music genre: between the commercial genre on the one hand and the progressive genre that by definition remains more under the (sales) radar on the other. He also emphasizes that a lot is suddenly expected of them. He adds that they did not really see this huge success coming and that, for the time being, they can't be counted yet among the true music virtuosos like Cream or Jimi Hendrix. Those men of MC5? He doesn't take them to seriously at the moment ...

The team from HUMO is amazed. John Kay is clearly someone with a strongly founded vision and maturity. Not something you would expect at first sight when you see him as a wild rocker on stage. He never talks too fast either. Sometimes he hesitates and thinks first to find the right words. He wants to be *precise*. Therefore, the interview he gives is on a completely different level than those of many of his fellow music artists, who sometimes want to ridicule the ordinary things of life (and their interviewers). John Kay, despite his sense of humor, is a profoundly serious and educated man! Every person who has ever had an interview with him, even decades later (and still today), will tell you that John Kay is really a very amiable man. He's someone who puts you at ease in such a way as if you've known him for a long time. And he likes laughing ...

Jim Christopulos 'screenshots from the Recordings on May 23, 1969, in Mechelen, Belgium. John, Goldy and Jerry (top) and Michael and Nick (bottom) in the Mechelen sports hall at Winketkaai. Free advertising: on television the whole time for the Mechelen beer brand Lamot included. Three months later Michael will no longer be part of the band and one year later Nick also leaves the band (again). (Copyright VRT Belgian Television)..

A few weeks after the Mechelen gig, the interview appears in full in HUMO. The Steppenwolf guys got the benefit of the doubt and HUMO was very much convinced of their musical qualities which was quite clear from their comments.

After their performance in Mechelen, Steppenwolf goes to the Paradiso Club in Amsterdam and a day later they are welcomed in Groningen. The promotional campaign continues in Germany and there is one last gig in England on March 30. Then the band returns to its home base in Los Angeles. Steppenwolf is firmly on the map in Western Europe after this European tour of the spring of '69.

The band has enormous successes all over the world. Especially in Great Britain, Scandinavia and Germany, they remain extremely popular until 2018 (the final cessation of touring). In the Netherlands it's not that bad, but Belgium never turns out to be a breeding ground for lasting success of the band. It was as if there had been a general boycott here the whole time, so that their music was not played. Apart from their biggest hit *Born To Be Wild*, we have hardly -or not at all- heard them on our radio stations in the past 54 years. To be fair, we should mention that in the summer of 1971 Rudy's Club, Radio Oost-Vlaanderen (Radio East Flanders) devoted a whole Wednesday afternoon special to them and that was a huge surprise, but on the other hand it was a one-time occurrence that they received so much detailed attention on our radio. All Belgian radio stations continued to prefer home-grown music or the rock music that came over mainly from Great Britain. Jimi Hendrix never got a real sounding board here either, and his *Hey Joe* is played more in our classic top lists today than at the time it was released. By way of example, when Steppenwolf's promotional single *Ride With Me* from the new album *For Ladies Only* was released in the fall of 1971, it was only played twice on Flemish radio. Comment of one of our presenters at the time: *"We don't like this at all, but we have to(!) give it a chance."* Is it then up to them to judge those things? None of *them* are indispensable in the music world, while musicians are ...

The single *Move Over* from the album *Monster* was also played only once or twice in the autumn of 1969. Not coincidentally, that was also on Radio East-Flanders; the only station in Flanders that still gave them a little respect and attention. Just to mention: whoever holds the reins behind the scenes, determines who gets to be known somewhere and who is allowed to become successful. The incident with Michael Monarch and the American flag is, despite the fact that the boycott of *Rock Me* is due to their own misconduct, perfect proof of this. That song was really great and at that time a real breath of fresh air between all the softer pop songs. But Steppenwolf was banned because of a stupid incident, also in the US by the operators of the many AM stations. Now, Steppenwolf never really needed Belgium and/or Europe in any way. Not back then and not 50 years later. They have been a tremendous success in the US and that has continued for more than 50 years ...

There is no time to relax after their European tour of May 1969. The ambitions change another gear. Only Michael is looking back for just a moment. Is he thinking of that mini romance he (apparently) briefly had in Copenhagen during their tour? Is this true or not? We don't know for sure ... Only he has the answer ...

Steppenwolf is immediately under contract to play at some larger festivals, including the very prestigious Newport Festival. On June 20, 1969, they are at the gigantic horse racetrack at the three-day musical event at Devonshire Downs in Northridge, California. Some 200,000 people attend to admire Ike & Tina Turner, Creedence Clearwater Revival, The Byrds, Steppenwolf, The Jimi Hendrix Experience, Janis Joplin, Johnny Winter, Eric Burdon, Love and The Rascals and Marvin Gaye (the one and only Marvin Gaye who- in the eighties- lived in Oostende on our Belgian coast, until he died).

On June 23 during that same summer (with their overflowing schedule) of the year 1969, the movie *Easy Rider* is promoted. A film that had been shot the year before and that puts *Born To Be Wild* and *The Pusher* at the forefront of the film's sound recordings. Laszlo Kovacs

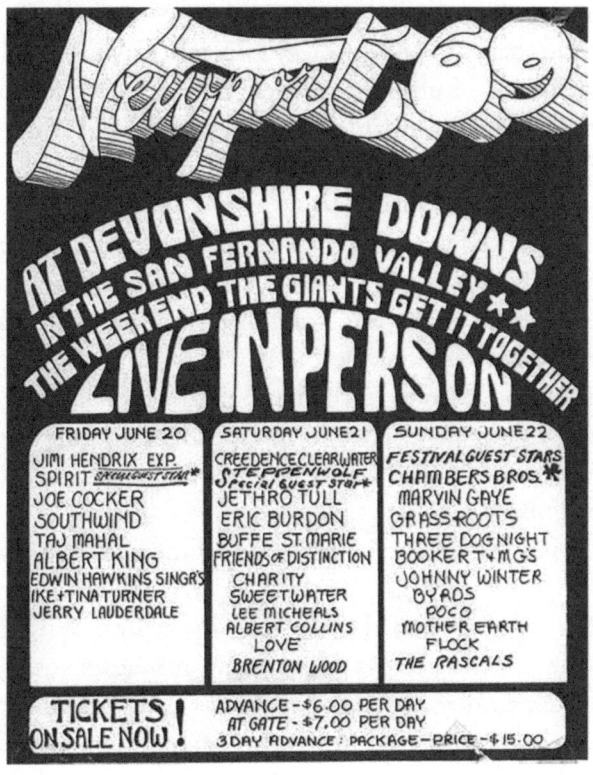

June 1969. The Newport Festival. A ticket for three days costs $15. Jimi Hendrix walks away with the highest fee there. He gets a whopping US$ 125,000, which up to that point is the highest amount ever paid to a rock artist for a single performance.

and Dennis Hopper have their eye on Steppenwolf's music. The first reason is to create a sense of freedom in the audience and among viewers by playing this music when Peter Fonda and Dennis Hopper tour the American roads on their Harley Davidsons. From the release of *Easy Rider* to the present day, *BTBW*, by the way, is invariably associated worldwide with every next generation of men and women who ride motorcycles. *The Pusher* in turn alludes to the drug scene and the negative consequences for those who let it rule their lives.

Another reason Steppenwolf is chosen is apparently because director Laszlo Kovacs really liked John Kay's life story. After all, Kovacs, like John, is an Eastern European refugee. During the Hungarian uprising of 1956, he had been able to flee Budapest and had even smuggled out home-made recordings of the ruthless crushing by the Soviet Army of the uprising, just to show to the Western world. He knew well enough himself what the road to freedom cost and what both he and John Kay had once had to do for it. Laszlo felt connected to John Kay and especially to his life story. The only problem was that the filmmakers ... had no money left to pay Dunhill to use Steppenwolf's songs in that film. However, the band members felt that this was an opportunity to put themselves in the spotlight and they urged Dunhill to work out a compromise. And so it happened, much to the relief of both parties ...

After *Candy*, *Easy Rider* is the second film in which Steppenwolf can promote their musical talents via the silver screen. Later on, their repertoire is regularly called upon for other films. With *Easy Rider*, however, the effect in terms of publicity reaches a totally different dimension. *Easy Rider* not only becomes a cult symbol for motorcyclists. It also becomes a kind of relic for a generation of young people who like to associate themselves with freedom and rebellion and dare to oppose the establishment. The fact that drugs are often part of their normal life pattern and many of them are no longer inclined to earn their living by the sweat of their brow is sadly too often considered the norm. Fortunately, towards the end of the film it is made quite clear that in the long run heavy drug use does not only destroy those around them and their immediate family, but also themselves.

But the publicity that Steppenwolf provides with its contribution to the film, sparks the desire for much more success. *Easy Rider* works worldwide as an exponent for the group's popularity and *BTBW* is already reranked in some charts barely one year after it was first released.

BTBW becomes a gigantic financial success and the biggest one ever for Steppenwolf. Mars Bonfire will never have to work on an assembly line in a car factory, something he had feared for a while when he

hung up his guitar and said goodbye to Sparrow in the summer of 1967 ...
Easy Rider *featuring Dennis Hopper, Peter Fonda and Jack Nicholson enjoying freedom to the full. (Photo Wikimedia Commons)*

A subsequent -never to be equaled- opportunity to optimize their success, however, is woefully missed. Deliberately even, because they prefer to continue with their normal program. At the time, they had no idea of the scale of the success of the summer festival that was about to begin, but in retrospect their refusal was not a good strategic move. Considering the enormous publicity that the festival still radiates even more than 50 years later and the enormous amount of beautiful reviews that the performing artists have received, they will probably regret forever and ever that they were not there in the meadows of WOODSTOCK, against their better judgment.

Also, Steppenwolf was indeed asked to play there in August 1969. You cannot predict the future, unfortunately, but the business manager of Steppenwolf will certainly have had a lot of sleepless nights because of it. Possibly, however, another detail influenced their decision not to go to Woodstock ...

After all, Michael Monarch did get himself completely entangled in all kinds of unpredictable acts in that summer of 1969. In fact, he is becoming the victim of his own immense success. The handsome young man who, with his spontaneous laughter, had already melted so many girls' hearts during the band's performances, is now hopelessly bogged down in his own improprieties. The problem with Michael is, that his success was just thrown into his lap and that he doesn't seem to realize it. At seventeen, the (music) world was already at his feet, because Steppenwolf is doing extremely well in the US, but Michael still has not yet the maturity to deal with that success. Drug use makes all that much worse, as his sense of responsibility ebbs away completely. There are more arguments between him and the other members of the band and especially with John he often has serious arguments. He becomes more of a rebel within the group's own cocoon, and sometimes he is unmanageable. At times, he refuses to play the guitar on stage when it is expected of him. It even happens once that he puts down his guitar and just walks away from the stage. Michael becomes completely obstructive and his behavior also affects the credibility of everyone else. In the end, he brings about his own dismissal.

Indeed, enough is enough and Michael is shown the door. (However, some insiders declare Michael left the band himself). According to John, his unprofessional behavior has gone on long enough. Later on, Michael Monarch readily admits that his drug use was the real cause of his arrogant, unpredictable attitude and that it was the main reason for his derailed behavior. Does he regret it? Of course, he does! If only he could go back in time and correct the things that went wrong because of him. He would certainly not make the same mistakes again.

Michael Monarch has so many different skills and even more than 50 years later that is still evident. The musical project with his band Detective was perhaps not as *successful* as Steppenwolf, but it was still very good. And even today, in his seventies, he still is a very busy and talented man. Playing music and kayaking worldwide are a few of his passions, and he shows his natural talents from time to time even on the dance floor.

So, Michael leaves Steppenwolf and ... T.I.M.E. is contacted again. After Nick, a few months earlier, now Larry Byrom is also released from that band to join Steppenwolf. Starting in August, "Alabama beast" Larry will play from now on alongside Nick, John, Jerry and Goldy. He can already focus on the next Steppenwolf album which is almost finished. An album that will cause a lot of controversy in the American musical and political world: the controversial Steppenwolf album *Monster* ...

With Larry Byrom in the band, John Kay indeed gets all political in September 1969. (Although, is seems Michael still did the guitar works for the song "*Power Play*"). Following some earlier slightly veiled political messages, he now attacks the establishment and the wide-spread corruption in the US head on. With *Monster*, Steppenwolf kicks in a few open doors, although their firm statement also antagonizes many Americans. Of course, to start with, these are all the people who feel targeted, including members of the political elite in Washington D.C. The truth hurts and in *Monster* those haughty politicians are confronted with the facts. For although the US highly prizes such symbols as democracy, freedom and justice, in practice things have been going completely wrong for quite some time. And mainly because these politicians, who are supposed to protect the people and to serve the country, think primarily of themselves and want to secure their positions. John Kay masterfully touches the sore spot and appropriately denounces the corruption and carelessness of the very people who, by definition, should be fighting those wrongs. It is clear that John has studied American history very well before venturing onto this thin ice. His music is rough and hard, extremely hard indeed.

But instrumentally also very clever and balanced. The real message however is of course in the lyrics. He says bluntly what the problem is and insists that the way politics is done in America, can indeed best be compared to a runaway monster that constantly spies on society in order to devour them as a defenseless prey. Several songs on the album deal with the chaotic situation in which the US found itself at the end of the 1960s. In the pilot single *Move Over*, John Kay apparently alludes to the mismanagement of then President Richard Nixon and makes it clear that it would be best for him to step aside. But the lyrics of the song could also give the impression he is lashing out ... against the recently fired Michael Monarch.

The album causes a national shock in the US. As expected, the band unintentionally sows discord with their statement. Many Americans like to associate themselves with the militant statements John Kay sings bluntly through the microphone and they are glad that someone is finally making a clear statement on this issue through music. Others turn away and find the criticism expressed inappropriate. Moreover, what the opponents of his statements see is a huge show of ingratitude on John's part towards his host: the USA. Didn't that German John Kay get every chance here in the US, which he criticizes so openly here? Would he have had those opportunities in his old homeland of East Germany? No Way! Is it really up to him to criticize a democratic regime so much, while he himself is a descendant of the extremist Nazi regime? And what if he had indeed stayed in East Germany? If he had expressed such criticism of the regime there, would he not have been immediately interned or even eliminated?

John, however, declares with conviction that the song *Monster* certainly does make a statement, but that it is actually not a protest song. Rather, he sees *Monster* as a *love* song, that he wrote to express his gratitude and profound respect toward the US, but that he hates to see it ruined by negligent or corrupt politicians.

"Many things go wrong here, but there are so many good things worth cherishing as well. And I love the United States so immensely, that I hate to see it broken down by the mistakes and self-centered behavior of a few politicians who don't have the best interests of the people at heart."

The triptych from that album *Monster - Suicide - America*, followed by the decidedly anti-militaristic *Draft Resister* and *Power Play*, causes a lot of people in the US to change their minds. For those vehemently opposed to the US Vietnam campaign, it is very welcome. But as is so often the case, an (anti-)political message, whether or not delivered through music, only has any effect if there are shifts in long-term policy. After all, the US remains tied up in the Vietnam War for years to come and President Nixon remains in office. Time for a global change? Not yet! *"Il est temps pour un grand changement"* is also a popular slogan in student jargon in France during this period. Capitalism must be overthrown! But also in the French student movement, where the heavy protests at the Sorbonne from 1968 lingered on for a long time, the sympathy for Steppenwolf's protest texts is for many only a temporary phenomenon. Once those same students graduate a little later and smell big money, most of them are no longer charmed by their previous ideals of a more balanced policy. The people who wanted to change everything once and for all during the massive protest marches at the end of the 1960s, both in the US and in Europe, very quickly adjusted their own "priorities" and their revolutionary ideas faded away. Jan Palach, the Czechoslovak who set himself on fire in May 1968 in Prague for more freedom and as a protest against Russian oppression, could have spared himself his own gruesome death and the jerrycan with that very expensive fuel.

The Monster *album from the fall of 1969 that would cause a lot of controversy in the US. Very loud protest songs against the establishment, the abuse of power, the corruption and especially against Uncle Sam and the Vietnam war.*

Monster - September 1969
John Kay, Jerry Edmonton, Nick St. Nicolas, Larry Byrom and Goldy McJohn.

Once the religious, the hunted and weary
Chasing the promise of freedom and hope
Came to this country to build a new vision
Far from the reaches of Kingdom and Pope

Like good Christians some would burn the witches
Later some bought slaves to gather riches

And still from near and far to seek America
They came by thousands, to court the wild
But she patiently smiled, and then bore them a child
To be their spirit, and guiding light

And when the ties with crown had been broken
Westward in saddle and wagon it went
And till the railroad linked ocean to ocean
Many the lives which had come to an end

While we bullied, stole and bought our homeland
We began the slaughter of the red man

But still from the near and far to seek America T
hey came by thousands to court the wild
But she patiently smiled and bore them a child
To be their spirit and guiding light

The Blue and the Grey they stomped it
They kicked it just like a dog
And when the (civil) war was over
They stuffed it just like a hog

But though the past has its share of injustice
Kind was the spirit in many a way

But its protectors and friends have been sleeping
Now it's a monster and will not obey

The spirit was freedom and justice
Its keepers seemed generous and kind
Its leaders were supposed to serve the country
Now they don't pay it no mind
Cause the people grew fat and got lazy
Now their vote is a meaningless joke
They babble about law and 'bout order
But it's just the echo of what they've been told
Yes a monster's on the loose
It's put our heads into the noose
And just sits there watching
The cities have turned into jungles
And corruption is strangling the land
The police force is watching the people
And the people just can't understand
We don't know how to mind our own business
The whole world has to be just like us
Now we are fighting a war over there
No matter who's the winner we can't pay the cost
Yes a monster's on the loose
It's put our heads in a noose
And just sits there watching

American where are you now
Don't you care about your sons and daughters
Don't you know we need you now
We can't fight alone against the monster

The political message John Kay and his mates deliver in September 1969 is still very much alive more than 54 years later and the same message applies to the current political situation. Not only in the USA, but in every country and in every political party where democracy and free speech are a priority on the agenda and where politicians are so eager to put these values forward as their party's *own* trademark ... but as a goal it is not so simple to achieve. There is still plenty of corruption and injustice. Impulsive thoughtlessness, insecurity and/or incompetence in making political decisions still negatively affect the life pattern of the average person in the twenty-first century. Whether the politics are left-wing, right-wing or in the middle and Democratic or Republican: politics are and will remain a power play. The proclaimed philosophy is still far too often flouted by its own members and exceptions to rules are often made for themselves. And that happens about anywhere in the world! Fortunately, in countries that like to call themselves "democratic" you can usually express your opinion without being persecuted and that is not possible everywhere in the world. But that all-consuming Monster is still lurking everywhere ...

In the middle of this politically sensitive period, Steppenwolf's militant lyrics increasingly draw opposition from the established services during their live performances. This often involves conservative Americans, fanatical believers in God, who literally follow today that 2000-year old bible, written in the times when the earth was flat. And also, some leaders of indoctrinated sects, who saw the band's lyrics as an indictment of the values and standards they previously acquired with difficulty. Throughout its own tumultuous history, the average American has learned to respect all that, and they feel that Steppenwolf's acts are deliberately divisive. In Winston-Salem in the state of North Carolina, a peculiar incident occurs in that respect. The band is supposed to perform there, but is already met on arrival at the airport by the local mayor accompanied by the county sheriff. They come with a direct warning to the boys and their management that there is a notorious pastor active locally who is strongly opposed to their lyrics. That powerful man apparently opposes very vehemently all their "vulgar and blasphemous" lyrics. This reverend has a lot of fanatical followers in the region and in order not to stir up the heated tempers, the group is urged NOT to perform certain songs from their repertoire that evening. The guys think it will be just a warning and they are intended to ignore the message. Until, just before the concert starts, they receive a visit from the police in their dressing room. This with the intention of making sure that they do indeed censor their own repertoire of songs that evening. Some songs they are not even allowed to perform that evening by police order. The band members, however, do not allow themselves to be lectured to and there is a heated discussion behind the scenes. They are told that they will not even be allowed to perform at all if they are not prepared to remove inflammatory and/or drug-related songs such as *Don't Step On The Grass, Sam* and *The Pusher* from their playlist. They risk being arrested for the intentional use of inciting language before the show even starts.

In the end, a compromise is reached. It was against their will, but they gave in so as not to disappoint the thousands of people in the audience on the one hand, and so as not to end up behind bars for a night themselves on the other hand. After much discussion, they are finally allowed to perform the anti-drug song *The Pusher*. In that song, *"God Damned"* is often used and they have to delete that curse. However, in the context of that song, "GD" only means *"May God curse the pusher for the misery he causes to other people."* But the local representatives of the law don't understand that.

"God Damned will NOT be spoken here tonight, or we will immediately unplug your amps and you can spend a night in jail!"

So, every time "GD" should be sung in *The Pusher*, they are not allowed to pronounce that word.

They have to come up with their own solution if they want to perform that song anyway ...
The concert starts and the police immediately takes up their positions behind the scenes, with the firm intention to intervene from the moment someone's swearing on the microphone. The guys then decide that every time the word GD is to be used in *The Pusher*, a screeching sound from Larry Byrom's guitar, somewhat resembling the bellowing of a siren, will be heard. John is lucid enough to announce this in advance to the massive audience of over 5,000 people over there in Winston-Salem ... Derisive laughter from the boys

and their management a bit later, though. When GD is mentioned in *The Pusher*, Larry plays his siren strings as agreed. John Kay then wisely remains silent for a moment ... but every spectator present (more than 5,000 people) in the packed hall sings "GOD DAMNED" at the top of their voices, as loud as they can every time the words should be pronounced, instead of the inwardly smiling and satisfied John Kay. The orderlies behind the scenes are speechless and powerless, and obviously cannot hold a jam-packed venue accountable for their swearing. To their own surprise, Steppenwolf have the final say here ...

"Very special people there in North Carolina," John Kay laughs later on about this incident.

The *Monster* album itself may have struck a chord when it comes to the statement it makes, musically it certainly won't be their biggest success. Not in the US and even less in the rest of the world. Despite a few musical masterpieces it contains, many fans long back to the swinging, rocking and bluesy sounding songs of their first two albums. The band seemingly deviates a bit from their own style after all. The much shortened version of *Monster*, which also appears on single a little later, doesn't do well and only just reaches the top forty in the US.

That 45-rpm version is not consistent enough in itself, because it contains too many completely different musical elements that are -in the opinion of this author at least- only appropriate for the LP version. Its B-side, *Berry Rides Again,* seems to be a return to the swinging genre of not so long ago ...
    But in the halls, the live audiences continue to flock. In the spring of 1970, their double album *Steppenwolf Live* is released, most of the songs having been recorded at the Civic Auditorium in Santa Monica. But studio work will be added that has absolutely nothing to do with the live performance. The studio recording of *Hey Lawdy Mama*, promoted as a single, will be included on that live album and the studio songs *Twisted* and *Corrina, Corrina* get a place on that live

album as well, although some artificial applause is added to make it sound somewhat "live". This artificial applause sounds very bizarre when you compare it to the other live recordings on the album. According to John, the live performance also didn't go as planned all the time.

To start with, there is a misunderstanding (or is it a technical malfunction?), so that the heavy curtains on stage do not open while the band is already playing. Jerry starts the intro of *Sookie, Sookie*, followed by the announcement by the local manager, saying "Live in Color ... Steppenwolf" and John Kay continuing with *"Let it hang out baby ... Let it hang out, now na-na now "* ... and still the curtains do not open. They play on stage like this for over half a minute behind closed curtains. If you pay very good attention, just before he sings *"Sookie, Sookie, Sookie, Sookie, Sookie, Sookie, Sue"* for the first time, you hear him yelling very vaguely -away from the microphone- in the background *"Open those curtains"*. A very funny sight probably for the audience, but it doesn't really look very professional. Apparently, more imperfections in their performance pile up that evening and fortunately they are covered with the cloak of charity. The audience doesn't seem to care ...

Meanwhile, Steppenwolf is experiencing an absolutely glorious period on and off the scene. Three of their four albums have so far reached gold and the dollars are flowing in. This gives Goldy McJohn a chance to pursue his eternal hobby horse: buying a Porsche. (By the end of 1975 Goldy will have ... twelve Porsches). It is and it remains arduous work and unfortunately Nick, following Michael's example, is now starting to loose it. "Medication" use is the cause he can no longer behave as he should. It also has a detrimental impact on Steppenwolf's appearance on stage.

A maverick and a joker Nick always was, but he starts acting really weird now. His strange behavior begins with his chosen outfit during performances. At first, he dresses like a regular rock star, just like the others. Now he increasingly walks around in extravagant robes that are somewhat at odds with the image a hard rock band essentially

The recordings from January 22 (poster left) are the main ingredient for the double live album that appears in April 1970 (photo below). There is also a single LP version of the Live album in which several songs have been skipped.

John and Jutta somewhere in the '70s

conveys. This clearly annoys the other band members. What's more, from some film footage of Nick, shot somewhere backstage during that particular period, you can directly infer from the rigid look in his wide-open eyes that he is not doing very well. He took some kind of drug, is totally dazed, and wanders around like a zombie, throwing himself down somewhere, completely stoned. John, as the leader of the group, feels urged to tell Nick that things are about to go totally wrong.

When they have to perform together with groups like Led Zeppelin in New York in April 1970, things *really* go wrong. This time their tour manager is also going mad, because at the moment the boys have to perform, they are suddenly nowhere to be found. Their manager goes to their hotel room and finds some of the band members, including Nick, playing hide and seek with some female fans through the corridors and in the rooms of that hotel ... naked! ..

"Are you going to play or what?" shouts their manager angrily ...

...When they finally start performing later that night, Nick walks on stage with Bugs Bunny ears, like the Playboy magazine symbol. Nick has apparently found a little too much inspiration in those cute, young centerfold girls from the Hugh Hefner shows. Besides those rabbit ears, he is only wearing his mini briefs and otherwise he is as naked as the Red Hot Chili Peppers many years later at some live performances, when their only item of clothing was a black sock around the genitals. John's fuses are about to blow. Apparently, John was already in a very bad mood that day, and enormously annoyed by the inappropriate behavior of a friend of Nick, who was with them in New York and who was getting on the nerves of the others the whole time...

Nick starts playing, but something sounds completely wrong and John immediately stops the performance. Out of necessity apparently, he quietly says to Nick, *"Nick, you're out of tune."* Some noise ensues and while the local presenter is clearly embarrassed with the whole incident, John makes it clear that he is not amused by Nick's performance, nor by his outfit. *"It's Easter; that's why I wear those ears"* Nick says to defend himself, arguing that those Bugs Bunny ears had prevented him to stay in tune. But to no avail! His excuse isn't accepted and Nick ends up paying the bill and is kicked out of the band. Nick, that charming German guy man who had been resurrected only a year before and had been called back to the old nest to the relief of both him and the four others, is now necessarily pushed aside. He, who knew John Kay from the early days at Sparrow and who, a few years ago, had in a way also played his part in John and Jutta's meeting, feels that beautiful friendship slipping through his fingers. One German no longer giving the other German any credit. Much later, Nick will declare that he felt betrayed and especially abandoned. Goldy later tries to mitigate the events related to Nick somewhat by declaring that "someone" had given him too much LSD. To Goldy's credit, he stood up for Nick, but he also knew well enough that things couldn't go on like this. Nick is replaced by George Biondo, the bass player from … T.I.M.E. … yes, of course, who else?

That group has had enough of being the organ donor for Steppenwolf and quits in defeat. George commits himself and his dedication is really beautiful and admirable. He also has a good voice and from now on, he will sing the songs that are not really John's cup of tea. George is a man of not too many words, but he is someone who faithfully toes the line and spontaneously does what is expected of him. John is the actual leader of the pack and George is aware of that. Nick by the way, will join the band Blue Cheer for a while a few years later … and we will see him again -by surprise- in *another* band as well. Just wait for it …

Steppenwolf's success continues and their "Wolfpack" continues to expand. By the summer of 1970, tens of millions of LPs have been sold worldwide. And their next album, *Steppenwolf 7*, is another masterpiece. In it, John makes a strong reference to his escape from East Germany with the brilliant song *Renegade*. The bass accompaniment by George Biondo on that song is quite amazing.

Front cover of the album
Steppenwolf 7.
Design Tom (O'Neal)
Gundelfinger

The album also includes another anti-drug song in the form of *Snow Blind Friend*, like *The Pusher* again a song written by old friend Hoyt Axton. *Who Needs Ya* becomes the pilot single, but scores rather poorly especially again in Europe. The other side of the single is *Earschplitten-loudenboomer*. In the song's introduction, John shows that he is still fluent in German.

From the photo shoot for the promotion of Steppenwolf 7. *Goldy McJohn, Jerry Edmonton, John Kay, Larry Byrom and George Biondo. Bass player George Biondo, here on the far right and replacement for Nick St. Nicolas, would sing several songs himself including* Fat Jack *and in their next album* Jaded Strumpet. *He also sang a duet with John in* Who Needs Ya *and* Foggy Mental Breakdown *among others. George was also the first backing vocal on quite a few other songs. He was always a loyal wolf.*

Besides some compilation albums like *The Best of*, *Portrait of* and *Steppenwolf Gold*, Steppenwolf's last album from their first period from 1967 to 1972 appears in the fall of 1971 and is titled: *For Ladies Only*. The personnel changes don't stop there and by now guitarist Larry Byrom has given way to Kent Henry.

Pilot single is the rock-solid *Ride With Me*, again written by that old faithful Sparrow guitarist: Mars Bonfire. Again, a song with a clear life message. All the other songs are also great, and George Biondo repeatedly shows that he has a good voice. The song *For Ladies Only* itself is also incredibly good, with beautiful piano work by Goldy and a very appropriate percussion there from Jerry. Unfortunately, the same mistake is made as with *Monster* by turning the handsome and long album version into a compressed, somewhat disjointed single version.

For Ladies Only. *The last album from the first period. The song* Ride With Me *is released as a pilot single. A shortened version of the song* For Ladies Only *itself also follows on single.*

For many loyal fans, this bizarre single remix doesn't sound quite right. They seem like mere details, as they don't actually get in the way of the actual success. But what is much worse is that the smooth resilience gradually dissipates from the group during that period altogether. Not that they are arguing again, but there is someone who has run out of energy and therefore wants to take it a little easier. Someone who has always worked hard, but is now putting a focus on something else. Indeed, Steppenwolf seems just about past its prime in the late fall of 1971.

The closing song of the album, *In Hopes Of A Garden*, sung by George Biondo, does sound a bit melancholy and towards the end it seems to drift off into thin air. The short song seems to convey a sad message and one can suspect that another bleak announcement will soon follow. Steppenwolf is indeed quitting. John Kay is going solo. As outsiders, from our position in Europe, we can only assume that John Kay may have been walking around with these plans for some time. He himself claims that he has completely run out of energy. (A burn out *avant la lettre*, we presume)

From a February 1972 newspaper. There are some mistakes in this article though. At the time of this (first) split, Nick and Michael had long since ceased to be part of the band. Moreover, there would be no double album at all and the two members that John brought along in his solo project were Kent Henry and George Biondo.

In his own words, he is constantly expected to take on the heaviest part of the job and to keep coming up with new songs and lyrics at short notice. He wants to go a little slower and uses his new project to release existing and older folk and blues songs as musical covers. A question of recharging the batteries first and then evaluating everything again. *For Ladies Only* was to be the last highlight and on February 14, 1972, it was announced that the band was splitting up. It sounds a bit paradoxical, but Valentine's Day, lover's day worldwide, is also the day that the relationship and the phenomenally successful (though also very turbulent) period ends for all the members of the band. Goldy McJohn and Jerry Edmonton first join the group Seven and a little later they found Manbeast. John Kay in turn is able to convince his Steppenwolf bassist George Biondo and guitarist Kent Henry to join his new solo project. The name of his new band sounds unoriginal, though. It will simply be "The John Kay Band". John counts on his fame to launch himself into the music world with new zest.

September 1972. Entry ticket for the old and new band, touring together. That day they perform in Bavaria, Germany.

Devoted fans of the former heavier Steppenwolf work, however, are somewhat disappointed in the first album that John is releasing under his own name as a solo artist: *Forgotten Songs & Unsung Heroes**. For many, it is not at all what is expected. Real swinging rock like we have been used to from him so far, doesn't appear at all on the album. Only with *I'm Movin' On*, a cover of Hank Snow, does John Kay refer to the rock music the band valued so much for five years and which had brought them so much success. John Kay clearly wants to go in a totally different direction for a while and return to the very beginning of his musical existence, even before he played with Steppenwolf or Sparrow.

---

* *Still remains one of Jutta's favorite albums to this day.*

Concert hall Paradiso in Amsterdam. Steppenwolf performed here several times to a full house of enthusiastic people. John Kay also came here with his new band.

Hank Williams' *You Win Again,* a 1952 song, even refers directly to his own first musical notes played on his "K.A.Y. guitar." The other songs on that album are clearly an ode to other older glories and once again a reference to his own beginnings in music, when he played the acoustic guitar and harmonica in coffee houses, bars and small parish halls. The title of the album, by the way, is a direct reference to that homage. It all sounds a bit folksy & bluesy, but too many ex-fans who like everything Steppenwolf used to make, are disappointed. A year later, his second solo album is released under the name *My Sportin' Life*, with some very nice songs like *Moonshine (Friend Of Mine)* ...

But after releasing two solo albums, during his tour with the band, John begins to long back for the old days. He's certainly happy with the work of keyboardist Hugh O' Sullivan and drummer Pentii Glenn, but he also misses his good friends Jerry and Goldy ... and it also becomes clear that not only himself, but also a lot of other people yearn for the earlier, rougher work and for that old, howling and grinding Steppenwolf. And he is looking forward to it again. The batteries will soon be fully recharged. Just a little more patience ...

In the Early Mornin' Rain, Corsica, end of October 1973.
The split in the early spring of 1972 of his favorite musical group is not doing yours truly's mindset any good. He is absolutely devastated. The album *Rest In Peace* that was released during that same summer of 1972, is not at all a consolation prize, quite the contrary. It is nothing more than a compilation of existing songs and its release only serves to deepen the pain. John's first solo album *Forgotten Songs & Unsung Heroes* was eagerly awaited. In the fall of 1972, it is finally in my possession. At first, however, disappointment got the better of curiosity, because I have to be honest and say that the album doesn't live up to my expectations. John Kay's solo project cannot charm me as yet. There are also doubts about the album *My Sportin' Life* that was released the following year. Those softer and sometimes purely blues-tinged songs cannot convince many Steppenwolf fans, partly because it is a musical genre that is not so popular in our regions at that time, and certainly not among the younger people. We especially miss the "strikingly coarse" and typical organ sound of Goldy which so distinctly makes its mark on the other albums. In 1972/73, in our circle of friends, we don't linger too long, and the focus is shifted a bit more towards British hard rock. The deep interest of Blue Cheer and Steppenwolf fans, among others, we had until then, shifts towards Uriah Heep, Led Zeppelin, Yes, The Who, Deep Purple and the better Dutch groups such as Sandy Coast, Thijs Van Leer with Focus, Golden Earring and last but not least the absolutely excellent band Earth & Fire. Groups like Shocking Blue, The Sweet and David Bowie are OK in some way, but their music sounds just a bit "too soft" for us. James Brown and a still very young Michael Jackson are successful with a certain audience and Junior Walker & The All Stars' music is especially popular in discos. Barry White is starting to appear on the horizon and this typical soul/Philadelphia sound will soon have a chance of a real breakthrough. Reggae is also pushing forward

more strongly and British glitter rock is in full bloom, while Annafrid, Björn, Benny and Agnetha (ABBA) will soon be ringing the doorbell with *Ring, Ring*. But most genres are more likely to be popular with a completely different audience than with the group we like to associate with. We, with our (very) long hair, jeans, fringes and wax army coats prefer to associate ourselves with the rougher rock scene. Slade is also becoming extremely popular in our parts and their album *Slade Alive* is also good. *Born To Be Wild* by the way is used by them as the closing song on that live album. But in all honesty, I have to formally state that there are no better versions than the Steppenwolf versions, both studio and live. Many later versions of *BTBW* (and in 2002 even one by the then Miss Belgium Tania Dexters) prove beyond doubt that *BTBW* can only really be performed by one person and that is not Noddy Holder or ... Tania Dexters, but Joachim Fritz Krauledat alias John Kay.

But life goes on. As a young man of almost eighteen, yours truly has to join the Belgian army on March 1, 1973.

First, I join the Special Forces on a voluntary basis at the Second Commando Battalion in a Belgian place called Flawinne,* at the time, called the *commando-paratrooper*s (Green Berets). For the reader this may be somewhat unnecessary information, but I mention it, because it was during this period that, by meeting a few American soldiers on the Island of Corsica, I also heard a different view about John Kay's profound protest songs ...

In October 1973, in the mountains of Corsica, I happened to talk to a platoon of American marines. They are all experienced veterans, having just returned from combat zones in Vietnam, where the war was still raging at the time. They had also lost many good comrades in the jungle fighting the Vietcong rebels. Recently, they had been relieved in the jungle of Vietnam and after a two-week vacation, they came to us in Marche-Les-Dames (Belgium) to learn our Belgian commando techniques. Together with us, they will head into the mountains of beautiful, rugged Corsica at the end of October for a

---

* *This is followed by my career in the Belgian Air Force.*

while. According to these Americans, the Belgian paratroopers enjoy great prestige in the US and these marines definitely want to see (and feel) for themselves whether all this is justified. After they had shared their joys and sorrows with us for about four weeks, they finally paid us a compliment "you Belgians are the best soldiers in the world".

In the mountains, near Monte Incudine, a fraternization between some US Marines and Belgian para commandos occurs. The conversation begins spontaneously after the singing of their distinctive marching songs. One of them is quite striking and it constantly catches our attention: *"In the early mornin' rain ... With my bottines(?) full of sand ... I'm a long, long way from home, and I miss my loved ones so"*. We thought this was a fun sing-along song while marching and wanted to know where they got it from.

"The song you guys sing so often, who is the original from?"

Early Morning Rain *is a song by Gordon Lightfoot. Gordon, however, is not American, but Canadian. He's from Toronto."*

"Ha, Toronto, that's also where John Kay comes from."

"Do you know John Kay, from Steppenwolf?"

"Yep, I've been a big fan of Steppenwolf for years!"

I learn from these long-serving marines that songs like *Born To Be Wild*, *Magic Carpet Ride* and other Steppenwolf songs were very popular with them too. Over there, far away in the murky swamps of South-East Asia, this music kept them mentally afloat during the most difficult moments. Celebrating Christmas in the pouring rain in the jungle, overwhelmed by misery and despair and the loss of some mates, is hardly any fun. Among giant leeches and venomous snakes, in a period full of death and misery, they certainly felt supported by rock & roll music. They even had small portable 45-rpm record players in their backpacks, sometimes playing a nice record between two battles, while the casualties and the wounded were evacuated in helicopters.

From 1970 onwards they also had small cassette players with them. A true case of combining business with the (un)pleasant.

"Death and music went hand in hand in Vietnam. It sounds weird, but we got used to extremes over there. Rock & Roll helped us get through the more difficult days."

However, they speak of that extremely politically engaged *Monster* album with much less praise. As professional soldiers they cannot agree with songs such as *Draft Resister* and *Power Play*, because they believe that every American should defend the values of the US by all means, if necessary, at the cost of their own lives. They also consider *Don't Step On The Grass, Sam,* a direct insult to themselves. Of course, not everything in the US Army goes perfectly smoothly, but they see the US army as the most efficient tool for defending democracy in the world. According to them, the rotten regimes of the Nazis and Japan could only be defeated in 1945 by fighting against them with all possible means and not so much by singing or protesting about them. They also find it somewhat ironic that John Kay, *a German,* came to the US to lecture them *in* the US about their own very controversial history. And this while in Germany there had never been any serious form of democracy until those American (and British) soldiers got rid of the totalitarian regime. It was not just sweet talk that brought worldwide liberation or saved some peoples (such as the Jews) from total extermination.

"No, democracy was only saved by soldiers armed to their teeth, tanks, planes with bombs and heavy weapons and by using all possible means to overthrow those totalitarian and destructive regimes."

So the views of the marines are totally different from the views of pacifists and demonstrators who believe that you can't solve anything with violence but only with words and negotiations. Words are stronger than the sword? Forget it! According to them, young people who protest against everything have become much too spoiled and pampered during the last decade. Those marines also believe that the stressful political situation in the US at the time (i.e. in the early 1970s) is certainly not only a consequence of deep-seated corruption, as John Kay claims in *Monster*. It is at least as much a consequence of the excessive use of drugs everywhere in the US, a cause of decadence for many years and many things going wrong. The "Summer of Love" which, according to them, began in San Francisco in 1967 with "love & peace" and a flower in your hair was soon turned by the same people into an intoxicating cloud of hash & pot. Furthermore, they had absolutely no desire to get a job and earn a living of their own. All this did, according to them, much more harm than good. After all, work was not considered necessary, because through excessive drug use people often floated in a haze of sweet dreams which they confused a little too often with hard reality. That is certainly one of the reasons why the average American has become "fat and lazy" (literally the words of John Kay). The people who only protest while otherwise sitting on their lazy backsides are just being part of the problem. There are plenty of them, by the way, who protest against everything and who need to smash things up in the street at the same time in the name of equality, instead of rolling up their sleeves themselves. Some of them, by the way, have arrived on an island in the Mediterranean not too far from here with a lot of money from home. (He meant Ibiza, but I didn't know that at the time). They think they have rights, but when you talk about duties, they are stone deaf. Moreover, John Kay expressed plenty of criticism at the States and the way the police try to contain demonstrations and serious riots. All this while he himself left a country where not a single demonstration was allowed (the GDR) and where any criticism on the government was suppressed. Literally, if necessary. To his credit, he has studied American history very well and his texts are also quite accurate, but his views are, in our opinion, rather one-sided and certainly not everyone shares them.

"By the way, did you know that many of those who in 1970 started protesting out loud against the establishment in the US, after obtaining their degrees, without hesitation became part of that same establishment? Isn't that a bit hypocritical?"

So, these marines clearly have quite a different view on things that are going wrong in the US. According to them, many critics of the corrupt regime are themselves part of the problem.

Probably understandable from their point of view. Because it is exactly these soldiers, who after long periods of political naivety and gullibility in the eyes of the good citizen, are sent out by their government to solve wrongs with military means. There is often more than one truth, and you need to have more elements at your disposal than the words of one person on the one hand and the conviction of another person on the other. Usually, the truth lies somewhere in between. All this just as a note in the margin ...

Nevertheless, John Kay has been able to build up a strong and exceptionally good relationship with war veterans, and there has always been a great mutual respect. Many years later he still gives them the respect they never received when they returned home after their service in Vietnam, often mentally confused. In 1990, as a tribute to the scary war experiences of those Vietnam warriors, John wrote an absolutely wonderful song. That song is included as *Rock'n Roll War* on the fine CD *Rise & Shine*. A very moving song, which perfectly describes the confused feeling of the Vietnam war veterans. In some way, *Rock'n Roll War is* a detailed sequel to the earlier song *None Of Your Doing* from their 1968 album *The Second*. During that song, when guitarist Rocket Richotte is playing his guitar to the max and you allow your thoughts to wander, you automatically go back in time. You see those horrible black and white television images from the Vietnam War before you again: B-52 bombers dropping napalm bombs, a burned Vietnamese girl Kim Phuc and her screaming friends, the all-destructive Agent Orange and the loud protests against the war everywhere ...

Reborn to be wild. But now, let's get back to the music and a new era for John Kay and the band. John reforms Steppenwolf in 1974 and a second period dawns with an immediate awesome album. *Slow Flux* brings back the sound fans had been looking forward to for a long time.

Steppenwolf is again that vigorous rock band from the early years, although they have polished their biker-appearance and you can clearly see that in the pictures inside the cover. They have tidy hairdos and are fashionably dressed. Goldy, Bobby Cochran and Jerry even wear a nice tie. But the songs are once again rock-hard and *Gang War Blues* is a prime example. It reminds us a bit of the song *Ball Crusher* from the album *Steppenwolf 7*, which conveys an equally extreme statement. By the way, that album includes another American top 50 hit, *Straight Shootin' Woman*. The cover song of Albert Hammond's *Smokey Factory Blues* is a nice bonus. Goldy conjures up the fabulous *A Fool's Fantasy* out of his curly hair and John cleverly plays the mouth harp on *Jeraboah* which was a while ago too. George Biondo and Bobby Cochran, nephew of the one and only Eddy Cochran whom we know from the original *Summertime Blues* once covered by Blue Cheer, confidently support the other songs. *Slow Flux* is the album we have been waiting for.

1974 lineup of a reborn Steppenwolf. John Kay, Jerry Edmonton, George Biondo, Goldy McJohn and Bobby Cochran.

The new outfit suggests that they have traded in their wild hair and trendy clothes for the fashionable mid-seventies trend. But make no mistake, the album itself is a rock-hard album.

Unfortunately, that renewed glory doesn't last very long. One of the three performers of the first hour, old and faithful Goldy McJohn, gets serious behavioral problems due to drug use. Goldy already has those "issues" for some time. Apparently, during the recordings of *Monster (autumn 69)*, he was already "absent minded" from time to time. But this time, it's all going completely the wrong way with him. John doesn't want to give up on him and asks him directly if he can control his "problem," at least for those moments that they have to appear on stage. Then Goldy suddenly breaks down completely. He is no longer himself, starts threatening the others and his angry reactions degenerate into a big quarrel. Goldy, in turn, is banished from the group and replaced by Andy Chapin. It is clear that Goldy has lost control and is driven by evil spirits haunting his affected brain. Goldy, however, will not simply ignore his dismissal and is looking for a way to assert himself in some way. We will soon find out when he goes on tour again, without John Kay ... and with a band under a name that will make someone *very* angry ...

Surely, after *Slow Flux*, two very good Steppenwolf albums appear, first *Hour Of The Wolf* (1975) followed by *Skullduggery* (1976). Andy Chapin, the new keyboard player, decides to give it all up very soon. Because he doesn't like touring, he quickly passes the torch to Wayne Cook, who takes care of the keyboards on the album *Skullduggery*. These will also be the last albums to be released under the name Steppenwolf. Andy Chapin dies unexpectedly some ten years later. On their way to Dallas with Ricky Nelson's band for a one-off performance on New Year's Eve, December 31, 1985, their plane crashes. The man who was afraid of long distance road trips for fear of a fatal collision somewhere at night in a faraway place, finally looses his live in a plane crash ...

Then, in 1977, their producer of early Steppenwolf days Gabriel Mekler is killed in a motorcycle accident. The man who had baptized Steppenwolf and had put their career on the rails, is suddenly no longer with them. The man who, on the cover of *At Your Birthday Party*, was dressed in a gangster outfit and was wearing a hat and black sunglasses to become their fifth man, and who on the studio version of *Magic Carpet Ride* played rhythm guitar on that one occasion, very unexpectedly and much too soon says goodbye to this world ...

From 1977 on John Kay has to recover from all the emotions and stressful situations he had gone through. He is working again on a solo album that is released in 1978: *All In Good Time*. It seems that Steppenwolf then definitely ceases to exist.

During that period he also has other serious problems to deal with. From all that arduous work, he has been able to save up a decent penny, but to the great indignation of his wife Jutta and himself he discovers one day that he is as good as bankrupt. Their "investors" have taken too many big risks in all kinds of real-estate and oil-industry investments. Combined with their gullibility and inexperience in this kind of business, this wipes out all of Jutta and John's efforts over the past ten years in one go. They are especially afraid of the impact this may have on their daughter Shawn. Now, he is not the only (famous) person in history to fall victim to such wrong and bad investments. Johan Cruyff, Ajax player and famous Dutch soccer player who had earned big money especially in Barcelona, had stopped playing. However, he had to go back to playing soccer after a huge financial loss in order to make up for his losses. But that he put on the jersey of ... arch-rival Feyenoord Rotterdam in 1983 was very painful for many people in Amsterdam. Niki Lauda, famous Formula 1 driver and already world champion twice when he stopped racing, was later forced to get back behind the wheel of a racing car to get his ailing airline Lauda Air and himself out of the red. He, who miraculously escaped death in 1976 after a terrible accident at the German Nürburgring, became Formula 1 world champion for the third time in 1984. He was very generously paid for this by main sponsor Marlboro and a little later he finally quit racing and went to live in Ibiza on his spacious private property.

Retirement is clearly not yet in the pipeline for the Kay-Maue family and there is not much time for John to despair. He will have to get his act together and try to build some kind of musical empire again.

Music is all he has, so it *will* have to be music. Will he once again resuscitate his brainchild Steppenwolf? No, he considers that out of the question! Many great memories on the one hand, but also heavy disappointments on the other. The end of his friendship with his old mate Goldy still hurts him a lot! The earlier breakup with Nick, who had even introduced him to his great love Jutta in Toronto, had also been hard on him. But as the leader of a band that enters into commitments and has to honor contracts, he had to take unpopular yet necessary measures. Someone has to be at the helm in order to avoid collisions. In a musical group everyone is supposed to behave responsibly. This is just the same as in team sports: you are only as strong as your weakest link. To put it in John's own words, *"It's a band and not a kindergarten"*. John also doesn't feel he has to bear the responsibility for the stupidities of others. Moreover, he completely regards anyone who tries to fool him in any way as his enemy and even his good friend Goldy has experienced this personally. Apart from the many beautiful things they have experienced together, tough decisions had to be made at times. John, along with Jerry Edmonton, would incidentally make a firm allusion to Goldy's "behavior" in the song *Someone Told A Lie* on the 1975 album *Hour Of The Wolf*. The previous statement he made *"Don't let me pay for your mistakes, I have to pay my own"* in the song *Move Over* was not only aimed at President Nixon, but could just as easily be reflected in full on Michael Monarch.

The best thing for John to do is to start all over again with a clean sheet and perhaps also choose another group name. Will he definitely say goodbye to Steppenwolf and perhaps join the group Tall Water, the group of his friends the Palmer Brothers? If needed even as a lead singer? For the future, he is looking for members he knows he can trust, and with whom he won't have any problems off stage and certainly not *on* stage. In short: he wants men who have the same vision as he does, and both musically and ideologically are on the same page. Let the old Steppenwolf rest in peace. Rest in peace for the second time ... Amen!

But while he is forging new plans, one day John Kay gets another nasty surprise. It turns out that there is a band -apparently even more than *just one* band- that simply calls itself Steppenwolf which is touring the US and even the European continent. John frowns, though that is a serious understatement. He is indeed furious. What or who could be behind it? His indignation grows when he discovers that these few bogus bands have been created by a couple of ex-members of his old band. Nick St. Nicolas, Goldy McJohn, Kent Henry, Rushton Moreve (who apparently lives in California again) have formed their own Steppenwolf and are performing everywhere in that capacity. They have asked a few other musicians to join them and they are now functioning under the wings of a few managers, who somehow see (financial) opportunities in this situation. It is abundantly clear that they are doing this because they have recently or long ago been embarrassed in one way or another by John Kay and are now looking for some kind of revenge. They assume, that they have as much right to use that name. But then they don't know John Kay very well. If you try to fool him, you will soon and for the rest of your life have to live with the results.

For all those different bands which all of a sudden perform under the name Steppenwolf, things are not going as smooth as people might think. Their performances are a far cry from what people expect from a band that in all vanity calls itself "Steppenwolf". The fine reputation that was so cleverly built years ago with a lot of effort is now badly affected. Apparently "Rest in Peace" for the dead-and-buried Wolf is out of the question and the good name of yesteryear is being dragged through the mud. Everywhere these guys perform they arouse mistrust among organizers and disappointed fans alike. Some fans in the audience even demand their entrance fees back. The explanations given are not well received. The organizers themselves sometimes feel cheated and so do the fans. In a few cases it even comes to a scuffle between the management of the fake bands and the humiliated organizers. At one of the concerts, someone shouts from the audience:

"Is this Steppenwolf? We don't recognize them! And where is John Kay?"

To which a look-alike acting as a singer replies:
"John Kay? He is dead!"

Is John Kay dead and buried? Forget it! They are wrong, completely wrong. For John is alive and well and they will soon realize. Although he may have dozed off a bit, there's no better way to wake him up and spark his motivation again than to present him with a *fait accompli* in this way. Besides, any group that dared to call itself Steppenwolf, but without John Kay as a member, was not really Steppenwolf at all, and surely, they should have known that. Too bad, because these guys could certainly consider themselves good musicians and they did not need the name Steppenwolf at all to get noticed. However, it is abundantly clear that the previous members of the band deliberately wanted to put a spoke in John Kay's wheel. John Kay does find full support in his former drummer Jerry Edmonton. Neither of them can manage this situation and they eventually decide to file a lawsuit. In a way, they feel sorry for Goldy. The three of them had been through turbulent times together, but at this very moment they see no other option ...

Someone as experienced as Goldy McJohn certainly had no need to use the group name Steppenwolf for personal purposes. He had already proved that in the band Manbeast and his own later performance of, for example, *Sookie, Sookie* was certainly not without Steppenwolf quality. For a while he had also been a member of Steve Marriot's group Humble Pie. Talented as he was and, thanks to the financial support of his wealthy parents, having received musical training since the age of four, he could have easily gone his own way without jumping on the bandwagon. He would abundantly prove that later on. Too bad he was clearly only filled with resentment at the time instead of going his own way. There is one thing ALL bogus Steppenwolf bands should have known anyway. Even if you combine all the people who have acted as temporary surrogate singers, from Tom Pagan, Peter McGraw, Tom Holland, Bob Simpson to Larry Green (to name but a few) and you look at the result, you might have a very good lead singer. And maybe you'll create some kind of wolf, but still not ... a *Steppenwolf*.

Because it is exactly John Kay who makes Steppenwolf what it is. HE is the wolf and nobody else. And of course, you may like John Kay, or not at all. You can even curse him and completely disagree with the statements in his political lyrics. And you can, if necessary, even wish him to hell and accuse him of being a blind (pun not intended) opportunist. But what you CANNOT do is *replace* him as the singer of Steppenwolf and nobody can change that. All the look-alikes who tried to do so between 1977 and 1980, experienced this first-hand and were ultimately forced to keep their heads down and to shut up …

By the way, the court ultimately ruled in favor of John Kay. He and nobody else is now allowed to use the name that he and his then manager/producer Gabriel Mekler had given to the group. But he is not sure what to do …

One of eight(!) bogus lineups that briefly operated under the name Steppenwolf between 1977 and 1980. We clearly recognize Goldy McJohn, Kent Henry and Nick St. Nicolas in this photo.
They assumed they could continue to use the name Steppenwolf, despite previously agreements to the contrary.
This band also went to Breda, the Netherlands during its European tour. The story of all the fake Steppenwolfs was not a successful one and shortly afterwards they one by one experienced their swan song.

In 1980, John Kay is faced with a rather challenging task. A lot has gone wrong in recent years -financially as well- and it will take him a lot of time and energy to get everything back on track.

The whole thing inspires John after all to use the name again himself and he decides to come up with a new Steppenwolf. But to avoid any misunderstanding in the future, he is legally forced to add his own name. The group he put back on the map in 1980 will thus go through life as John Kay & Steppenwolf. No more misconceptions in the future with some John Kay look-alike on stage and with furious local managers managing the contracts ... and the pennies.

But John Kay is forced to build everything back up from scratch. He still has his fame and that is an advantage. The easy life of touring around the globe in a luxury jet is no longer possible because of all the financial problems. The band travels around the US in a large, second-hand van, in which they can barely fit all their equipment.

Travelling along the long, dusty roads reminds John of the early days, when he and his mates still had to prove everything. Life is sometimes hard, but it is now up to him to show that he still has it all.

Jutta believes in him, she always has and just as his mother Elsbeth always has as well. The financial blow has hit him awfully hard, especially because Jutta and he also blame themselves. After all, it is partly due to their own gullibility that they have ended up in this financial dip.

But come on, cheer up! There are far worse things in life! Jutta does resolve to keep an eye on things from now on and to occupy herself a bit more with the overall management of the band. Daughter Shawn is now perfectly capable of taking care of herself. Jutta also continues to perfect her skills in the sport of judo. She promptly gets her black tie. Does she have mischievous plans with any rogue elements in case something goes wrong behind the scenes?

It is somewhat surprising that Jerry Edmonton and George Biondo are not included in John Kay's new band. The true reason for this I am unfortunately not aware of, for neither of them ever had anything to do with the bizarre situations of rebellious ex-members. Jerry and

George were always loyal followers of the pack leader (John). Admittedly, they too wanted to start a band, but it is a bit of a mystery to this author, that they were not asked in 1980 to accompany John Kay in his new band. John then gives the reason himself: Jerry has started a photo business and wants to devote all his energy to it. Apparently, that's why he doesn't want to go on long and distant tours. Possibly it is indeed Jerry's and George's own choice. But a little later, they themselves found Steel Rose, assisted by the ladies Laurie Richardson and Heli Hewko. This band will already cease to exist in 1984. Jerry *then* becomes a full-time professional photographer and George dives deeper into the studio for producer work. George Biondo and Jerry Edmonton remain eternally loyal to the original Steppenwolf by never joining one of the bogus groups.

The renewed Steppenwolf (with the one and only John Kay) immediately crosses the Atlantic in 1980 and will perform for three days in France. In 1981 they are in Europe once again and the band records their first album *Live In London* under the name John Kay & Steppenwolf. No new songs yet, but a live CD with the best-known songs. New studio work appears a year later with the album *Wolf-Tracks*.

In one of the songs on that album John lashes out hard against the bogus bands of the past years with all the fake situations. *Five Finger Discount* refers to all those who wanted "a free-ride".
  But John Kay himself is also still experiencing negative after-effects of the problems of the past. Sometimes it is back to square one. At times, the band is forced to change in a far too small room or even in the bathroom and to perform a little later in some dilapidated barn. His new band members, such as the Palmer brothers and Michael Wilk, who are the first to support his new John Kay & Steppenwolf, had also imagined certain things a bit differently. Back to the absolute basics, and for the most part that can be taken literally. One day during a gig somewhere in the back of beyond, John is even directly reproached by a spontaneous young man:

"You are not John Kay! He would never perform in such a dirty hole!"

John is surprised by this remark, but he realizes that the boy may have a point. Indeed, is it all worth it? A year ago, he was on cloud nine, and now he has lost virtually everything. Brick by brick he tries to rebuild everything. But performing in small venues and using the kitchen or even the toilets as a cloakroom out of necessity? Can he still bring himself to do that? He stands in front of the mirror, has a good look at himself and makes the serious reflection:

"Joachim Fritz Krauledat, you have indeed just performed in an old, dirty and dilapidated barn! And you ask yourself if you still want to do this. But look here, man! There were over six hundred people here and they were very happy to see you perform. And if that rundown barn is good enough for them to see you, why shouldn't that old barn be good enough ... for your to entertain them, huh?"

John obviously saw more in that mirror than his own face. He looked far beyond his own dark eyes. He was able to draw this sober conclusion in all honesty by looking directly into his own soul in this desolate place. He suddenly rediscovers himself. Because didn't it all start this way in 1965? On the one hand, he realizes he still has a long way to go to return to that old level of success. On the other hand, he feels that he can now find his way back to the old driving force that got him started in the music industry: the passion for music itself and not the "$ sign". Besides, if the gigs are good, the necessary pennies will also come again. We'll get through this! But the situation with all those fake bands still continues to bother him. After some gigs he referred to all those bands who, according to him, gave Steppenwolf such a bad reputation. He finally has a clear message for all those deceitful elements who dared to question the credibility of his own and Gabriel Mekler's brainchild. As already cited, he files a lawsuit, and he will win hands down. The words he sometimes uses afterward are full of irony:

"Court has taken them out of the highway ... and out of their misery."

Many decades later all of this may sound laughable, but that whole bogus legacy must have been very hard on John and left a few scars. But John Kay wouldn't be John Kay if he allowed himself to be pushed into a corner for a long time as a result. He stands up and fights like a devil in a holy water font.

And the 1980s, meanwhile, go by like an express train. There are constant personnel changes in the band. Michael Wilk, who joined the band in 1981, will stay until the very end in November 2018. That, by the way, is the longest period for anyone other than John Kay to stay in the band. Michael Wilk's comrade Ron Hurst, who joins the band in 1984, will also remain a long time, until their last performance (together) in October 2018. Rocket Richotte on guitar stays until 1993 and is then replaced. First by Steve Fister for a while (two years) and then by an old friend of Rick Derringer, Alice Cooper and Rod Stewart: Danny Johnson. Year after year they tour very frequently, especially in the US. Sometimes the schedule is so full, that John and the others are only home for Christmas. It is hard work, but it pays off. They are often asked at festivals of motor clubs and eventually they also found their own annual "Wolf Fest", which the fans are always very enthusiastic about. In 1987 the album *Rock & Roll Rebels* is released. That way, the '80s are gradually ending. But in the last year, something special is happening, and it will make a very deep impression on Steppenwolf in general and on John Kay in particular. A very bizarre day at the end of that very bizarre decade of the turbulent "eighties". Once again, we cross the Atlantic Ocean, but this time we do so without John Kay and his band. We head for Germany and soon we will experience an incredibly unique event:

November 9, 1989. A milestone in history … and certainly in the heart of our protagonist here. A wall is pulled down, literally and figuratively.

Four CDs from the eighties. On WolfTracks *(1982, top right) John gives his own opinion on the meaning of* Five Finger Discount.

A Crack in the Iron Curtain

"Wall of bitter tears, wall of chilling fears, You will never keep me here ... "

November 9, 1989. Annemarie Reffert is just a normal GDR citizen. She has no lofty ambitions to put herself in the spotlight, but we will see in a moment that on this day she will nevertheless somewhat unexpectedly go down in history as an icon. If things had gone wrong there, she would have been yet another martyr ...

9 November 1989. People of East and West Berlin together on the Wall. (Creative Commons CC PDM 1.0.)

1989. The GDR, loyal satellite state of the USSR, is celebrating 40 years of statehood. But *is* there anything to celebrate? The regime has kept the people under strict control the whole time and systematically and increasingly strengthened the East/West border to prevent people from fleeing to freedom. According to the GDR regime this border was guarded so fiercely in order to prevent terrorist attacks from the capitalist West. In this way they could "protect" their own people more easily and in 1961 they had also built the accursed double wall in Berlin: to give their people a more secure feeling and to protect them from Western depravity and fascist ideas(?).

Transparency and objectivity have never been symbols of communism. People have long been fed up with the fact that since the end of the Second World War, they have continuously been lied to and they were never allowed to express their own opinions about the things of life. Fleeing to the West is therefore a dream for many people. Besides, between 1948 and 1961 almost 10% of East Germans would (try to) cross over to the free West risking their lives, which means that they knew well enough that elsewhere things were completely different and above all much freer. Barbed wire and wooden watchtowers with machine guns on the eastern side were supposed to prevent this, but for too many, the urge to get away prevailed over the fear. Elsbeth and Joachim had done the same in 1949, just in time before it became almost impossible ...

It is true that the communist system also has its advantages. Everyone is entitled to a roof over their heads and health care is basically free. (In Cuba, for example, the health care system still functions very well). However, it should be noted that East German doctors and nurses are well aware that there are many more opportunities in the West to realize their scientific ambitions and that, above all, with their practical medical knowledge they can earn more (money). After all, in a communist state, the care given by the medical profession is not reimbursed in proportion to studies and training.

But in the everyday life of the *healthy* GDR citizen, none of this is a priority. They are indeed not immediately concerned about the imposed political views, and the total lack of freedom of expression in the first place either. What they find much worse is that the shelves of their stores for basic necessities are usually empty and that the range of available foodstuffs is constantly far too limited. For example: today no bananas, tomorrow no pears and the day after tomorrow no oranges. After all, according to the regime, these are "luxury products" that are only occasionally available ... and even then, in very limited quantities. *If* bananas are available at all, a family of five has to make do with just two bananas, for example. Excuse me? Do you want one banana for every person? Are you mad? You won't get them, even if they happen to be on the shelves! There will be other customers, and we'll have to share ...

Moreover, everyone is thoroughly tired of having to do *Schlange stehen** in the *Magazin Organisazion* stores every day, where most things that in the West have long been regarded as products for daily use or consumption are not available. It seems at times even worse than during the war. Ordinary coffee beans have not been around for many years and they have to content themselves with "malt coffee", a coffee substitute made from malted barley. And all this while they are well aware that in some nearby East German *Intershop* luxury stores (yes!) everything is available, as long as it can be paid for ... with Western currency. Of course, THEY do not have Western currency themselves, so the shop is exclusively reserved for Western visitors, such as Western sports clubs who come to play European matches in East Germany. The communist regime of course blatantly contradicts itself in this way and most people are sick and tired of it. And the East Berliners who watch (secretly, because it is strictly forbidden) West German television channels, are beginning to realize one thing: they have heard nothing but lies for 40 years!

All that anti-Western propaganda that has come from the SED party for so long! It's enough! For 40 years they have been fooled, looking on powerlessly and in the long run even apathetically ...

A majority of (East) Germans wants to get rid of the GDR regime. They have been dreaming of reunification between East and West

---

* *A long queue of people waiting patiently.*

World-famous photo of an East German border guard escaping through the barbed wire to the West, throwing away his submachine gun in the process. (Creative Commons CC BY-NC-2.0 License Annalisa Ceolin.)

Germany for decades. When West German Chancellor Helmuth Kohl makes a clear allusion to reunification of all Germans and that this new Germany in exchange wants to finally recognize the disputed Oder-Neisse border, a reunification of the two Germanies might be a possibility in the opinion of the Western world. All we have to do now is wait and see how the Politburo in the Supreme Soviet reacts to this … and whether Erich Honecker's own GDR party is willing to give up its position of power just like that …

For the time being, the Soviet Union is shrouding itself in a mysterious silence. This may seem positive, but it certainly does not offer any guarantees. After all, didn't they intervene firmly in Berlin in 1949 and 1953, in Budapest in 1956 and in Prague in 1968? Indeed, every uprising against their regime was immediately crushed, time after time. Most of the older generation have not yet forgotten the bloody crushing of every opposition to the regime, and people know that even now it can still end badly if they dare to revolt. But the heavy, rolling war equipment of the Warsaw Pact remains in the barracks for the time being. Would US President Ronald Reagan go down in history as the great peacemaker after all with his words:

"Mister Gorbachev, open that gate. Tear down this wall!"

Indeed, with those words, US President Ronald Reagan addressed Soviet leader Mikhail Gorbachev earlier (on July 12, 1987) at Berlin's Brandenburger Tor. He made this hopeful appeal to the entire Eastern Bloc, to finally eliminate the very hostile atmosphere that had been dragging on for about 42 years between the East and West power blocs. The West spontaneously sought the cautiously outstretched hand of Soviet party leader Gorbachev, who had already promised a little more transparency in the future from the Soviet Union, with Perestroika and Glasnost.

The two (world) leaders of the US and the Soviet Union had already met several times. In Geneva for the first time, but that meeting was rather clumsy and seemed a bit forced. At the next two meetings, things went more smoothly, and mutual trust grew gradually. In Reykjavik, Iceland, one year before Ronald Reagan's visit to Berlin, the two leaders had already paved the way for even warmer relations. And one year later, in 1988, they would also sign a far-reaching disarmament agreement. It seemed as if some thaw was finally occurring in the frozen relations.

Ronald Reagan was not taken seriously at first as a presidential candidate. A Republican cowboy actor in the White House? You're joking! He was known as a fierce anti-Communist, and many Americans feared that he would go full blast in the arms race with the Soviet Union. Yet, he had become US president in January 1981 because the average American citizen had noticed that his Democratic predecessor Jimmy Carter had been a far too weak and indulgent figure during his time in office. A literal translation of a Dutch proverb "soft healers are making stinking wounds" had apparently been very applicable to Carter and he was judged accordingly. Hopefully, history will not repeat itself and the US will once again not play it *too* softly against potential enemies who want to wipe Israel off the map and, by definition, wish all Jews and Americans to hell anyway. But both the Left (Democrats) and the Right (Republicans) in the USA collide every four years with their own limitations. A democrat becomes president after the people often denounce a policy that is too right-wing. After all, this often shows that entire population groups, especially the weaker ones, are at risk of being left out in the cold. A Republican, in turn, becomes President because a Democrat too often shows that he does not have the courage to make firm decisions and also uses well-meaning people who work hard to get on in life to bear the suffering of the whole population ... including the "suffering" of those who ... do not *want* to work. In the words of another former president J.F. Kennedy, "democracy is not perfect." No, not even in the land of the free, the US.

But in Carter's case it was above all the crisis in Tehran in 1979, where American diplomats had been scandalously held hostage for months by the Iranian Revolutionary Guard, which exposed Carter's limitations in a most pitiful way. The helicopter raid that he finally, in all desperation, ordered to free the hostages, came much too late and ended in a complete failure, much to the amusement of this new ideological archenemy Iran.

American citizens were so bewildered that many were eager to flatten all of Iran at once. Jimmy Carter and the parliament, however, did not take any action and henceforth Iran would treat the USA without any respect whatsoever ...

After Carter, America apparently needed a strong(er) guiding hand to deal with extremist and/or religious regimes that were at odds with the US. So, in 1983 the Americans were once again led by a Republican. From the start of his time in office, Reagan was criticized -again by definition- by many democratic opponents in America for his clearly right-wing views. He was even accused by the Left of being a shrewd warmonger. But Reagan would certainly not let himself be dominated by spiritual leaders like Ayatollahs or by some Kim Jong's or any other power-hungry figure with bad intentions. In the periphery of his convictions, he even thought it fair to sell arms a little later to a so-called moderate (secret) wing within Iranian politics and channel the proceeds in US $ to insurgents in Nicaragua, a Central American country under communist rule. Doing everything possible to avoid getting a second Cuba crisis in the vicinity of one's own homeland. But what if the weapons that were sold to Iran, eventually fall into the wrong hands in Iran? The US would also sell weapons to the Taliban in their fight against the Russians who invaded Afghanistan in 1980. However, post factum it is clear that the Taliban is ideologically much more dangerous than the Russians and their entire communist political system. Irony at its finest, because to this day those weapons sold by America at the time, are being used in Afghanistan in full against American soldiers ...

But on 12 July 1987, supposed warmonger Reagan caused, ironically enough, a definitive thaw in those so badly strained East-West relations; in spite of all the white doves and archangels who had preceded him in the interest of peace. In fact, J.F. Kennedy, former president and democrat to the core, had had a hell of a job as a preacher of peace, to prevent a third World War after the incident-rich period with Russia, Cuba and the events at the Bay of Pigs in the early 1960s.

John Kennedy's legendary statement at the Berlin Wall later, in 1963, had incidentally made the Communist Eastern Bloc even more determined to persist in selective deafness. Other presidents had also failed to live up to their peace and other ambitions. Lyndon B. Johnson, another Democrat, failed to build up a good reputation because of the far-reaching American involvement in Vietnam and had caused a great deal of division within the US: some were in favor and others against war in Vietnam. Johnson's approach simply could not succeed, because the American soldiers were placed under too many restrictions. You can't win half wars anyway. So, when you dig into a hornet's nest, immediately throw out the political interference and dig on, or you will fail. Johnson continually stepped up the war effort and did not admit defeat. He did, however, eventually forego a possible extension of his own term in office. Indeed, he did not run for president again after his first full four-year term. His successor Nixon, a Republican again, had to deal with the ever-growing opposition in his own country to the Vietnam War. Not only in the US, but also in major cities like Madrid, Paris, London and Sydney, resistance against US intervention in South-East Asia was growing. Nixon, together with Henry Kissinger, sought a solution to break the deadlock. He would get credit for slightly improving relations with China, but that was essentially nothing more than kowtowing to Chinese President Mao Zedong. After Nixon's visit to China, Mao promised to ensure that the North Vietnamese troops and the Vietcong rebels would respect the limited parallels and to leave the South Vietnamese alone, *after* America's withdrawal. When the Americans left South-East Asia, the conscience of the masses in the West opposed to the Vietnam War was somewhat appeased and the protests in the major cities faded away. The problem was "solved" for the average US and world citizen. Only the heavy financial burden still lingered …

But if you are too confident in international politics, you will be cheated. Indeed, because the *real* impact of the American withdrawal, was essentially as predictable as it could have been.

Most Americans don't even know this to this day, but not even two years later, that South Vietnam was overrun without any mercy by the troops of North Vietnam. All this under the approving eye of … Chinese leader Mao Zedong! In the process, many thousands more innocent people were bluntly slaughtered, because they had no protection left. Would the average American citizen (or others), so adamantly opposed to any American interference, have problems with his conscience as a result as well?

Nixon had finally pulled the Americans out of Vietnam and by giving China free rein in South-East Asia he allowed the people there to "solve" their own problems. He did, however, nail himself to the cross a bit later in the bizarre Watergate wiretapping scandal.

But high time now to go back to the Berlin of the late 1980s. So, what about this former movie star Ronald Reagan as a president? That somewhat timid person with his modest acting talent. According to the then Libyan leader Muammar Gaddafi, he was no more than even a "shadow figure from the third row of second-rate actors". But Reagan achieved more than that. He, who was not taken seriously by everyone, even brought about the end of the Cold War worldwide to everyone's surprise. Thanks to Mikhail Gorbachev, who paved the way by playing his cards openly, but who also took a huge gamble in the Kremlin's own head quarters. After all, it was far from certain that the Supreme Soviet would support Gorbachev's progressive political views. Many of them had associated themselves all their lives with Stalin's strict schooling and would not deviate an inch from it; often indeed because they themselves did not even know any better and were stuck in their own narrow-mindedness. Gorbachev's innovative approach therefore raised heavy and dark-haired eyebrows among most conservative party members in the Politburo. But the trend toward relaxation had begun, thanks to an objective minded Gorbachev, and that trend was apparently irreversible. It looked very much as if the rigid relations that had developed between the two superpowers USA and USSR immediately after the Second World War would be much smoother in the future. For that to actually happen, however, we had to be patient ...

True, there had always been deep folds in that Iron Curtain of Eastern Europe during those 40 years. But the Moscow of Stalin and his successors always put things in order, and time after time after every pinprick -from the inside as well as from the outside-, the Curtain was tightened again. We had already seen the discontent of all Berliners after the blockade of Berlin in 1949, which had led to a further expansion of the fortification of the East-West border line, a full-blown Berlin revolt in 1953 and a bloody Hungarian uprising in 1956. Budapest was crying out for Western help, but an intervention by the West had undeniably led to an armed conflict between the superpowers, possibly even a Third World War. In this regard, American President Roosevelt had been very categorical in the spring of 1945: Hungary, according to the Potsdam agreements, fell within *the Soviet Union's sphere of influence ... forever*, and the West could not intervene. While the Hungarian uprising was literally crushed, the West turned its head. Then there was the construction of the Berlin Wall in 1961 (to curb the flight of many fortune seekers from East to West) and the speech that then-American President J.F. Kennedy delivered there in 1963 for the occasion. We had the Prague Spring in 1968 and later the Polish uprising against the communist regime, which started at the shipyards in Gdansk (Danzig) in 1980 under the leadership of union leader Lech Walesa. Repeatedly, the resistance against the communist regime in one of the countries under Soviet influence, was mercilessly thwarted and the path to more democracy and political achievements was resolutely blocked by the Kremlin. Also, in 1980 in Gdansk (Danzig), Poland, where General Wojciech Jaruzelski took over all power, outlawed the trade union and even imprisoned Walesa for a time. The rigid Soviet regime curiously made an exception for President Tito's communist Yugoslavia. Russia had always felt a kinship with the Slavs and for that reason the Balkan countries had always been able to count on Russia's support in history.

In fact, this was one of the reasons why the First World War had erupted on July 28, 1914, when Austria-Hungary had presented Serbia with an ambiguous and impossible ultimatum. Yet in Yugoslavia from the 1950s onwards, President Josip Tito had always steered a somewhat idiosyncratic course, and it is highly curious that the Kremlin never vetoed it. Would the Kremlin really not have known that Tito secretly sent his air force pilots … to the United States to undergo specialized training on new types of fighter planes? Or did the Kremlin tacitly allow that too in the hope that they could extract secret information? Who knows, but the story was confirmed to me personally and wholeheartedly by Steven (his full name is known to the author), a former Belgian F 84 fighter pilot. He was trained in the USA at the end of the 1950s along with Yugoslav pilots in all secrecy. For about 40 years, it was kept a secret for the entire world …

So, in the mid-1980s, communism did not fold as yet, and according to Moscow, living according to that rigid pattern of life was still the only way to consider all people as equals in a state with a growing population … and to feed them. Any relaxation or concessions, in their view, would ultimately lead to laxity and decadence. That was one of Karl Marx's main maxims and since Lenin had overthrown the corrupt regime of the Czar and taken power, there was no room for private property and corruption ... at least in theory. Indeed, it is an open secret that in *every* nation around the world where communism is preached, since time immemorial, the party members themselves have been made exceptions in the practical application of those principles. *"Everyone with property, is a thief"* said Marx, but all so-called "socialist" party leaders enjoy exceptional luxury and have valuable private collections, which was at odds with the overall philosophy they themselves confidently proclaimed to their supporters. Gorbachev could not stand this any longer, and bided his time nervously but firmly. A little further into the 1980s a pale sun began to shine more clearly in the murky world of rigid communism, thanks to Reagan and Gorbachev.

In Hungary, thirty years after the bloody riots of 1956, a cautious attempt was made to bring about more openness, and this time in a very strange and subtle way: through Formula 1. In 1986, the Hungarian president succeeded in bringing the Formula 1 car circus to Budapest, and even getting the race on the permanent calendar in the future. Enterprising business people immediately saw opportunities to commercialize everything. McDonald's restaurants, shops, boutiques, and other capitalist trademarks emerged for the occasion and that was unheard of in a country that lived under a strict communist dictatorship. Therefore, it was feared at first that Moscow would put a big stop to this extremely capitalist event. Curiously enough, there was no Soviet intervention at all. Bizarre! The folds in the pattern were accompanied by deepening cracks in the reinforced concrete of communism. Communism was faltering and the solid Berlin Wall was about to collapse.

The pressure for more openness was continuously increased internally, and it gradually appeared to be paying off. Soviet Party leader Mikhail Gorbachev is therefore of a vastly different caliber than his predecessors Stalin, Khrushchev, Andropov and other Brezhnevs. He realizes that his own regime has by now committed suicide and that socialism as written by Karl Marx and imposed on the people by Vladimir Lenin is out of time. In particular, the corruption within the Communist Party's own leadership has bothered him for much longer. Enjoying benefits thanks to the party card was thumbing a nose to ordinary citizens for a long time. Everyone who has finally figured out this deceptive game is tired of the hypocrisy of nepotism and lies. All the people behind the Iron Curtain are fed up with their so-called "democratic" system in which they have no say whatsoever.

It looks as if in a few months the way will be opened to the miracle that has been impossible in the past 44 years. On November 9, 1989, that time has come. East Germany rebels against its own regime, and in Berlin people climb the 45-kilometer double Wall of Shame en masse. However, most citizens of East Berlin still fear that their protests and their enthusiasm in the drive for freedom will once again end in failure. GDR party leader Honecker makes one more supreme attempt to save his swaying bastion from capitalist ruin. He even orders to shoot the whole crowd, anyone who dares to climb onto the Wall, with war ammunition …

Honecker's orders are -fortunately- flagrantly ignored by the country's security agents, for they too believe that the era of rigid communism is history by now. The people absolutely want to make their way to freedom. Even literally if they have to, and if necessary, even at the cost of many people who will fall under the bullets if fire is still opened. The East Germans have smelled freedom and there is no turning back now … Honecker's power is collapsing completely. He soon finds himself even forced to hurriedly flee to Moscow and he is helped in this by a few loyal collaborators of the last hour. There he receives the promise of lifelong asylum from the Soviet authorities. "For years of faithful service as our most loyal marionet", they must have thought, although they already know that not only the GDR, but also the Soviet Union and the other Eastern Bloc countries will soon cease to exist under this current communist form of government.

Meanwhile, on that day of the turbulent year of 1989, East German radio broadcasts messages that are difficult to catalog with complete precision. On state television, the East German politician Gunther Schabovski even tentatively said that the free movement of people across the East-West border might be possible soon for East Germans.

In East Germany, this suddenly creates a euphoria. But people are still too scared to *dare* to believe it, and the message does not immediately sink in with everyone ...

It does, however, get through to Annemarie Reffert and her fifteen-year-old daughter Juliane. They want to see it all with their own eyes as soon as possible. With that in mind, Annemarie, born in 1943 and exactly one year (and *one* week) older than John Kay, is driving toward the town of Mariënborn on November 9. A little after 9 p.m. she arrives at Checkpoint Alfa, the border crossing between the two different worlds. It is, as usual, very heavily guarded and she is stopped by force. Bright spotlights are promptly directed at her, so that she is briefly blinded ...

"Nothing has changed here! And now I will probably get arrested too!" she thinks to herself."

A very bewildered East German border guard steps up to her and asks what the purpose of her maneuver is. A little intimidated, but determined not to just let herself be drummed out, she opens the side window of her bubbling two-stroke Wartburg (built in the Wartburg factory of the same name in Eisenach) and she replies with conviction:

"Our political superiors have just announced on television that the border is open from now on. You must therefore let me through."

Her response may still be a tiny tad premature at *that* moment. Yet her determination makes an impression on the chief of security at the border post. He too is having some doubts after all the bizarre things he saw recently on television. He also thinks of all the demonstrations and the tense hope that people have that there will soon no longer be a border between East and West Germany. The man is still unsure of exactly what to do next. Nevertheless, several checks on both the vehicle and the person of Annemarie Reffert and her daughter follow first.

But to both their gigantic surprise, the light suddenly turns on green. She thinks it is a mistake ... or possibly even a trap to give the guards the opportunity to open fire for "attempted escape". She and her daughter then instinctively drive a few meters further, with beating hearts, through complete darkness and they reach checkpoint Alfa, the border guard post of that other world ... that of WEST Germany.

Her daughter is terribly scared, because she fears that they are not allowed to go any further and that they cannot go back either.

Annemarie drives on at a walking pace for another twenty meters and reads the sign "Helmstedt". Again, she gets strong bright rays of light in her eyes. She fears a second check. To her own great surprise, she suddenly sees photographers and journalists standing there, and instead of a 9 mm pistol (as she first thought), she gets a microphone pushed under her nose to tell what her first experience is. She has no idea at the time, but it turns out that she and her daughter are the first two people to have actually ventured across the border from East to West. She is asked if she wants to emigrate or if this is a one-time visit. She says she just wants to see what things are like *on the other side*. She has heard so many things and finally wants to know what is true about it. A final transition is not on the agenda for her for the time being, she says ...

Annemarie Reffert is the first to cross the border. Less than an hour later, the border crossings at Checkpoint Charlie in Berlin also open up and people everywhere no longer just crawl *on* the double wall as an expression of protest, but also *over* it to finally go from one side to the other unhindered. The wall is literally and figuratively being knocked down. Souvenirs in the form of concrete blocks and iron supports of the concrete reinforcement that came from the wall are taken away. Forty-four years of tension have ended, and the Cold War seems to be over. Along the entire double wall in Berlin and everywhere else on the border between East and West, great euphoria spontaneously arises on November 9.

People are frenzied with joy as they realize that soon they will be able to see their families again without problems and without being closely followed and spied on by the STASI* in East Germany.

---

* *Staatssicherheitsdienst, the East German intelligence service.*

A little later, long lines of puffing "Trabi's" (Trabants) equipped with a prehistoric two-stroke engine in a huge plume of smoke from burnt oil and gasoline are lined up at the open border. Young people in particular want to finally see this other Germany.

Until then, they had known nothing but an East and a West Germany. That West Germany, which they only know from hearsay and of which they assume that the people there have everything and they themselves nothing. And the elderly people? They spontaneously go searching for their relatives. Finally, people see their parents again, their cousins or their siblings. For so many, the last time they saw them, was already before ... 1945.

Not only in former East and West Germany there is plenty of euphoria in November '89. Now the other countries that are part of the Warsaw Pact, established in 1955, also suddenly feel a great relief. They immediately see useful opportunities when it appears that freedom, money, and individual property are no longer taboo and free movement becomes possible everywhere. Poland, Czechoslovakia and Bulgaria followed suit, and in December of the same year Romania, too, finally made a clean sweep by getting rid of its own corrupt rulers who had kept the ordinary man in the street as dumb as possible for far too long under the guise of so-called equality. There, too, President Nicolae Ceaușescu, like Honecker, made an ultimate attempt to get the "Securitate" to do his dirty work. However, they also turned against him, and his empire was over. Together with his wife he was executed for his years of authoritarian rule in which repression, mismanagement and personal profit had been the order of the day for decades.

The tension between the former communist countries behind the Iron Curtain and the NATO countries, just about all capitalist countries, ebbs away. Communism in Eastern Europe is collapsing completely and people are delirious with joy now that they are free. The mutual distrust between East and West is abating and it suddenly seems as if the world is awakening from a long, evil dream ...

Anno 2013. A part of the authentic Berlin Wall. Ideal setting for graffiti artists. The rows of barbed wire that were on top have been removed everywhere. (Photograph by the author)

USA, November 9, 1989. Close to the town of Franklin in the state of Tennessee, located about thirty miles south of the slightly more "notorious" city of Nashville, is a luxurious mansion near a lake. It is inhabited by a 45-year-old man and his wife Jutta. They moved up here from the American West Coast a few months ago. The man is an (East) German who emigrated to Canada in 1958 and who has been living in the USA since 1963. He is following the developments in Berlin with great interest. He feels enormously involved; even more so than anyone else ...

He is not the only one who is interested as a result of that bizarre autumn day in November. The whole world -the USA included- is naturally curious about the further developments of the situation in Germany. After all, the Cold War seems to be coming to an end and it looks like at least some of the American occupation forces that have been in Germany for so long to protect the West may soon and defin-

Annemarie Reffert was the first East German citizen to search for freedom in her two-stroke Wartburg, but it is the Trabant that is the actual, true symbol of the fall of the Berlin Wall. People from Belgium and the Netherlands even went to Berlin to help people flee. With this car, the East German couple Rosi and Christian, their three-year-old son and three-month-old daughter fled to the West. On the western side they were welcomed exuberantly. The joy was indescribable. (Authentic car, photograph by the author)

itively return home. John F. Kennedy's legendary 1963 speech in Berlin at the Brandenburger Tor is finally having success 26 years later. But the events there make an enormously deep impression especially on *this* man, who is sitting quietly in his seat here at home in the US, far away from Berlin, following the news on TV. The living room is, as always, very dimly lit, and according to his old habits he is wearing slippers at home. He is completely overwhelmed by the bizarre news report about something that is actually happening more than 12,000 kilometers away. He can hardly believe what he is seeing and hearing. Isn't this all fake? But the images prove it! People are crawling on the wall in Berlin and are chopping small pieces out of it, as souvenirs. It seems as if that almost 3.5-meter-high double row of thick concrete blocks, adorned with all those crosses and all those names of the unfortunate ones who had paid with their lives in an attempt to escape, will soon no longer be there. From his seat, the man continues to gaze at these strange images. A bit apathetic, he is uninterruptedly staring at the screen, and it dawns on him more and more: this is really happening! His mind fills up at the sight of all those people whose happiness cannot be described in words.

He takes off his dark glasses and tries to rub his eyes dry, but it doesn't seem to help. His wife Jutta asks him what is wrong. Of course, she knows all about his flight as a little boy and the dangerous circumstances in which it took place some 40 years earlier on the border between East and West Germany, near the town of Eisenach. She herself is German, from Hamburg. No one knows better than she about the enormous differences between German citizens in East and West Germany; the freedom they enjoyed themselves as West Germans compared to those poor former compatriots who had had the misfortune to end up in East Germany after the war.

John Kay looks again -almost pleadingly- at his wife Jutta Maue with those striking, dark, piercing eyes which are so characteristic on him. He cannot say a word nor answer her question. His eyes are suddenly all swollen and bloodshot, while thick tears well up over and over again. Those weak eyes of his, which have been a burden to him all his life, let the tears run freely. He can hardly see through those tender eyes, but through those same dark eyes he has been able to show his emotions better than anyone else his whole life. You would not immediately associate a man who shows his emotions in this sensitive way with the image he has had for more than two decades as a militant-sounding rock singer. Everywhere in the world where he is known, he symbolizes the cliché image of a few slightly rougher sections of the population. By now by a third generation worldwide he is associated with, among others, macho bikers, solid hard-rockers, bike chain swingers, roadhouse "visitors", experienced Vietnam veterans and other soldiers, in short: the tougher guys. Usually dressed in black leather himself, heavy boots with heels, with his long chestnut brown hair and his very distinctive singing voice that is somewhere between a grinding saw, an old diesel engine and a roaring 305 mm fortress gun. On top of that, he invariably wears dark glasses that make him somewhat mysterious and even a bit terrify.

He has indeed been the incorrigible leader of his own "Wolfpack" for more than twenty-two years. A real pack leader, that's what he is. But there is more to him than that. He also has a softer side, he pleads with conviction for human and animal rights and doesn't hide his sympathy for people who oppose any form of violence. With his lyrics he supports conscientious objectors, draft resisters and anti-war demonstrators while also protecting the 'wretched of the earth'. At those sensitive moments, the tears flow naturally as well. Jutta finds this so admirable about him and it is, in fact, one of the reasons why she fell for him so readily at the time. On the one hand, he is a real man; an "alpha male" that women often look up to or fall for with spontaneous admiration. He is hard on others, but even more so on himself and he has unlimited energy. On the other hand, however, he is so incredibly sensitive, melancholy and … Ooooooh My God so tenderly fragile. Since she met him in 1965 in Toronto, Canada and married him a little later, Jutta has always sensed his deeper feelings much better than anyone else. Even better than his own mother Elsbeth, who could not always judge exactly how John absorbed the things of life. He does not have to answer Jutta's question, because his facial expression immediately tells her everything he feels. She supports him and understands him. Words are superfluous, but understanding and already comforting, she caresses his shoulders and kisses him on the cheek ...

Later that night, when they turn off the television and both go to sleep, John is still upset about all the turmoil on the other side of the Atlantic. He cannot sleep and thinks constantly of his early childhood. The events that he had experienced a long time ago as a four-to-five-year-old child, pass his sensitive retina again tonight in all vividness. He was indeed only a little boy then, but you never forget such scary experiences. He vaguely remembers his old home at Obere Weiße in Arnstadt and the whole area which had been flattened by bombs and where his mother and he had been given shelter by the generous Frau Kranz for several years.

There, in the city of Erfurt near Arnstadt, his serious eye problems were also diagnosed and treated for the first time. A treatment without any success, however, so that Elsbeth finally made a drastic decision. Now, on this overwhelming and exceptional night of November 9/10, 1989, when he thinks back to that one cold evening in the year 1949, he feels the same chills of 40 years ago all over his body again. He sees those grim images which were stored far away in his subconsciousness over and over again. He also feels the icy, misty chill and is facing again all those long rows of terrifying barbed wire, those bright floodlights scouring the border line uninterruptedly, the piercing barking of German shepherds, the clatter of machine gun fire, men to his left and right falling under bullets as they flee, his mother Elsbeth's frightened and grim cries in the icy misty darkness:

"Joachim, wo bist du?!" (Joachim, where are you?)

He doesn't talk much about that period anymore, but as a German he felt always some interest in the political situation in Germany. As a Westerner today, he could go and visit East Germany, but he knew well enough that he would not be given a moment's rest by the East German Stasi. In his mind, all those nasty things from 40 years ago never quite went away ...

John feels the urge to grab pen and paper, to sort the things he has just seen on television and to describe them in depth in lyrics for a new song. He would love to write a kind of sequel to the much earlier written *Renegade* from the album *Steppenwolf 7*, released in the summer of 1970, in which he describes his flight to the West. The flight itself was also preceded by a turbulent history, as we have already seen. Towards the end of the year of revelation, 1989, John Kay will write a very profound song that clearly expresses his feelings about the fall of the Wall.

That wonderful song *The Wall* appears on the next CD *Rise & Shine*, in the fall of 1990. It partially incorporates J.F. Kennedy's 1963 speech in Berlin ...

The fall of the Berlin Wall in 1989 is certainly a milestone for John Kay as well. He never thought he would see this happen ...

Brandenburger Tor in Berlin. J.F. Kennedy and Ronald Reagan, among others, made their appearance here. (Photograph by the author)

Communism in Eastern Europe is ebbing away completely from 9 November on. Long after the fall of the Wall, however, the feelings of many Germans -both from East and West Germany- are still very much divided. Some are happy to have finally escaped the yoke of communism.

There are also people who are not yet convinced, but they accept the situation as it is and are patient, hoping that all will be well some day, while others are struggling with the new situation. This last group is especially extremely disappointed, because they had imagined that *everything* was great and fantastic in the western part of the country. They are even nostalgic for the GDR and would rather return to the situation that existed before 1989, where on the one hand they were given only just enough to live on but on the other hand there was a lot less work pressure.

In the open market economy of the West, however, it is not profitable to keep people working in factories or other state institutions just to *have* a job. After all, planned economies are not profitable and multinationals are quick to move when profits are down, or they threaten to relocate to somewhere in Asia, where labor costs are much lower anyway.

The old East Germany has, with the financial support of Europe since German reunification, developed many projects to improve their stagnant and run-down situation, especially in terms of infrastructure. The corporate sector, too, is investing heavily in the technologically backward area of former East Germany. However, not all Westerners are happy with that, they feel that too much is handed out for free, while they had to work hard for decades. The difference between the former East and West Germany as regards manufacturing efficiency is now levelling off somewhat. But the wage differences are still considerable, and an ex-West German will still earn, on average, (many) more euros than an ex-East German. Germany may have been reunited, but to this day it appears that complete equality in lifestyle has not yet been achieved.

It will clearly take some more time. Many people evidently also expected (too) much from the fall of communism, but as J.F. Kennedy pointed out in 1963, democracy is also far from perfect ...

Regimes, patterns of society, people: they all constantly evolve throughout history. Always and everywhere there will be people who are happy to thrive in a certain pattern and people who do not. While Europe is constantly striving for more unity, the British are leaving the European Union at the same time. There too, many conservative-minded people think that this will soon solve all their financial, political, migration and other problems ...

Another Berlin symbol: Checkpoint Charlie. During the Cold War, this was an extremely critical location between East and West Berlin. Several times in the '50s, '60s and '70s, Russian and American soldiers faced each other in full combat mode. Today, this location has become a tourist attraction with somewhat of a folklore appearance. (Photograph by the author)

Flowers at the Wall for refugees who didn't make it and an inscription against the breaking up of families. (Creative Commons CC BY-NC-2.0 License Peter Fechter.)

Photos of refugees who paid with their lives for their attempt to get over the Wall. (Creative Commons CC BY 2.0 License Ben 124.)

Feed the Fire

"For the sound of the crowd ..."

It leaves a deep impression on John Kay and his wife Jutta Maue to literally see the Berlin Wall crumble. Jutta is from a suburban town near Hamburg, so she has (fortunately) not personally experienced what it must have meant to live on the "wrong" side of the Wall. She does, however, know perfectly well how intensely her husband John feels about all this, even after so many years. But these miraculous events in his old homeland are also reawaking John and make him want to 'feed the fire' again. The enthusiasm and passion with which he has made it in the music world, needs to be stirred up a bit to keep the fire burning. The revolution in his old homeland gives him a lot of energy and he realizes, to his great relief, that his passion for music is still alive. But he also realizes that he will have to come more out of his shell again. John admits that he had fallen asleep a bit. So, in 1990, the band members want to put themselves back on the musical map resulting in the excellent studio album Rise & Shine. *It is a strong wake up call and also a confirmation to the fans -the Wolfpack- all over the world. It proves that they do not want to consider themselves yet among those groups whose fame is only based on former success. "Yesterday's glory won't help us today." Who wrote those wise words long ago for that critical song* Move Over *in order to wake up someone else? Exactly!*

So, John Kay, is the fire still burning? Yes, it is! Thank Goodness ...

"Every night you are lying' in a different bed, every morning don't know where you're waking." That's what we hear John sing in *Sound Of The Crowd* on the album *The Lost Heritage Tapes* (1997). Already then John alluded to his hectic life. Waking' up every day in another room in an unfamiliar environment, thinking: *"Where the hell am I this time,"* must certainly feel a little strange.

But John will go on doing his thing. After the turbulent '80s, his never-ending energy -fortunately- prevailed over the doubts he had about continuing. The fall of the Berlin Wall has not only liberated (East) Germans in their own homeland. He, too, feels liberated in a way, and he finds a lot of new motivation in the strange events of late November 1989 in Germany. With that in mind, in 1990 John Kay & Steppenwolf are touring Europe again with renewed energy, to promote their new album. In the song *Rise & Shine* from the CD (with the same name), John himself clearly indicates that he is once again full of musical passion. Will you *"Show your colors,"* John? Yes! The performances in November and December 1990 prove him right. He also comes to Belgium and in our country, Studio Brussel announces a concert for Sunday night, December 2 as the closing act of their European tour. But again, there is not much publicity. Many people will unfortunately only learn later that the band ... had been in Belgium in December. A missed opportunity, as has been so often the case. Steppenwolf and their public relations in Belgium: it doesn't work. It never worked and it's even downright dramatic. It was not going well at the end of the '60s and more than two decades later, it is still not good. Their mega hit from 1968 *Born To Be Wild* is released again in the autumn of 1990 and it is also in the regular top 30 for several weeks. But there is no follow-up on our radio stations. They only score in our retro charts, but each time only with that old mega hit. Apart from that the band is totally ignored. So, John Kay & Steppenwolf are on the Vooruit stage in Ghent on December 2 of that year. Twenty-one years after their performance in Mechelen (with a completely different lineup at the time), they will finally be performing in Belgium again.

The lineup consists of John Kay: vocals and guitar, Rocket Richotte: guitar, Ron Hurst: drums and Michael Wilk: keyboards. Michael Wilk also takes care of the general bass line, which he simultaneously blasts into the air through his keyboards. Not until 2009 do we see a real bass player on stage again. That will be Gary Link, the bassist who accompanied them already for a while in the '80s. At that time, they had him temporarily "on loan" from the band of the excellent

American singer Rita Coolidge. Only then the band is again with five members, and it must be said: a real bass guitar on stage is something else than synchronized bass sounds via an electronic organ and that is how it should be.

Belgian hostess Chantal Pattyn from Studio Brussel first calls John Kay at the end of November of that year 1990 in his hotel room in Greece. Just to ask him directly what we can expect in Belgium a few days later. There is some interference on the line ...

Chantal Pattyn: *"Hello John. Steppenwolf has been a bit out of sight the last few years. Can we consider the new* Rise & Shine *album as a sort of come-back album?"*

John Kay: *"Well, I can understand why people in Europe at least to some extent could feel that way, because we haven't been in Europe for quite a few years. But actually, in the United States, I've been acting as* John Kay & Steppenwolf ... *since 1980, for the last eleven years. And we toured very frequently every year and in the mid-'80s we also had a new album." (Note of the author:* Rock & Roll Rebels*)*

Chantal Pattyn: *"John, how important is* Born To Be Wild *for the band?"*

John Kay: *"BTBW will always be to Steppenwolf what* Hound Dog *was to Elvis Presley and* Whole Lotta Love *was to Led Zeppelin. It is the song when you hear it, you think of Steppenwolf; that's quite normal.*

It's also the song that has now -at least- a second and maybe even a third generation of Rock & Rollers who have adopted BTBW *as their own anthem for rebellion and freedom. So, it's something that always will be with us, no matter what happens in the future."*

Chantal Pattyn: *"But don't you think Steppenwolf is depending too much on it's former success?"*

John Kay: *"I see things very simply, which is that I make music for a living. I have had the luxury all my life since I left school to express my opinion in my writing and in my music. And the rest of the stuff, I leave to those who analyze and think about it all and what does it mean and how important success is. To me, that's just the packaging, the "window dressing", the consolation prizes. Although, BTBW is the song that most people want to hear when they come to see us and that doesn't worry me. Because if that makes them happy, I'm not going to argue with them."*

Chantal Pattyn: *"In the seventies, John, you had a few solo records. So, what about your own career now? Does it definitely belong to the past?"*

John Kay: *"At the moment and for the last eleven years, our act is called John Kay & Steppenwolf. So, I don't feel any need to go and do something separate. I just do what I like to do at any given time."*

Chantal Pattyn: *"You are still on tour in December, and you're also coming to Belgium. So, what can we expect here in December this year."*

John Kay: *"Our tour will be, approximately, half songs from the early days and half songs from our new album* Rise & Shine. *And the songs will alternate. In other words: we'll do an old song - a new song - an old song - a new song. And that way we won't bring too many new things at once, but also not too many older things and get bored. So, we try to make everybody happy."*

Chantal Pattyn: *"Ok, thank you John! Good luck over there! Bye bye!"*
John Kay: *"Bye bye!"*

After which, on Studio Brussel, the rock-hard introduction of the promising *Let's Do It All* sounds. The first song, clearly based on a passionate love affair, from the new and powerful album *Rise & Shine*. Their passion is unabated and the songs swing like in their glory days. *Rise & Shine* really is a great album that reminds us of that glorious period of the good old times.

Although he clearly indicates in his introduction at the *Vooruit* venue in Ghent on December 2 that he is now very tired from all that touring, the band gives the people more than what they came for: an exceptionally good performance. It includes all their nice classics interspersed with new songs, as John had already indicated in his interview. *The Pusher* is the final encore.

The exceptionally good 1990 CD Rise & Shine *has some surprising songs. In* The Wall *John Kay refers to the fall of the Berlin Wall. In the song* Rock & Roll War *he describes the traumas of many Vietnam veterans and the tricky situation they had to face when they set foot on American soil again. He also expresses his concern for the environment in* Do or Die. *(See Chapter The Jutta Maue-Kay Foundation)*

On a chilly, drizzly Sunday evening of December 2, 1990, Steppenwolf takes the stage at the Vooruit venue in Ghent (Belgium). John Kay and guitarist Rocket Richotte here in full action. John went full blast to give the people an enjoyable time. (Photograph by the author)

On almost every European tour, John Kay also likes to visit his old homeland Germany ... and not just to perform. Between a few performances in November 1990 in Germany, Italy, Greece, Austria and Switzerland, he will cross the old East-West German border to visit a few people. But there is a substantial difference now. The extensive list of formalities to complete if someone wants to visit that part of Germany is gone. From now on there no longer is an East and a West Germany either, but it simply is a "Germany". For John, this is a peculiar experience. No more blockades at the eastern border, where you risk being mowed down by machine gun fire if you try to go from one side to the other. So, John has the opportunity now to say hello quietly ... to his pseudo-grandmother: Frau Kranz in Arnstadt. After all those years, he is also extremely glad to meet the other members of that helpful Kranz family and his former neighbors over there as well. He had not seen them since his escape to the West in the late 1940s. That's 40 years now! What an amazing experience! What a joy!

The fall of the Wall and to be able to do just what you want to do, without being constantly followed, can have an enormous impact on someone's mindset. John expresses his feelings about all this each time he performs that beautiful song *The Wall* on stage. The lyrics (which he wrote) hit him emotionally straight in the heart. The passion of his total experience can be read from his facial expression the whole time. He realizes that he owes his freedom to the cool-headed actions of his mother Elsbeth and her courage and conviction to go through the barbed wire, way back then. That he honors his mother so deeply, will also become very clear later on in the song *For The Woman In My Life* on his much later solo album *Heretics & Privateers* ...

Almost every time he comes to Germany John will also try to visit ... his mother and stepfather. Elsbeth and Gerhard are now both back staying in Germany. Yep! They are indeed enjoying their retirement in the city of Aachen, close to the Dutch and Belgian borders. They were already in their forties when they emigrated to Canada in 1958.

On the day they stopped their professional activities, the idea arose to return to the old *Heimat*. Elsbeth has family living in the region of Aachen and the prospect of seeing them more often, in combination with the beautiful nature of the magnificent triangle Germany - the Netherlands - Belgium, made them decide to spend their days in the old homeland. Jutta and John often visit them over there. John and Jutta will also visit John's aunt Inge from time to time, the woman who took care of him in WestKirchen at the moment his mother Elsbeth was looking for a place to stay in Hannover. They do this all rather incognito, for fear that there would be too much interest, if their German fans knew they were in the neighborhood. John Kay & Steppenwolf indeed still have many fans in Germany.

During the '90s after *Rise & Shine* only one new studio album is released by John Kay & Steppenwolf, *Feed The Fire* in 1996. However, there are only two new songs on it; the other songs are all previously released songs. The song *Feed The Fire* itself is a symbol of their everlasting motivation. Other compilations appear on CD as well. The band tours continuously throughout the year and it is clear that the fire of their passion for music is still very much alive. When you have a look at their packed agenda and you keep in mind that they are getting older, you can only admire them. However, guitarist Rocket Richotte is making room for Steve Fister in 1993 (for about two years) and he in turn for Danny Johnson (from 1995 on). Rocket lives in LA while John and the management live in the Nashville region, that was hard to combine ...

What has been noticeable over the years, is that John Kay is wearing his dark glasses less and less, even on stage. When I asked him one day if he had undergone eye surgery, he replied in the negative. But he pushes himself more to train his light sensitivity by limiting the wearing of those glasses as much as possible, despite the pain and discomfort. *"Sometimes that works, sometimes it doesn't,"* he says. But living totally without dark glasses, is not possible.

In 1992, a certain Charlie Wolf quits his job at the US Air Force and he will soon become the band's new tour manager. Later on, Charlie will also manage the official website and the fan shop. Charlie is a very helpful guy, who -in my personal experience- will always communicate smoothly with the Wolfpackers or other enthusiasts worldwide.

In 1993, unfortunately, there is some awful news. John's very close friend Jerry Edmonton is killed in a car accident in Santa Barbara (LA). John and all the others who know Jerry, are really devastated.

In fact, to this day, Jerry is still missed by everyone. Especially by those who have (or had) something to do with Sparrow or Steppenwolf, either up close or from afar. Notwithstanding the fact that he had been a professional photographer for over ten years, he made an incomparable contribution to the worldwide mega success of Steppenwolf. Jerry was someone who, from his central position as a drummer, made the band progress each time by pointing out the things that went wrong sometimes during a previous performance. He was concerned with the overall arrangement.

After the death of Gabriel Mekler (†1977) and their original bassist Rushton Moreve (†1981), both in a motorcycle accident, and Andy Chapin (†1985 in a plane crash), this was yet another black page in the history of Steppenwolf.

Ironic detail about Jerry's accident is that he was on his way to a funeral at the moment he crashed …

Jerry Edmonton, at the heyday of his career with Steppenwolf.
After 1985, Jerry took care of Andy Chapin's widow.

In 1994, the band is exclusively touring Germany between the first and twelfth of June. They visit Heidelberg, Homburg, Zwickau, Trier, Arnstadt, Pforzheim, Reutlingen, Kitzingen, Germesheim, Rockenhausen and Jüterbog. In Arnstadt, he again meets some of his old friends.

A few years later, in 1996, John Kay is inducted into Canada's Hall of Fame. As yet, he does not receive this recognition in the United

States. The reason for this is inexplicable to his millions of fans worldwide. However, my suspicion (I have no proof) is that possibly what he sang about the USA in, among others, his 1969 album *Monster* has not yet been completely digested to date. It is a personal hypothesis, but I cannot think of any other reason. In the US he -with his group or not- has been among the absolute top for several decades. He has toured the US and the rest of the world with immense success during that entire time. In the US, he is perhaps as well known in the blues and rock scene as illustrious blues legends like BB King, Howlin' Wolf, John Mayall and John Lee Hooker, to name but a few. Whatever the reason is, his achievements in music are enormous, especially in the US.

They continue touring the world and they very often visit Europe. Eight years after their performance in Vooruit in Ghent, they are performing in our (Belgian) region again. In the spring of 1998, they first played at Den Atelier in Luxembourg City and the day after they were present at the Boogie Town Blues Festival in the Walloon town of Louvain-la-Neuve, on the university's site. On May 2, they will play at The Splendid in Lille* and on May 3 at Ris-Orangis near Évry, just south of Paris (île de France). Their presence at the university site in Walloon Brabant, Belgium on May 1, 1998 is the result of a rather peculiar and funny course of events ...

The managers of the Walloon Boogie Town Festival were already looking in the autumn of 1997 for the best groups to include in their annual blues festival in the Louvain-la-Neuve. The websites of a lot of bands were visited and the organizers also ended up on the website of Steppenwolf. The band is one of the absolute favorite blues/rock bands of local chief organizer Frédéric Maréchal.

Unintentionally, Frédéric sends a blank e-mail message to Steppenwolf's tour management in Franklin, Nashville in November 1997. There, Jutta Maue and Charlie Wolf manage the group's tour schedule. Frédéric Maréchal suspects that this accidentally sent blank e-mail will just vanish into cyberspace without any reply. He forgets

---

* *That performance has been cancelled.*

about it, and he focusses on other names of potential candidates to complete the list. Until suddenly, he gets an unexpected response from Steppenwolf tour manager Charlie Wolf:

"Hello, Belgium! You have sent me an e-mail, but it was empty. Perhaps you have something to tell me?"

"Well, I am very sorry. It was a mistake. We are indeed looking for a good band to complete our Blues Program on May 1 next year, but ... I've sent you that e-mail by accident."

"Oh, I see. No problem! But please, listen! We have not been in Europe for a while. And we have many loyal fans in Brussels. So, if you like us to come?"

"We would love you to come, but we will have to negotiate the price. We absolutely cannot pay the same royalties as you get in the United States. Steppenwolf is much too expensive for our small budget."

Step by step, the parties come a bit closer. Thanks to a coincidence, John Kay & Steppenwolf are on the bill that May 1, 1998, as headliners, along with blues icon Jimmy Vaughan. John Kay & Steppenwolf are on their way to Europe for the umpteenth time. John himself, however, is not too happy about this, because on the very same day he had agreed to come and play in his own backyard in Robinsonville, Mississippi (he had also played there on April 4). That venue is located just about 300 kilometers from his then hometown of Franklin, Nashville. At exactly the same time as Boogie Town, a festival (Blues Aid) is held there too to benefit musicians who could never have made a big name for themselves, but who do all the same make very good blues music nevertheless. It is mainly those musicians from the Mississippi-Delta, located even further south, who never had the luck that John Kay once had himself. John realizes that he owes a lot to the blues music that had sprung up especially there in the greater New-Orleans region and this was his way of giving something substantial back to those people. But his tour manager Charlie Wolf has other plans. A lot of mileage plays no part when it comes to cashing in on success continuously. So, they would play a few days in a row in Europe and then immediately travel on to South America. The next gig *after* Europe has already been scheduled, even before they travel to Europe. On May 14, they will play in Peru, South America in the "Estadio Manuel Bonilla" in the capital Lima.

Upon his arrival in Belgium, John Kay was asked to give an interview in the Belgian (French-speaking) RTBF radio studios. On Wednesday, April 30, the day before his performance in Louvain-la-Neuve, he is a guest on the program Rock a Go Go at the radio studios at Boulevard August Reyers in Brussels. However, the car that was supposed to pick him up at his hotel broke down and it was feared that the program which was already quite tightly scheduled, would be ruined. Moreover, it is feared that this incident is very unpleasant for John and that it might affect his mood. But they needn't have worried, on the contrary. Half an hour later than expected, John Kay finally enters the RTBF studio ...

"Hello John Kay, good evening!"

"Bonsoir mon ami!" says John spontaneously in French.

So that earlier breakdown with the car has not affected his good mood. Jacques de Pierpont (aka "Monsieur Pompon") and working for the Belgian French-language station RTBF as the regular presenter of Rock a Go Go, asks him to speak some more French.

"Encore quelques mots en Français?" *("A few more words in French?")*

"That's easy for you to say, but that is unfortunately where my French stops."

Whereupon John himself spontaneously bursts into a merry fit of laughter ...

Once again, John Kay has to tell his life story there. In all likelihood, he must be bored to death by having to answer the same questions over and over again. In an interview lasting about an hour, he has to answer all the questions he has been asked for the umpteenth time in his life. He smoothly talks about East Prussia, Hannover, his first "K.A.Y" guitar in Canada ... He never gives the impression that it bothers him to have to tell the same things over and over again. Occasionally the interview is interrupted for a moment and Steppenwolf songs are played in the studio, such as *Move Over*, *Hoochie Coochie Man* and *Rock Me*, all three versions from the double Live album *Live at 25*.

One copy of that anniversary album, by the way, is won by a certain Claude from Mont-sur-Marchienne, as he is the first to call to say that before Steppenwolf, John Kay's group was called Sparrow. Their first studio version of *The Pusher*, recorded with The Sparrow in New York City in 1966 is also played on that Thursday night on RTBF. *Somebody* from his first solo album and *Corrina, Corrina* from the May 1967 live album *Early Steppenwolf* follow too.

John also tells us that with his first solo album he consciously went back to his own early days in music, when he was staring at Hank Williams' score with his bad eyes and with his Wollensak tape recorder ready to go, trying to make the chords on that first "KAY" guitar. He also says that, after the first period of Steppenwolf (1967/1972), he was a bit jaded and that with his first solo album, he chose to go back to his early days in music: Folk & Blues. The album *Forgotten Songs & Unsung Heroes* is a mixture of some of his own folk and blues songs, together with a few songs by other and lesser-known artists he dusted off for this album. John is open about himself and how things have gone in his life. He makes it quite clear that he realizes how lucky he is. For him, the American Dream did not remain just a vague dream. He, who lay in bed every night in Hannover pondering how he would get to the other side of the Atlantic, eventually made the American Dream his own. He is also grateful that after so many years he is still being asked to perform in so many places around the world and he is grateful that he was able to realize his childhood dreams. But he also notes that adults often break something in the minds of children when they want to curtail their imagination because it is thought to be unrealistic. John argues that it is wrong to do so.

"We often extinguish something in children's imaginations when we try to talk them out of things that are important to them. Look at me! My dream was also totally unrealistic and even though it required a long run-up and even involved a lot of risk, I was extremely lucky to be able to realize it ..."

Since Louvain-la-Neuve is mainly about blues music, John's connection to blues is also regularly questioned. He tells us that he very often participates in such blues events in the US as well, along with other typical blues and rock groups such as ZZ Top and Canned Heat. Billy Gibbons of ZZ Top once whispered quietly into the ears of guitarist Danny Johnson on one occasion:

*" That John Kay, he really **is** a sneaky bluesman, isn't he?"*

Suddenly in the studio, John Kay himself asks if he can say something: *"I would like to add something here myself. We are incredibly happy to play here at Boogie Town and we are looking forward to having a wonderful time with our friends here. But at the same time, I had actually agreed to play at Blues Aid, in Robinsonville. The event there aims to raise money for those many "starving" musicians who never made it out of the Mississippi Delta and never became famous, but who play very fine blues music."*

But his manager Charlie Wolf had other ideas this time and John complied. After all, that's what managers are for ...

The final question:

"John, you as a true blues lover, will you play until you are deaf?"

Well (while he's still laughing), *I'll certainly keep playing as long as the fire keeps burning ... and of course first and foremost as long as they keep paying us so lavishly to perform. That's the difference between us and the many bands who are struggling to pay their bills. We do what we love to do, and we are handsomely rewarded for it. And that's a very difficult combination to beat."*

Jacques de Pierpont then wants to play a song from the *Live at 25* album, but his studio assistant Jean-Paul points out that the program is over, and it is too late to play anything else.

"John Kay, thank you, very, very much!" says Jacques.

And as always in his enthusiasm and spontaneous friendliness, John Kay concludes the interview:

"Ooh, it was a pleasure!"

Boogie Town 1998, Louvain-la-Neuve (Belgium)

On that soaking wet Thursday of May 1, 1998 -Ascension Day- he played, more or less unexpected, on the drenched campus of the University of Louvain-la-Neuve close to amusement park Walibi near the Belgian town of Wavre. Together with Belgian blues band Give Buzze, Drippin' Honey, 13 & Lester Butler, A.J. Croce, Omar & the Howlers, Jimmy Vaughan, Gary Primich and Big Sugar.

For eccentric blues man Lester Butler, by the way, it would be his very last performance ever on our Mother Earth, as only a few days later, on May 9, 1998, he dies in Los Angeles as a result of an overdose ...
The fire is still blazing and during the RTBF interview John also tells us that he has twelve new blues songs of his own ready to be worked on. He's not sure yet if it's going to be a new CD, but it would be a pity if it wasn't. He says it's really going to be something to look forward to. According to him, it will be something "to sink your teeth into".
John Kay is indeed a 'secret blues man' in the words of Billy Gibbons of ZZ Top, and he always will be ...

About three years after their performance in Louvain-la-Neuve, the then already vaguely announced new solo blues album *Heretics & Privateers* is released, in which he once again emphasizes how deeply rooted the blues is in him. It is an incredibly good album, with many surprising personal touches and in which he also -once again- shows his sensitive side. Especially in the song *For The Women In My Life,* so full of gratitude. In that song -a real masterpiece- he honors his mother Elsbeth and his daughter Shawn in a very emotional way. He never forgives himself for not being present when daughter Shawn was born at the end of March 1968. He was so busy with himself and the band, that he had to hear about the birth of his daughter over the phone by Jutta, while he was in San Francisco, about 600 kilometers from the place he perhaps *should* have been. He likes to emphasize his love and pride for daughter Shawn. But in the song, he also emphasizes -especially- the admiration he feels for his wife Jutta, and with it, he offers her unbelievably beautiful (lyrical) flowers. As if he wants to say a deeply meant *sorry* in some way. Just as the lyrics in the song

You're The Only One from the album *Paradox*, may tell, he tells her frankly there is only one woman he absolutely loves. He realizes that she was very often alone at home, while he was on tour for a long time ...

As we grow older, all those things become increasingly obvious to anyone who has children and grandchildren.

This is clearly no different when your name is John Kay or Jutta Maue. One day, when someone asks Jutta what the real secret of their long and steady relationship is, whereas many other popular singers go from one relationship to the other, she takes the naughty questioner aside. The latter thinks that she will now reveal a big secret to him, but Jutta simply answers:

"Our big secret is ... that we love each other and, consequently, have never been separated."

While she says this, she spontaneously smiles, and that broad smile is the best answer she can give.

John's last(?) solo blues album Heretics & Privateers *was released in the year 2000.*
The original color photograph (used in black and white for the CD) was taken by his wife Jutta at Hollow Lake.

Touring the USA and the rest of the world has become ordinary routine by now. The planning in their diary for 1998, during which they also visited Belgium (see tour guide 1998) was still somewhat limited. That year they stayed mostly in the US and they decided to take it easy for once during the month of December. When on tour, they also often show their human side. On June 5, 2002, they perform in Copenhagen, while on June 7 they are scheduled to perform in Stockholm and the following day -June 8- in his old hometown of 1958: Hannover, Germany. On this occasion he will also visit his old flat in Kronenstrasse. It appears that not much has changed in that apartment building since he left. The city itself, nevertheless, has become totally unrecognizable to him. No more ruins where he could have romped and cycled all the time as a child.

On his only night off, between two gigs, John Kay gets into a bumper car in Copenhagen with his local Danish tour guide and friend Flemming Hjöllund. Flemming, great inspirer of the successful Facebook page "John Kay & Steppenwolf - The Fan Base" describes this bumper car ride afterwards as *"the most terrifying, hellish ride I have ever taken in any car."*

In August of the same year John Kay is once again in Europe. First in Kaiserslautern, Germany, and the following day in Calw, Baden Württemberg (Black Forest). In Calw he is invited to a memorial ceremony in honor of Hermann Hesse, the author of the world-famous book *Der Steppenwolf*. The book that made both the author and John Kay so famous. Hesse once lived in Calw and there is a wonderful museum dedicated to him and his works. John goes there and is interviewed by local reporters. He clearly shows them he is still fluent in German, his native language.

June 6, 2002. John Kay (on the right) at the wheel of a bumper car at Copenhagen's Tivoli amusement park. On the left is his local friend Flemming Hjöllund. (Photo Nicolaj Enig, Copenhagen, Denmark)

The Hermann Hesse Museum in Calw, Germany.

John Kay on June 5 in 2002 in Copenhagen. On stage, he wears his dark glasses less and less often. In his own words, he forces himself to better control his sensitivity to light. (Photo courtesy of F.H. Pedersen)

John Kay and Jutta Maue at one of the annual "Wolf Fests" in Nashville. For the photo, they both pose on a Harley Davidson. Posing only, because John is not allowed or able to ride because of his bad eyes. The original HD logo on the gas tank has been altered. Someone told me the bike belongs to Steppenwolf's drummer Ron Hurst. I wasn't quite sure, but Ron's wife Angela confirmed me this definitely was Ron's Harley. Ron sold it some years ago....

John Kay & Steppenwolf 1998 Concert Tour

March 7	Daytona, FL	Adam's Mark Hotel
April 3	Muskogee, OK	Civic Center
April 4	Robinsonville, MS	The Horseshoe Casino
April 30	Luxembourg City	Salle "Den Atelier"
May 1	**Louvain-la-Neuve**	**Boogie Town Festival**
May 2*	Lille, France	Le Splendid (*cancelled)
May 3	Paris, France	Le Plan
May 14	Lima, Peru	Estadio Municipal De Miraflores
May 16	Oxnard, CA	California Strawberry Festival
May 30	Las Vegas, NV	The Maxim Hotel
June 3	Montreal, Quebec	Molson Rock Fest
June 5	Caruthersville, MO	Casino Aztar
June 6	Tupelo, MS	The Oleput Festival
June 11	Santa Fe, NM	Camel Rock Casino
June 12	North Bend, OR	The Mill Casino
June 13	Piercy, CA	The Redwood Run
June 19	Trempealeau, WI	The Historic Trempealeau Hotel
June 20	Rice Lake, WI	Aquafest
June 24	Kalamazoo, MI	Kalamazoo State Theatre
June 25	Oshkosh, WI	Riverside Park
June 26	Rockford, MN	Acapulco Club
June 27	Bottineau, ND	The Wildrose Amphitheatre
June 30	Milwaukee, WI	Summerfest
July 4	Farmington, NM	McGee Park Coliseum
July 5	Dulce, NM	Apache Nugget Casino
July 10	Arnolds Park, IA	Arnolds Amusement Park
July 11	Walker, MN	Moon Dance Ram Jam
July 17	Moncton, New Brunswick	Magnetic Hill
July 18	Paradise, Newfoundland	Paradise Park
July 26	Centralia, IL	Chicken Ranch
July 27	Green Bay, WI	Oneida Casino
July 31	Rock Springs, WY	Sweetwater County Fair
August 1	Buffalo, WY	The White Buffalo

August 2	Wagner, SD	Fort Randall Casino
August 4	Billings, MT	JD's Club
August 5	Sturgis, SD	Buffalo Chip Campground
August 6	Denver, CO	The Grizzly Rose
August 8	Sparks, NV	Victorian Square
August 12	Anaheim, CA	Knotts Berry Farm
August 15	Las Vegas, NV	The Maxim Hotel
August 16	Ventura, CA	Ventura Theatre
August 18	Solano Beach, CA	Belly Up Tavern
August 21	San Mateo, CA	San Mateo County Fair
August 22	Hollywood, CA	House of Blues
August 28	Vincennes, IN	Watermelon Fest
August 30	Oklahoma City, OK	In Cahoots
September 3	Bristol, CT	Sports Rock USA
September 4	Essex Junction, VT	Champlain Valley Expo
September 5	Darien Lake, NY	Darien Lake Arts Center
September 6	Naperville, IL	Naperville Last Fling
September 11	East Ridge, TN	Jordanfest
September 12	Allegan, MI	Allegan County Fair
September 20	Lobau, Germany	Festzelt
September 26	Nashville, TN	Riverfront Park
September 27	Corpus Christi, TX	Bayfest
October 2	Yakima, WA	Central Washington State Fair
October 3	Gretna, LA	Gretna Heritage Festival
October 4	Mobile, AL	Bayfest
October 17	Coachella, CA	The Spotlight Casino
October 24	Port St. Lucie, FL	Rainbow Fest
November 11	Wichita, KS	Cotillion Ballroom
November 12	Dodge City, KS	Civic Center
November 13	St Petersburg, FL	Ribfest
November 25	Lorain, OH	The Palace Theatre
December 21	Miami, FL	Bay Front Park

John Kay and his band Steppenwolf still go on tour each year. The long list of scheduled concerts on their once so overcrowded agenda is gradually getting shorter. In 2007 they decide to stop. The endless travelling is starting to have a negative impact on their bodies and they are obviously not getting any younger. Although they own a very luxuriously equipped and comfortable tour bus, they decide to call it a day. Soon they realize however that they haven't quite run out of energy. Barely two years later they announce that they miss the whole thing and that they are going on tour again. One of the reasons for their comeback might be that they can do some extra fundraising for the growing Maue-Kay project.

Old faithful Gary Link also returns and the five of them continuously tour the world. They do, however, definitively denounce overloaded programs. Their annual "Wolf Fest", where the fans can have a good time in Nashville, Tennessee and where everyone can communicate with everyone while taking pictures if they want to, makes up for a lot. John and Jutta also have more time together. Not only to commute between their residence in Franklin, Tennessee and a second residence in Montecito, Santa-Barbara, California. Jutta starts her own project as early as 2004. She feels that the time has come for her to make her mark and leave her own footprint in the interest of the planet. Not only by protecting the environment and climate, but also as an advocate of general animal welfare and human rights. (See chapter *The Jutta Maue Kay Foundation*). John will help her as much as he can …

In 2011, John Kay will play *Snow Blind Friend* at a Wolf Fest in memory of his good friend Jerry Edmonton, their very first drummer who was killed near Santa Barbara in a car accident in 1993. For the occasion … old hand Goldy McJohn is playing keyboards. Yep! Goldy certainly thinks it's appropriate to join in the tribute to Jerry who once was a very good friend of his. It seems that the folds between John and Goldy have (finally) been ironed out. This will give goose bumps to the first generation of Steppenwolf fans. And in all honesty, as a complete outsider I think, that this must have been equally true for both of them. *"Goldy, it's so good to see you here"* says John as he strums the intro to that mellow and philosophical song about drugs *Snow Blind Friend* on his guitar. John's gesture to Goldy also sounds really genuine and is met with a spontaneous applause from the crowd. John's dispute with Nick will also be settled. And the one with Michael? I am not quite sure about it, but he was invited at some Wolf Fests and he was there. He and John even hugged each other. So, I suppose his youth sins are forgiven …

Some of the band members indeed caused a lot of trouble. Despite that fact John must have realized that they also had a large share in the overall success of the band and that he, in his youthful enthusiasm, might have been a bit too hard on them at times when he made drastic decisions.

John wrote the song *To Be Alive* for his first solo album *Forgotten Songs & Unsung Heroes*, referring to his own conscience that wasn't quite clear at a certain moment. He could barely look at himself in the mirror and was even afraid of his own reflection.

Self-knowledge has undeniably always been one of John's greatest life skills. And when getting older he perhaps also realized they could have settled their dispute at the time in a slightly different way than by sabotaging each other. Like grey hair, wisdom comes with age for most people. That incident with Goldy and his broom during one of the Wolf Fests: we will give Goldy the benefit of the doubt and classify it a typical "Goldy- joke." Therefore, in retrospect -again as a complete outsider- I can perhaps presume that all the members who have ever been part of the Steppenwolf family led by John Kay (we are not talking here about members of the bogus bands), have indeed contributed to its overall heritage. And as for Goldy McJohn, fortunately John and Goldy were finally able to settle their quarrel. Indeed, there wasn't much time left by then. In the summer of 2017, when Steppenwolf celebrates its 50th anniversary, one of the great icons of the original Steppenwolf leaves this earth. John Raymond Goadsby, classically trained keyboardist by profession and occasional songwriter for the band, dies on August 1, 2017, from the effects of a heart attack while recovering from a stroke. Despite the falling-out between Goldy and John in 1975, it cannot be denied that Goldy had a huge part in the band's mega success with his unique keyboard work. By the way, Kent Henry, Steppenwolf guitarist on the album *For Ladies Only* in 1971 and who accompanied John Kay on his first two solo albums, passed away in 2009.

In 2012 at the age of 68 John Kay (& Steppenwolf) will play one more time on Belgian soil and again at a blues festival. Blues Peer will be their last show in Belgium. The bill includes some well-known and some lesser-known names, some of which will raise eyebrows among blues fans. Besides Steppenwolf there's Howlin' Bill, Helmut Lotti(!), Roland Van Campenhout, Nick Lowe, The North Mississippi All Stars, Hamilton Loomis, BB King, The Bottle Comets, The Devilles, 24Pesos, John Mooney & Bluesiana, Keb'Mo' Band, The Soul Rebels, Kenny Wayne Shepherd, Philippe Menard, Lightnin' Guy & The House Rockers, Ten Years After, El Fish, Jon Amor Blues Group and John Fogerty. Unfortunately, it's not going to be a pleasant Saturday night on the totally drenched meadow of Peer/ Belgium in April that year. It's a bit sad to realize that several bands have come from halfway around the world to play in the chilly, pouring rain. The weather is awful, with incessant lightning and thunder. Strong winds make the tent tremble dangerously and it is impossible to step outside without being blown over. Because of that terrible weather it is understandable that not too many people show up on the evening John Kay & Steppenwolf play in that sodden meadow in Peer, Belgian Limburg. By the time the band arrives on the scene quite late at night, the peo-

Former Steppenwolf legend Goldy McJohn at the time For Ladies Only was recorded. His gigantic Afro hairstyle will later make some room for wise, gray hair.

Goldy passed away on August 1, 2017, just as Steppenwolf celebrated its 50th anniversary.

ple who are present, have become a bit fed up with the whole "thing" and this manifests itself in the very lukewarm enthusiasm of the audience. Actually the response of the audience towards the musicians has reflected the chilly weather outside. Even though, according to faithful Danish Wolfpackers Nicolaj Enig and Lars Christensen who were there, the band was exceptionally good that night. Indeed, the band members are not put off balance for one moment. Professional as they are, their performance is as it should be, although they do not get the cheers they are used to and deserve.

The audience is unfortunately more affected by the terrible weather conditions, and some want to go home as soon as possible, instead of fully enjoying this exceptional musical experience ...

This performance in Nashville symbolizes Steppenwolf's 50th anniversary in August 2017. This poster from a performance at the Ryman Auditorium bears the signatures of the final lineup: Gary Link, Michael Wilk, John Kay, Ron Hurst and Danny Johnson.

It could be taken as a tribute to Goldy McJohn who passed away shortly before the performance.

So, as already touched on briefly, Steppenwolf will celebrate its 50th anniversary in 2017 with a performance at the Ryman Auditorium in Nashville, Tennessee. The performance is scheduled for August 5, but it is unintentionally overshadowed by the death only four days earlier of Goldy McJohn. John Raymond Goadsby's health had not been good for some time. His life companion Sonja was very optimistic at first that he was recovering well from a stroke when he suffered a fatal heart attack aged seventy-two ...

John Kay and Danny Johnson during one of their last performances with John Kay & Steppenwolf in 2018. Coconut Creek Casino, California. (Licensed by CLender with CC BY 2.0. Creative Commons.org)

Then, in 2018 on October 14, there is the very, very last performance by John Kay & Steppenwolf. It wasn't planned that way, but in November John Kay announces that the October gig in Baxter Springs- Kansas had indeed been their final farewell show together. However, once again, it would NOT have been the final highlight, if Lady Fortune wasn't missing her engagement this time. And it was one of the only times she would not assist John in his life…

In the spring of 2019, John Kay is contacted at his residence in Montecito, Santa Barbara by Peter Fonda, the man who starred in the 1969 film Easy Rider with his Harley Davidson. Steppenwolf provided the music at the beginning of that film. As a souvenir John has a large poster at home in his living room of Peter on his motorcycle, the gas tank of which is decorated with stars and stripes. Peter Fonda asks if John would be willing to meet up again on the occasion of the 50th anniversary of that film and relive the music from that film together ... live on stage! Will John Kay & Steppenwolf be back on set barely a few months after officially parting ways? John asks for a moment of reflection. At first, he still thinks to himself *"No way, not again!"* But he keeps seeing that life-size poster of Easy Rider on his wall. On it, at the very bottom, is the message, "Peter Fonda and John Kay, for ever." John feels the nostalgia bubbling up from his mind once again, and he says: *"Peter, I'm in. Let's do this!"* Anyone willing to participate will soon travel to New York, where this special event will take place ...

John *will* be on stage with an occasional line-up. But unfortunately, Peter Fonda couldn't enjoy this event the way it was planned by him. Not even two months after asking John to do this, he already dies of cancer. John regrets he didn't think of helping his old friend earlier with his last request on earth. After all, he indirectly contributed to the enormous success of Steppenwolf.

John Kay himself continues to make music in 2023. During the Covid 19 crisis, things were a bit awkward, and all the safety regulations were followed very closely. Now, fifty-eight years after his debut performances in coffee houses along the American West Coast, he is back on stage with an acoustic guitar in his hand and a harmonica around his neck, just like he started out in the mid-'60s. There are no more tough concert schedules now, and no more big business plans either! Just playing a relaxed gig now and then for his biggest fans who still make the effort to come and listen. He is still a real bluesman, as real as all his musical ancestors who once upon a time sprung from the gloomy swamps -almost literally- in the Mississippi Delta and who will not put down the guitar until they themselves ... right! He also likes to tell funny and juicy anecdotes between his songs. In 2021 he already performed at the Libero Theatre in Santa Barbara (LA) and the Virginia Street Brewhouse in Reno (Nevada) not far from Lake Tahoe. More acoustic performances are announced in September 2021, one of them in Arnstadt, Germany. Yep! Does this bring us full circle? Actually, he should be playing ... in his birthplace Sovetsk (Tilsit). I will suggest this to him. May we perhaps also expect a (final?) new CD from our eternal blues man John Kay in the future?

Final lineup in 2018: Gary Link, Michael Wilk, John Kay, Ron Hurst and Danny Johnson. (CC BT 2.0 License - Creative Commons.org - CLender)

Ticket for an acoustic performance in Arnstadt in November 2021.

However, it is a pity that Covid once again came and threw a spanner in the works across Europe in mid-November 2021. The planned performance in Arnstadt was postponed as a result. Many fans from Europe, from Scandinavia to the Mediterranean and from Great Britain via Holland and Belgium to Ukraine and the Urals, were looking forward to seeing John Kay perform again in Europe. Fate decided otherwise. During that same weekend, by the way, an amazingly special sculpture of John Kay was to be unveiled at Obere Weiße, just behind the market square and the famous Johan Sebastian Bach

Church, where John was to have his acoustic performance on November 26. Tour manager Charlie Wolf is very annoyed, but there is no denying that he made the right decision in terms of safety and for the good of everyone. Hats off to you for this surely courageous decision, Charlie! Although, of course, we would have much preferred to attend it all as it was essentially planned. But emergency knows no law and sometimes unpopular decisions have to be made in the general interest. None of the fans will blame John and/or Charlie for postponing this event to May 2022… and it was going to be fantastic …

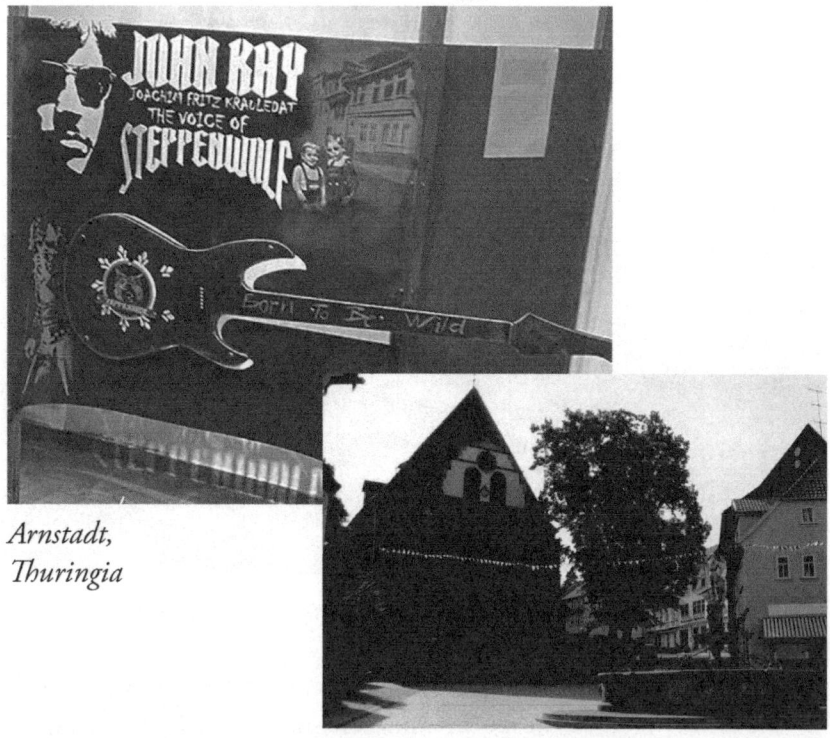

Arnstadt, Thuringia

Top: *Memorial plaque of John Kay under construction, awaiting its final unveiling in May 2022. John Kay added a text to it. The photo in the Dutch edition of this book was pretty much its world premiere. (Courtesy Charlie Wolf)*

Bottom: *Arnstadt City Center. The back of the JS Bach Church and the fountain. (own picture)*

Arnstadt, Thuringia, Germany, May 2022*

A nice small town of some 30,000 inhabitants in the German state of Thuringia is getting ready for a special event. The Maybach festivals are a recurring event, but this year it is followed by a rather unusual stunt: a performance in the Johan Sebastian Bach Church on Saturday evening, May 21 by a famous (former) resident and on Sunday, May 22, the unveiling of a special commemorative plaque for that same person.

Since last Thursday, May 19, there has been an increasing air of excitement. After a few very warm days, thick dark blue clouds are gathering everywhere between the hills surrounding the town. It's getting very dark in the early evening and the wind gets stronger and stronger. Suddenly, in quick succession, there are violent gusts of wind, a few flashes of lightning and infernal thunderclaps accompanied by a heavy downpour and a terrible whistling wind. Suddenly a very ominous veil descends on Arnstadt that evening ...

Members of the Wolfpack all know what this means: this ... is the hour of the Wolf. On this ominous evening, he must have arrived in Arnstadt.

Saturday, May 21, 07:00 p.m. About six to seven hundred fans of John Kay, coming from Germany, the Netherlands, Belgium, Denmark, Finland, Switzerland, Norway and Sweden are gathered at the entrance of the Johan Sebastian Bach Church. It is still a bit early, because the performance only starts at 08.00 p.m. Most people here have been strolling through town the whole afternoon. The small city center is very cosy; not too crowded and in a very pleasant atmosphere, perfect, as it should be on such an occasion. We expected Arnstadt to be overrun by people with heavy motorcycles on this Saturday night. However, that is not the case. Next to the entrance of

---

* *This chapter is not included in the original Dutch edition of the book.*

On every road to Arnstadt, we see this...

the church, we see a small stall with all kinds of gadgets and accessories. John's manager Charlie Wolf, assisted by Flemming Hjöllund, tries to satisfy the wishes of those people who want to take home a John Kay & Steppenwolf souvenir.

There are CDs, posters, T-shirts, plectrums with John Kay's signature, the updated edition of the biography *Magic Carpet Ride*, etc. ...

Charlie himself, in fact, has something special to celebrate this month, two things even! First: he has been John's manager for 30 years now. Second: at home in the US, one of his descendants is graduating at school. That's also the reason his wife Gloria isn't with him on this occasion. In some way, of course, he regrets not being able to be *over there* as well. Managers always have those difficult choices to make ...

My wife Linda and I have been in Arnstadt since Wednesday. We are both extremely interested in history. So, in this respect we already touched on the link in my book between John Kay and the wider (German) historical background in which he grew up (See Part I). We visited the site of Buchenwald (liberated by Americans on April 11/12 1945) on Thursday near the town of Weimar, about twenty-five miles to the north-east of Arnstadt. The old barracks in that camp in which political prisoners and the so-called *Untermenschen* tried to survive the terrible Nazi regime day after day way back then, do no longer exist. But there are still plenty of traces that blatantly refer to the horror that took place in those areas in the first half of the 1940s. As was the case in Auschwitz and Birkenau years ago, we are once again confronted with the disastrous human errors arising from some extreme and totalitarian ideology of the past. The current generation of Germans is well aware of their responsibility in view of what happened in the Second World War. Although confronting the past is obviously difficult for them, they are not inclined to minimize or belittle it in any way. Many people who once made the same mistakes (or are still making them), bite back rather fiercely when they are confronted today with the horrible crimes of their ancestors or their brothers. I am referring here directly to all those nations and population groups who hold in high esteem such fine-looking symbols as red, yellow, and green stars, hammers, crescents, half moons, and rising suns.

Most of them claim that their victims are the cause of them carrying out their acts of terror, but never they themselves …

The following day, Friday, we walked through the streets of the beautiful *Damenviertel* in Jena. We passed by the Arvid Harnack Strasse, where the Melzer family ran a large regional driving school for trucks before and even during the war. At that time, they also supplied the entire metropolitan region with all kinds of fuels and coal. It is also the location where Gerhard Melzer lived his whole life. This Gerhard was the man who provided us with useful information about the GDR in that (dark) period (see page 95) and who unfortunately passed away last year. By the way, Jena has regained some "color" since the fall of the Berlin Wall. The inner city looks really welcoming, and the buildings have had a fresh lick of paint, which can work miracles. During the communist era, everything there was dilapidated and drab, and people didn't have the money to buy "luxury products" like paint.

But of course, we primarily came to Arnstadt to live the present. The healthy excitement in the city center is increasing by the minute on this Saturday afternoon. The local brass band, playing to its heart's content on the little square a little further on, no longer gets any attention. A food truck that has set up right across the entrance of the church is still doing good business. Many visitors pass by for a real *Thüringer Bratwurst*. Besides the typical *Knödel* this is one of the local specialties ...

7:30 p.m. The doors of the little church open and people take their seats on the benches. Rumbling and murmuring echoes through the late medieval house of worship. Moments later, John Kay is announced and to loud applause, he walks in and places himself diagonally in front of the altar. In his usual warm-hearted way, he greets all those present and immediately gets down to business, playing *Walkin' Blues*.

It's not his fault, but one thing is immediately clear: the acoustics are not ideal, as was to be expected.

Between his songs, John tells all kinds of funny recent and not so recent anecdotes. A chair would not be an unnecessary luxury for him there, because we have the impression that John is a bit tired. Jetlag?

Probably, at least partly. His manager, Charlie Wolf, says he is also suffering from it. But John's enthusiasm and the passion he puts in his performance, overcomes it all. Towards the end, however, his fingers cramp up and he admits this in all honesty. He closes his initial playlist with *Down In The Bottom*. But there are always a few extra songs when John plays and the familiar audience has known that for years. If they just keep applauding long enough, he'll reappear on stage in a moment. As an extra, he first plays *Am Brunnen Vor Dem*

Tore, a popular German song written by Schubert. It's something he probably remembers from his early childhood years when he lived nearby in Obere Weiße, barely 150 meters from here. It is immediately followed by a song that has played an especially significant role in his long career as a musician: *The Pusher.* For myself it was back in ... 1998 that I heard him perform it live. And he's performing that song here, in the middle of the church; yep! The fact that he often uses the *"God Damned"* word in the process, doesn't seem to bother anyone in this church. In Winston-Salem, for example, that would be different ...

With *Got My Mojo Working* he ends his performance, and the over-enthusiastic applause is the best reward he can get. John is getting a bit tired, he indicates that he is getting a cramp in his fingers again.

After the performance, some people are already asking for a translation of this book *"Plectrum & Prikkeldraad"* in English or in German. A Dutch Wolfpacker, Mark Overbeeke, spontaneously offers me to help with the English translation ... if it will ever come to that.*
Meantime, some people go for a drink, others return home or to their hotel nearby. We all do have something in common this evening: a really good feeling. We all ask ourselves just this one thing: have we just been witnessing John's last performance here in Europe? It is only an impression that we have, but a strong one nevertheless ...

Sunday morning, May 22, the day after John's performance. It is 10:30 a.m. Already checked out at my hotel, I park my car right across the "Goldene Sonne Hotel" in the center of Arnstadt. I have an appointment with John Kay at 10:45 a.m., mainly thanks to loyal Wolfpackers Flemming Hjöllund and Lars Christensen and to John's always very busy manager Charlie Wolf. Nicolaj Enig and Bernd Kersten will also be there. Bernd has been the chairman of the German wing of the Wolfpack for many years. Unfortunately, Bernd's health is not at its best, but that performance by John Kay in his home

---

* *So, it* did *come to that...*

John Kay
Arnstadt, Germany, Bach Church
May 21st, 2022

Walking Blues
My Sporting Life
Going to California
Many A Mile
She's Got The Goods
The Balance
The Endless Commercial
Corinna Corinna
To Be Alive
Enough For Today
I Will Not Be Denied
Forty Days And Forty Nights
Kindred Spirits
The Back Page
Don't Waste My Time
Down In The Bottom

Am Brunnen Vor Dem Tore
The Pusher
Got My Mojo Working

Playlist on May 21st

country last night: he wouldn't have missed it for the world! Despite all his physical problems, he was possibly the most enthusiastic spectator of us all. Bernd sang along at the top of his (sick) lungs in that little church. Just for a moment, the poor guy felt completely liberated again …

The people I just mentioned have been very "close" to John for many years. They usually stay in the same hotel when he plays somewhere in Europe. These guys told him about me yesterday and also about the extensive background story that I have written about his life in my book "*Plectrum & Prikkeldraad* (Plectrum & barbed wire)

As far as that book is concerned, John already knew about my intentions for a while. After all, no one writes about anyone's life path without their personal permission, even though the book is certainly *not* just about him. He had also answered some of my questions before, because I was not sure about several things. Well, it is very hard to know everything that happened in the course of 78 years (John's age now). John himself could not answer all my questions either. So, as an author you just have to accept that, even if you write books that have a strong link with history, because otherwise you'll never get anything done. John also suggested in a friendly way not to ask any more questions, so as an author you have to respect that as well. We are not fanatical paparazzi and have no desire to use all (im)

John in the JS Bach Church. (Photo Thorsten Möser-Westkirchen)

possible means to find out just a little bit more …
For me, meeting John Kay is an incredibly unique experience. As a fan, I have known him since the summer of 1968 (from *Born To Be Wild* on) and I have seen him perform several times. But until now, I have never been able to have a conversation with him. Indeed, this is the first time I will be able to speak to him in person. By the way, 50 years ago I could never have believed that this would ever happen.

I step under the archway of the entrance to the sidewing of the hotel and enter a courtyard. I first meet Flemming, Charlie, Bernd, Nicolaj and Lars. A cheerful and spontaneous greeting and even a heartfelt hug I receive from each of them on this rather special Sunday morning. Although I have known them for a while through the Facebook fan page, it was only yesterday that I met these guys for the first time in person. Yesterday, I also had the opportunity to become acquainted with Wolfgang and Klaus Sander, Anna-Liisa, Harald, Patsy and Rolf; a few more loyal European Wolfpackers. Yet it seems as if we have known each other for a long time. That feeling of deep connection comes spontaneously and it's all because of that mysterious Wolf, you know. Yesterday we also strolled around Arnstadt all together and talked the whole time like old chatterboxes. We even had dinner together just *before* John's performance in the JS Bach Church, and *after* his performance, we sat together for a drink in a bar, somewhere in a cozy basement. An amazingly pleasant experience for us all …

Now, on this Sunday morning, Flemming and Lars had just spoken to John at the breakfast table and informed him of my visit to their hotel. At least: it turns out *John* had done most of the talking, and they had just listened obediently. John really likes to tell stories, and they would have enjoyed listening again.

"John knows you are coming, and he is quite curious to meet you. So, he will be here any moment now." says Lars.

I put a few copies of the Dutch edition of the book on a small table. John has promised Flemming and Lars to sign those for me …

A tall, slender, and self-confident man with sunglasses comes strolling very relaxed into the courtyard of the hotel.

"Hello, John! Good morning!" I suddenly hear Flemming say.

"Hello, you all. It's a nice and sunny morning, isn't it?" John greets us.

John immediately turns around and with a wide smile and a pair of mysterious eyes staring at me from behind his dark glasses, he says:

"So, you must be that Belgian guy who wrote that book?"

" That's right. I'm the one. … Good morning, John!"

"Great! Can I see it?"….

"Of course!"…

We see an even wider smile appear on his face. He looks at the book and we hand him a copy for himself and for his wife Jutta. He is pleasantly surprised and asks how many copies he has to sign for me.

"Only five copies? Well, I can do that, can't I?"...

I go with him to the small table in the courtyard, where he sits down and promptly opens a first copy, while asking where exactly he has to sign. Something immediately strikes me in the process, however. Something I have known for 54 years and thought it would not surprise me by now. And yet I am amazed ... Yep! Those weak eyes of his ... He has a tough time seeing exactly where to sign. He also asks for a better ballpoint pen, because he can barely see where he placed his first signature.

I thought: "*Poor guy, what am I doing to you.*" Feeling somewhat guilty already, I feel I must say something.

"Thank you, John, for giving color to my youth in the late sixties and the seventies. From the musical point of view, no one did this as much as you and your Steppenwolf did!"

"And I thank YOU for being one of those guys who loved us and supported us," was his spontaneous reply, as he looked at me.

Flemming and Lars take a picture for some further publicity and John has to go immediately. The other side of the coin of success for him: he is always in demand. Yet another press conference awaits him and then it's off to Obere Weiße, where his commemorative plaque will be unveiled at noon sharp.

"Sorry, I have to go. I see you folks over there?"....

"See you there in about half an hour, John..."

My wife Linda and I, we also leave that little garden behind the Goldene Sonne. Lars, Nicolaj, Bernd and Flemming spontaneously ask us

John Kay, signing some copies of the (original) Dutch edition of the book "Plectrum & Barbed Wire".

if we wouldn't like to come along with them to Obere Weiße. Of course, we will! Again, we meet Klaus, Wolfgang, Patsy, Harald, Anna-Liisa and Rolf outside the hotel and so we all walk together -once again- to the beautiful center of Arnstadt at our leisure. There is a pleasant bustle, and the weather is favorable. A nice spring sunshine provides the necessary warmth. After the rather chilly evening of Friday, that's a good thing. Along the way, several people join to attend the unveiling of John's commemorative plaque behind the JS Bach Church. There are even some children dressed for the occasion in T-shirts with the appropriate inscription *Born To Be Wild*. It's so adorable to see. Could they already be fans?

John Kay and Charlie Wolf have been on the road a little longer than planned. The whole time, they are followed by a camera crew, which doesn't leave them alone for a moment. We see that the commemorative plaque at Obere Weiße is still completely wrapped in plastic film. However, a sneaky person has already secretly caught a glimpse of what is to be admired under that plastic, as there is a large crack in the foil on one side. We are welcomed by a cheerful saxophone player. Bottles of foaming *Sekt* are chilled on the spot ...

John and Charlie arrive at Obere Weiße, followed by yet another camera crew. (Photo by the author)

Sculptor-artist Christoph Hodgson spontaneously welcomes the people and afterwards the mayor pays a large tribute to the only two persons from Arnstadt who ever put this town on the musical world map. The first one was a certain Johan Sebastian Bach a few hundred years ago, and the second one is ... right: John Kay! Exactly where the house stood where he and his mother Elsbeth had lived with the Kranz family between 1945 and 1949, the commemorative plaque is unveiled to loud applause. *Born To Be Wild* is written on the stem of the granite guitar.

Bottles are uncorked and glasses are raised on this special occasion and to John's health. John sees himself morally obliged to address the people. While he speaks English from time to time, we can tell that his German is still exceptionally good. The crowd is enthusiastic, and they all come to admire that commemorative plaque, where, after his speech, John sits down at a table to start an autograph session. Everyone brought something to be signed by him: an old record sleeve, a photo, a T-shirt, a guitar ...

Toast at Obere Weiße, right where the Kranz family's house stood, where John lived from 1945 to 1949. (Photos Linda Van Gelder)

We decide not to stay here much longer and to have something to eat a little further on, in a small local Italian *Trattoria*. After all, there is another extended "Meet and Greet" with John Kay planned there in the city center this afternoon. We'll just have to wait and see where precisely that will be. Let's enjoy our meal first …

A little later, Charlie and John pass by the terrace where we are sitting.

"We are glad to find you here. Since we haven't found any suitable location, we would like to go back to our hotel. We will continue "socializing" and talking there. Please, feel free to come over when you have finished your meal!"

We finish our lunch a little later and go back to the Goldene Sonne. A little after 2 p.m., Charlie and John once again appear on the scene at the cozy courtyard behind the hotel. While John signs a few mini posters for each of the present Wolfpackers, he spontaneously starts talking about the things of life …

John goes back in time and tells us he was completely overwhelmed by the beauty of the Pacific Coast when he visited that region for the very first time with his friend Klaus many, many years ago. But these days, the Maue-Kay foundation is obviously his biggest concern. He talks about the support given to all kinds of organizations. Talking about elephants and other animals of the "Big Five" on the one hand and about his experiences during his visits to the Foundation's projects in Tanzania, Kenya and Cambodia on the other hand, has really become his favorite subject.

I suddenly feel that, perhaps, it would not be inappropriate to add something about this subject myself. Therefore, I start to talk about my youngest daughter Debbie and her adopted baby elephant Kinna from years ago. (See the next chapter *The Maue Kay Foundation*).

I further respond to the theme by referring to the wonderful "nature and animals" photos that John's wife Jutta keeps on her Flickr page and to the social media on which she also posts beautiful photos with some regularity.

John does not follow social media himself (and he says he never will), but he listens attentively to what I have to say about it. He nods approvingly the whole time when I mention the organization "Friends of the Elephant", the organization where my youngest daughter followed and sponsored a few orphaned baby elephants for many years. Quarterly, she was asked to donate a small amount of money. That way, she could follow the growing animals. From the moment the orphaned elephant arrived at the center and received its first porridge bottle until it was returned into the wild, all details were clearly recorded. Our daughter punctually received photos and an identification certificate of her baby elephant was sent to her.

It turns out that John knows this organization. He is also pleasantly surprised by all our positive reactions to Jutta's Foundation. When I show him some pictures of Jutta's own Flickr page (a few of which, by the way, appear in my book) his enthusiasm keeps growing. Once again, John shows his gratitude quite explicitly when he sees for himself what exactly I am talking about ...

4:15 p.m. Flemming Hjöllund says it's time for a little break. Everyone here is staying in Arnstadt until tomorrow, except my wife Linda and me. Because we have a long way to go, we indicate that we would like to say goodbye. So, these pleasant days and afternoon meeting session today, are gradually coming to an end for us. We were able to listen and talk well. It has been good, but now we have to call it a day ...

"So, you have a long way to go?" John asks.

"Mechelen, a small town right between Antwerp and Brussels. You even played there with Steppenwolf, a long time ago ... on May 23, 1969 ...

"Well, that's possible. Probably during our first European tour. And so, you came all the way down here?

"I guess it's about six hundred kilometers, John. So, it's no big deal. You did this for decades, and almost every day, when you were on tour with the band."

During our last minutes there, and while we are still chatting with the others, I tell John that in the package I gave him this morning, besides *Plectrum & Prikkeldraad* (Dutch edition), he will also find a USB stick. Along with some publicity slogans, a few videoclips and some pictures, there are a few PowerPoint presentations I used a few weeks ago when I presented my book about him in public. One of those presentations is a brief biography of him, with *Feed the Fire* playing in the background. The choice of that song is very obvious (at least in my opinion). Watching that "rewinder" and listening to *that* song at the same time, is an emotional experience for people who know about his amazing life story …

"When you are home again and have a quiet moment, will you please have a look at it?"

*"And I **will** do that!"* he says very convincingly.

There is a brief silence, and then I resume with:

"John. I have no more words. Thank you SO much … for EVERYTHING!"

John now approaches me in a very decisive manner, looks me straight in the eye, spontaneously extends his hand and gives me a very firm handshake. I am somewhat surprised, because up to now, he has been rather reserved in this respect because of the Covid threat that is still present. He gives me even more than just a handshake. He doesn't let go of my hand, grabs my thumb and we make with each other's wrist for a few seconds that globally known gesture of deep and mutual appreciation, as if we have been brothers for years.

This feels a bit strange to me. After all, he is without any doubt my greatest youth idol. For many, many years I was crazy about his music and even today, I still play John Kay and/or Steppenwolf on an almost daily basis. But while many other European Wolfpackers went to the Wolf Fests near Nashville from time to time, I never went to any of them. I admit: deeply to my regret today. The fact I was always too busy with lots of other things is just my explanation to it, but it is absolutely no excuse. Bernd Kersten even made a funny allusion to that, saying frankly *"You have been a Wolfpacker and a fan since 1968, but I never saw you over there"*. This doesn't mean of course that I wasn't a fan of the Wolf all those years. Because I admire John Kay enormously for his music and even more for the deeply human person he essentially is. So, writing this book could be -in some way- the consolation price to express my feelings. Respect and admiration, that's what I have for this man. But I don't *worship* him the way some fans dare to worship their idols almost literally. I therefore think that in other circumstances and in another lifetime, we could have been good friends indeed. We obviously feel a deep mutual respect and we don't need too many words to understand each other …

Did I possibly miss an opportunity somewhere in my life? Maybe I shouldn't have just *imitated* him in front of the mirror in my youth, just like he had imitated Elvis Presley and Little Richard in the 1950s in the Kronenstrasse in Hannover. Instead of just *playing* Steppenwolf records at the time, wearing dark sunglasses, holding my head back a bit and standing in front of that mirror singing *"God damn the pusher man"* myself, I should have practiced hard enough on some musical instrument, so one day I could cross that Atlantic Ocean to do over there what he had done, or perhaps even play in a (his) band …

Says John still very sincerely to us at the moment we leave:

"I am very grateful as well. And on your way home; please be careful! Let all those rushing people go ahead."

My wife and I say goodbye to all those nice people we met there a few days ago. Anna-Liisa, her daughter and both her adorable grandchildren. We also say goodbye to Patsy, Harald, Bernd, Lars, Flemming, Nicolaj, Rolf, Klaus, Wolfgang … all so truly kind people. We get another heartfelt hug from Charlie Wolf. *"Say hello to Gloria at home, Charlie"* …

A little later, we are in the car, driving towards Belgium. I still find myself somewhat in a dream mode ... Thank you so much Flemming, Lars and Charlie to make this happen ...

"Arnstadt 2022. Was all this just a dream or reality?" I ask Linda.

"What do you think yourself?" she replies immediately...

Heading home, a little later we already pass Eisenach. On the left and on the right of the highway, we see the remnants of obstacles that marked the border between East and West Germany until November 9, 1989. South of the highway, the medieval Wartburg Castle stands undisturbed on that high hill. For centuries, it has been watching over this entire region. That was also the case in 1949 and 73 years later, nothing seems to have changed. At least what that castle is concerned, because the East German border guards with their machine guns have disappeared. Indeed, fleeing from one side of Germany to the other with the real chance of losing one's life, is fortunately no longer necessary in 2022. While we are crossing that old border, I'm shivering. I go back in time for a moment and think again of a boy called Joachim Fritz Krauledat, who 73 years ago as a five-year-old boy crawled through the barbed wire with his mother Elsbeth here nearby, on the way to eternal freedom. It is really unbelievable how his life and the overall political situation has changed ...

Around 7:30 p.m. we decide to stop somewhere along the road. In a restaurant near Siegen, I look at the menu, searching for that typical German *Strammer Max*, but they don't know it here. Yet we are in the heart of Germany, aren't we?

Does everything become more universal here in Europe, including the menu? Ha, here we have something typically German, *Kartoffelsuppe*. Potato soup it is then ... and also a *Thüringer Bratwurst* to go with it ...

Now it's starting to sink in. I have just experienced something incredibly special. In fact, I have been experiencing it all weekend. After my marriage, the birth of my three children and my seven grandchildren, this is definitely a new milestone in my life. And tomorrow, moreover, is the 23rd of May. Isn't that exactly the day, 53 years ago, that I was not allowed to see Steppenwolf in Mechelen? (See introduction)

"Mechelen ... How far from here?" I ask Linda.

"Let's see ... We still have about 380 kilometers to go..." she says watching the board computer.

"Windows down and we both sing "Head out on the highway?"..."

"... You wish! Just relax and put the air-conditioning on, please!"

... The day after, John is already having several appointments in Berlin ...

Wartburg Castle in Eisenach.

*A few Wolfpackers in Arnstadt, with Bernd and Lars in front.
(Photo F. Hjöllund)*

*Bernd Kersten, president of the German Wolfpack.
Bernd passed away on July fourth 2022, only a few weeks after his visit to Arnstadt.
(Photo F. Hjöllund)*

Lots of credit to both these guys. Flemming and John in 2022. (Photo F. Hjöllund)

The Maue Kay Foundation

"Let us be the voice for those creatures who have no voice."

The musical career of more than 50 years Steppenwolf ends on October 14, 2018. On that day, John Kay gives his final performance with the band. A much earlier announcement in 2007 to stop was abandoned, because some time later the band was touring again. But at the end of 2018, the curtain seems to have finally come down. And that's OK! It is not so much the energy itself that is running out, but rather ... the body that has to generate that energy. So, let the Wolf finally rest in peace, he deserves it. In 2018, John is 74 years old, and he has some other projects to focus on from now on. But he will probably never be able to stop performing completely. It's clearly in his blood, it always was, and it always will be. With some regularity, he is now on stage exactly as he started out in the early sixties. John Kay, just as the person he is. During the Covid crisis everything comes to a standstill, of course. But he will continue to play anyway and as befits a true "bluesman", that will probably be ... until he is completely deaf, as a matter of speaking. In this last chapter, we are introduced to his new engagements. This time, though, it is his wife Jutta Maue who is at the center of these fine initiatives, although for his 1990 album Rise & Shine *he had already written a song to express his concern about global environmental problems ...*

In *Do Or Die* on the 1990 CD *Rise & Shine* John Kay & Steppenwolf sings very convincingly about his deep concern for the ever-increasing environmental problems and he openly expresses his support for Greenpeace in their titanic battle against the gigantic garbage dump the world is becoming. Of course, John Kay is not the first to address these issues through music. In 1968, long before *Do Or Die* appeared,

British singer/presenter Wally Whyton wrote the song *Leave Them A Flower* pointing out that the world was going in the wrong direction with the environment. And in 1971, Cat Stevens repeats the call for a better environmental policy with his brilliant song *Where Do The Children Play?* from the fine album *Tea For The Tillerman*. Cat Stevens, the man who later converted to Islam and took the name Yusuf Islam in the process also draws attention to this problem in a sensitive way.

Has anything changed today? Today's youth may find this hard to believe, but four to five decades after Cat Stevens and Wally Whyton released their protest songs, the situation has certainly improved in many places in Western Europe. The water in many rivers here is now much cleaner than it was back then, and industry has managed to reduce the emission of harmful substances. So, some investments in that area really do pay off. Thanks to greatly improved waste management, Western countries are succeeding in sorting waste on a massive scale and many different products that used to be simply dumped are now being recycled. Of course, the mountain of different types of garbage has increased enormously. The main reason for this is that plastic is massively used, especially in the food industry, to preserve food longer. Unfortunately, far too often this plastic ends up in the ocean and the ecological balance and fish stocks suffer greatly as a result. We can also hope that this problem will eventually be solved and that most of the developing nations will soon be able to use the necessary resources to help ensure that their waste is processed in a better way. However, there is still an awfully long way to go in every respect ...

To be honest: when it comes to the protection of the environment, we need to have to look at the whole picture. After all, the industrial revolution of the 19th century first brought us enormous progress and unprecedented wealth. There were many opportunities and practical advantages and the ever-growing industry gave an unprecedented boost to basic human comfort. Progress knew no more bounds. From the mid-1980s onward, digitalization further reinforced people's overall comfort and data management grew exponentially. In fact, today it seems highly likely that we have only uncovered the tip of a gigantic iceberg of possibilities in the material and digital world.

The other side of the coin of all that formidable comfort, is that we consider it all perfectly normal in our everyday life today. It seems as if this enormous material evolution in 2023 is flagrantly overshooting its initial goal. The unpleasant side effects are now reflected in an increasingly unbalanced quality of life on this planet. It is no longer about convenience and progress in itself, but much more than ever before about the gigantic profits that most multinationals can reap through industry. In the process, environmental standards are often circumvented or flagrantly flouted, or the polluting factories are set up in countries where environmental standards have yet to gain a foothold. Politicians are often unable or afraid to take drastic decisions for fear of losing popularity. They do not always dare to scale back certain negative developments for fear of massive job losses in the sectors concerned and the collapse of the financial markets … or because, through a cumulation of all kinds of agreements they have gained interests themselves.

For the environmental problems, increased efforts are made, and solutions are sought, but meanwhile we are confronted worldwide with a completely different evil phenomenon that -surprisingly- is not even toxic in itself: the emission of carbon dioxide …

In the early 1970s, the emission of carbon dioxide was not yet considered to be a huge problem for the climate. In fact, carbon dioxide is not *directly* harmful to the environment. However, global deforestation results in reduced processing of oxygen and an excess of carbon dioxide inevitably warms the atmosphere. Add to that the fact that more and more people are present on our planet, and CO^2 emissions are now generally considered the main cause of climate change, with all sorts of bizarre consequences: the melting of Arctic ice and glaciers, abundant and concentrated rainfall here and exceptionally extended periods of extreme drought and heat elsewhere, or vice versa. There are plans, however, to collect carbon dioxide from the atmosphere on a massive scale in the future and to convert it organically into oxygen, in much the same way that trees and plants do. In Norway, there are supposedly already concrete plans in this regard. Hope springs eternal. So, what are we waiting for?

Today, many groups worldwide have good environmental management as the most important item on the agenda, and that -at least the idea in itself- is very commendable. Awareness is already a noticeable big step in the right direction. But if all those environmental activists stick to their own principles, we like to assume that they too will automatically and consistently distance themselves from the luxuries and comforts that result from all the things they are so fanatically protesting against. And that is a long list including many things these activists clearly do not always take into account. Many of them *are* not consistent with their own conviction, after all. Because protesting against something while continuously violating your own principles, is the same as protesting against your own lifestyle. Unfortunately, this is also happening in many places, consciously and unconsciously ...

Since his protest song *Do or Die,* John Kay's views on the environmental problem have by no means become less critical. But he now sees it in a much broader perspective. Starting in 2004, he, his wife Jutta and daughter Shawn began to accentuate their concern for the environment and their sympathy for animal and human welfare much more fervently. They set up a non-profit organization for the benefit of several charities around the world. Together they put their weight behind an admirable brainchild of Jutta's which she had for some time. Her initiative is not only related to the environment, but also involves worldwide animal welfare and the welfare of people who do not get the opportunities we consider *normal* in our Western world. Simple things like education and clean drinking water from the tap are not yet considered a matter of course for all children on our planet. Not even in the 21st century ...

Now that John has scaled back his musical activities considerably, given his age, he is more and more concerned with environmental issues. This may sound paradoxical to some critics coming from someone who has flown around the world for years. Many will find it a form of (self)deceit. But whatever it is and whatever people think: something has to be done worldwide to get rid of our gigantic mountain of waste on the one hand and to temper global warming on the other; it doesn't matter who is to blame and to what extent. The human race has indeed made a mess of things and the damage done to the planet may not be easy to mend in the next few decades...

The world will keep on turning, but it will take several generations of good management, at least, to reverse the overall negative trend. It is unfortunate, however, that our Western world too often takes up rather one-sided positions in this regard. Not so much by denying the problem, but by thinking that by keeping our own house in order, the (world) problem is also largely solved. By investing heavily in renewable energy and an environmentally friendly fleet of vehicles, we are paying through the nose to comply with strict national and local environmental standards. It clearly bothers us less that our own toxic waste is still being shipped by millions of tons to countries in Africa or Asia to be dismantled and destroyed. Often extremely poor children have to dismantle our gigantic waste mountain. And apparently, it also does not sink in enough that our polluting fleet of vehicles which is taken out of circulation here today, is exported to Africa next on a large scale. There, emission of CO^2 and nitrogen oxides is subordinate to the local way of life and economy, so all those cars that no longer meet environmental standards here, will find a new owner there. After all, no one there is bothered by environmental or any other standards and people over there cannot afford electric cars anyway. More important in those countries are the primary necessities of life, and in the first place this means ensuring security… by having some food on the table. Only when these primary necessities can be sufficiently obtained, there will be a possibility to invest in sustainability and a better environment. According to Darwin's doctrine and theory of evolution, this is basic logic. You have to first deal with the primary necessities before you can invest in something else …

The pressure to dismantle all nuclear power plants worldwide is also increasing and it seems that nuclear energy will soon be a thing of the past. For a long time however, it was thought that building more nuclear power plants would be by far the cheapest, cleanest and most efficient way to provide the world with sufficient *clean* energy. In reality, this is true, but the downside of this is and remains, of course, the continuous threat that emanates from nuclear power plants and the enormous problems that exist with the processing of nuclear waste.

So spurred on by the "green" political parties, we may soon be facing a total dismantling of nuclear power providers. Hopefully there will be sufficient alternatives, or we will have to use candlelight again and light the stove ... if that is still allowed because of the CO and CO^2 that even our most modern stoves will always emit. Solar energy or energy from our wind farms may provide a partial solution and there are also lofty expectations for research into the possibilities of hydrogen. And so, our conscience in the Western world is gradually being eased. The definitive closure of the nuclear power plants is indeed in the pipeline, and we are also striving for complete CO^2 neutrality (in Europe) by the year 2050 and the maximum limitation of the emission of all possible nitrogen and other harmful substances.

...However, all these promising projects will only succeed, if people worldwide are convinced they all *must* live together in peace, and when speculators or share holders/ managers who systematically abuse international crisis situations, have no longer any influence on the international energy prices... AND in the meantime, let's not forget eighter that pollution does not stop at one border or another, nor should we forget that animals worldwide are the victims of man's unlimited pursuit of profit. This not only has a negative impact on the climate and the environment itself. Many animal species are directly threatened in their survival by massive deforestation or ruthless hunting by poachers ...

The Maue Kay Foundation as already mentioned, addresses *general* welfare rather than the individual problems raised above. Human rights and support to Amnesty International and non-governmental organizations (NGOs) are equally high on the Foundation's agenda. Emphasis is also placed on the vulnerability of endangered nature and wildlife in Africa and Asia, where heartless poachers don't care about the rules and are active only to make more money. Jutta came up with the idea when she met some people in a Tennessee Sanctuary who were taking care of a herd of retired elephants who used to live in captivity. The idea to support the sanctuary came about in the period when she and John still lived almost full time in the town of

Franklin, between 1989 and 2005. She admired the initiative in which all the animals, which had had a pretty tough life in a circus or somewhere else, were allowed to spend a peaceful old age in Tennessee. She became so much involved emotionally, that she couldn't let go and decided to do more than that. She put the idea on the agenda at home to start something along these lines herself. Especially her daughter Shawn was immediately enthusiastic, and she really liked the idea. John also believed in her plans, but he still had too many contractual obligations with the band at that time. Since the band stopped touring and performing in 2018, he now supports the project almost full time and today he lends his powerful voice to all kinds of promotional films in the interest of nature and the Maue Kay Foundation. Jutta and John do not limit themselves to (passive) fundraising, by the way. Wherever those funds go they will also go to see what is done and how the pennies are spent ...

Worldwide, for several decades now, there have been several of these nonprofit organizations that are concerned with the welfare of wild animals. In this regard, I once had a funny experience myself with my youngest daughter Debbie, when one day she came home from school and told me out of the blue:

"Daddy, I have adopted an elephant and his name is Kinna!"

With that nice -but rather unusual- greeting, she came home from school sometime around the year 2000. I guess she had just turned seventeen. She spontaneously made me laugh because I thought she was joking, and I didn't exactly know what to think of it. I immediately told her that I didn't have a leash that was strong enough to take that animal out for a walk, but that I would ask what to do at the Côte d'Or chocolate factory (which has an elephant as its brand symbol) because they probably also had to walk it once in a while. But she looked me in the eye with a serious expression.

"A joke? No, Daddy! I'm dead serious! The money I will get from now on, will be spent to help that poor elephant and other animals to survive!"

She had indeed pledged to the worldwide appeal of the organization Friends of the Elephant, which is committed to the care of orphaned elephants in the jungles of Kenya ...

The adoption of that elephant was the final farewell of a family pet phase. When my children's continuous longing for *normal* pets like dogs, cats, guinea pigs, chickens and horses seemed to ease off, our youngest daughter suddenly announced that she had adopted an orphaned animal from the Big Five. Orphaned elephants, the parents of which had been mercilessly killed by poachers for the price of ivory, were being cared for in an asylum in Kenya. The aim of the organization was to find godparents all over the world, and through small regular donations, to give these orphaned elephants the opportunity to grow up in a shelter and to prepare them for a return to the wild. I admired her idea, and I fully supported her in this ... hence, my personal interest in wildlife grew even more, when I became aware of the Jutta Maue- Kay Foundation. When later on, I visited the exceptionally beautiful and private Flickr page of Jutta Maue for the first time, I was really flabbergasted on the spot. All those wonderful and unique photos she posted there: they are really beautiful! (I advise the reader here to visit that page.) But as already mentioned, the general welfare of our fellow human beings is also highly regarded by the Maue- Kay group. A range of projects is now supported by that foundation: African People & Wildlife, the Amboseli Trust for Elephants, Big Life Foundation, the International Fund for Animal Welfare, Lewa Wildlife Conservancy, Orangutan Foundation International, Saola Foundation, the Elephant Sanctuary ... all in the interest of nature, the environment or people who need a bit of support in life. John and Jutta also visit the locations they support. During the trips they take together to Asia and Africa they show their enthusiasm. In Cambodia, where one of their projects is located, there is a nice banner to welcome them with the words "Welcome to John Kay & Jutta Maue Kay". Nicely done by the people there to show their gratitude. These people, by the way, are still traumatized by crimes committed by the genocidal regime of the Red Khmer, a communist movement very much pro-China. Two million Cambodians (out of a total population of seven million) were mercilessly killed under the leadership of ruthless leader Pol Pot for the most idiotic reasons (or equally for no reason at all). Pol Pot used horrible torture methods to oppress and exterminate people. He didn't care about numbers because according to his philosophy those many dead bodies were good for the ecological balance and ... for fertilizing the soil. In the 21st century, some order has finally been restored in Cambodia, although the lawsuits against the former Khmer Rouge murderers are still ongoing in many cases and it is still striking how few older people from that period are still alive. Some of the local museums, by the way, completely expose that terrible period. Pol Pot's regime was apparently even more cruel than the totalitarian regimes of Hitler and Stalin put together ...

In Tanzania, East Africa, Jutta and John support a few schools and on their visit in 2004 to one of them, the Gijedabung School, they are also very enthusiastically received by the spontaneous singing of the children. Their honest expression of thanks arouse the emotions. Behind John's dark glasses, tears well up again seeing all these spontaneous expressions of empathy. All the more so, because he knows well enough that they are children who have to make a lot of effort just to go school. There are no parents there who take their children every day by car or bus. They have to walk several kilometers on foot -often barefoot- through the wilderness in order to get the basic learning material. And because they believe they can have better future than their parents, they all put a lot of effort into doing it really well.

As a VIP couple in the USA, Jutta and John are used to be in the limelight. Every year at their beautiful Wolf Fest they enjoy the exuberant excitement of the crowd and the people in Nashville and surroundings are very grateful to be able to experience this. But this is different, because the response of these grateful children comes straight from their hearts. Jutta addresses the children and gives them nice packages with all kinds of goodies, including coloring books, drawing paper, colored pencils and markers. This nice extra for the grateful children is, of course, completely separate from the much larger monetary support they are pumping into that project. Because the school there has no decent infrastructure and no canteen, they will also provide the necessary funds for that. Also, a better equipped play area can be built. The teachers in the schools are delighted, and the children are happy, while their dark eyes clearly show their gratitude. Children are easily pleased, and both Jutta and John are very much touched by the spontaneous, warm and generous response they receive. They are also amazed by the high level of their courtesy. These children have practically nothing materially, but they do have something that is clearly becoming increasingly rare in our cold world: they radiate honest warmth, and they show an incomparable gratitude for everything they have and get ...

Reception committee for Jutta and John at the Tith Mom School in Cambodia.

All this reminds the author of a special event in the year 1949, on Christmas Day in *Kronenstrasse* number 35/37 in Hannover. There lived a brave lady and her little five-year-old son at the time, who had also experienced a real adventure together by fleeing to the West. That lady's name was Elsbeth Zimmermann, and that five-year-old son was Joachim. Wouldn't John Kay himself, on seeing those images, have thought of his mother Elsbeth, who had given him more or less the same present in Hannover in 1949? Like these children here, they had also gone through a miserable period. Those little things not only brought him literally some color (as far as this was possible of course with his eye disease) and brightness into his life, but also figuratively. The only difference however is that from that day on way back then for Elsbeth and Joachim things would only get better and that is something that -despite all efforts and good will of third parties- still remains to be seen for these children. Also in Kenya, John and Jutta meet with a lot of gratitude from local wildlife-protection initiators. It is a unique experience for both of them to travel through the bush with their guides in a vehicle and observe the elephants and rhinos and they are even able to caress some of the animals. It all strengthens their conviction that the creation of their Foundation was one of their best ideas and initiatives ever. So, *Born to be Wild* takes on a totally different meaning than that megahit from Steppenwolf's repertoire.

As a last update in this chapter, we are glad to mention the UN-agreement from March 2023 in New York about the protection of the oceans worldwide. So it seems we are going in the right direction…

Jutta and John make beautiful reports of their travels to the countries where they support nature and wildlife projects. Their photos are posted on Jutta's FLICR pages.

John with local volunteers from one of their projects in Africa.

This little elephant has clearly found its godmother.

Epilogue

John Kay has been on stage (with or without a band) for over 57 years. The band toured around the world all these decades in many different lineups, as some members of the original band and others who joined later dropped out over time for several reasons. Apart from John, keyboard man Michael Wilk is by far the one who stayed with Steppenwolf the longest with 37 years of loyal service, followed by drummer Ron Hurst with 34 loyal Steppenwolf years.

Since 1996, John's name has been engraved on the Walk of Fame in Canada. So far not yet in the USA which we find hard to understand. But it is what it is and whining about it all the time won't help much …

Walk of fame Canada. John Kay's name immortalized in granite.

In 2021 John Kay becomes active as an advocate for the weaker creatures of this world, but he still has acoustic performances regularly. The intention is to give a live performance on average once or twice every three months. No more heavy-duty tours through the US or elsewhere in the world, with all that never-ending stress. The group itself, after those 50 years of multiple ups and downs and some painful splits, finally ceased to exist as an active performance band in October 2018. From then on, John Kay occupies himself more with the Maue Kay Foundation and he lends his powerful voice to foundation's promotional films. But his music lives on uninterrupted for multiple generations of enthusiasts and he, himself, is a living icon for a lot of people from various backgrounds, ages, income brackets and so forth. Even at the last performances in 2018, the halls were very well filled and there were fourteen-to-sixteen-year olds, loudly cheering the whole time. The further back you went in that frenzied audience, the older the age of the attendees, until you saw those rows of people who were pretty much the age of John himself. And ALL those people had one thing in common. They came to see the band and the singer who was (and is) the symbol of all those successive generations so eager to be identified with freedom and rebellion on the one hand and blues and hard rock music on the other. On hearing the first tones of *Born To Be Wild* no less than six generations of people from all social classes turn completely wild. Since that anthem about rebellion and freedom also featured in the 1969 film *Easy Rider* it has become the symbol around the world for every next generation of motorcyclists. But also many Vietnam veterans associate themselves for the rest of their lives with that song. It makes them think back to that cursed political situation in the tumultuous period of the late '60s and early '70s. When American soldiers were crawling through the treacherous swamps of South-East Asia, and music was pretty much the only solace to fall back on from time to time. Steppenwolf and Creedence Clearwater Revival in particular reflected their feelings. John stresses that post-traumatic feeling of many of these war veterans in his beautiful, compelling and straight to the point song *Rock & Roll War* from that fabulous CD *Rise & Shine* ...

Even today, especially the worldwide hit *Born To Be Wild* is still extremely popular. Whenever Steppenwolf's authentic and best-known hit is played anywhere in the world, people of the older generations promptly drop their walking sticks or shove their walkers aside and they spontaneously jump onto the dance floor (in so far as that is still possible). Some will string their ties around their (bald) skulls and play the air guitar enthusiastically, or they sink down on their knees or jump around and dance. From the first guitar riff they let themselves go with total abandon. In all that elated enthusiasm, everyone tunes back to the frequency of a long-forgotten youth, long hair and the almost carefree existence of yesteryear ...

As for the Netherlands, I don't know exactly how many times the band played there. They were also on a TV show in 1987 where they played *Hold On (Never Give Up, Never Give In)* and one of the eight bogus bands also visited once. John Kay & Steppenwolf visited Belgium about four times. In May 1969, Steppenwolf played in the sports hall at Winketkaai in Mechelen, on a rainy December evening in 1990 in the Vooruit in Ghent, at Boogie Town in Louvain-la-Neuve in May 1998 and the last time in August 2012 in terrible weather conditions at Blues Peer in Belgian Limburg. Unfortunately, in Belgium Steppenwolf's repertoire is not very well known and even less appreciated. Radio stations in Flanders, Belgium did not like these rough boys from the start at the end the '60s and fifty years later that hasn't changed, although there was one rare exception: the program Rudy's Club presented by Roger Troch on Radio East Flanders, who one Wednesday afternoon in the summer of 1971 devoted an entire afternoon to Steppenwolf ...

In the Netherlands and Great Britain Steppenwolf was a little bit more popular, but especially in Scandinavia and (West) Germany they were really hot for over five decades. And rightly so, because they had *so* much more to offer than that one, gigantic megahit from the spring and early summer of 1968 ...

Today, again residing almost full time on the American West Coast in Montecito (Santa Barbara), John Kay and his wife Jutta Maue are

John Kay had, apart from his wife Jutta, one more faithful companion throughout the years: his black Rickenbacker guitar that bears his signature ...

enjoying their well-deserved retirement. Deserved indeed, after an extremely turbulent life for both of them.

On April 12, 1944, in the middle of the Second World War, a certain Waquin Krauledaitis alias Joachim Fritz Krauledat came into this world in the town of Tilsit (East Prussia). A loud cannon shot ushered in his life, and that rumble was clearly heard in his voice throughout his whole life ...

Steppenwolf albums
Steppenwolf, 1967/68
Steppenwolf The Second, 1968
Steppenwolf At Your Birthday Party, 1969 Monster, 1969
Steppenwolf Live, 1970
Best Of Steppenwolf, 1970
Steppenwolf Seven, 1970
Steppenwolf Gold (compilation), 1971 For Ladies Only, 1971
Portrait Of Steppenwolf (compilation), 1971 Rest In Peace (compilation), 1972
Slow Flux, 1974
Hour Of The Wolf, 1975 Skullduggery, 1976

Solo albums John Kay
Forgotten Songs & Unsung Heroes, 1972 My Sportin' Life, 1973
All In Good Time, 1978
Lone Steppenwolf, 1987
The Lost Heritage Tapes, 1997 Heretics & Privateers, 2001

John Kay & Steppenwolf albums *Live in London, 1981*
Wolf Tracks, 1982
Paradox, 1984
Rock & Roll Rebels, 1987
Rise & Shine, 1990
Live at 25, 1995
Feed the Fire (compilation, except Feed the Fire), 1996 Silver (compilation), 1997
Live in Louisville, 2004

Exceptional releases
Early Steppenwolf Live, 1969
(As John Kay & The Sparrow in the Matrix San Francisco-May 14, 1967)
John Kay & The Sparrow, 1969 (Recorded in 1966 in New York City as demos for the Columbia label)

With thanks to:

- *John Kay & Steppenwolf Fan Base - Facebook page.*
- *Archives of VRT, Radio and TV of Flanders, Belgium.*
- *Belgian magazine HUMO.*
- *The Melzer family from Jena, Germany.*
- *The following people for their contribution and their enthusiasm:*

Charlie Wolf, tour manager and website manager of "John Kay & Steppenwolf"

Flemming Hjöllund - Denmark.
For his great help about my meeting with John Kay + all his pictures.

Paula Rodeiro - Buenos Aires, Argentina.
For her enormous enthusiasm about the band.

Oksana Linda - Ukraine
For her contribution about the Stalin regime.

Lars Christensen - Denmark
For his great general help and spontaneous friendship.

*Mark Overbeeke - The Netherlands
For his enormous effort by translating the
English edition of this book.*

*Klaus Sander, for his very useful contribution
with the day- by- day Steppenwolf calendar.
Klaus has made up the whole Wolf calendar
until February 2023. Unfortunately, it is
too voluminous for full publication in this
book*

And, of course, John Kay & Jutta Maue themselves, who were so kind to answer my questions and who gave me permission to use their beautiful photos.

The world is a better place with these two good people in it ...

For more information about the various projects of John Kay and Jutta Maue, visit the site: www.mauekay.org. *Also, the Jutta Maue's Flickr page is highly recommended.*

Website/webstore of the band: www.steppenwolf.com

John and his daughter Shawn

The Wolf, Charlie Wolf and another few Wolfpackers in Hotel "Goldene Sonne".

Our last farewell to Bern Kersten. Only a few weeks after John's performance in Arnstadt, Bernd leaves this world forever …
(Photos F. Hjöllund)

Alphabetic list by first names in the book story

Angela Hurst	Engelbert Humperdinck
Anna- Liisa	Eric Clapton
A.G. Croce	Erich Honecker
Albert De Beukeleer	Etta James
Albert Haesebroeckx	Fats Domino
Albert Hammond	Flemming Hjöllund
Albert Melzer	Frau Kranz
Alice Cooper	Frédéric Maréchal
Andy Chapin	Friedrich Paulus
Annelore Melzer	Fritz Krauledat (Krauledaitis)
Annemarie, Reffert	Gabriel Mekler
Arthur Harris	Gary Link
Barry White	Gary Primich
BB King	Gerhard Kyczinski
Benito Mussolini	Gerhard Melzer
Bernd Kersten	General Chernyakhovsky
Bill Haley	George Biondo
Bill Utley	Georges Clemenceau
Billy Gibbons	Georgy Zhukov
Bo Didley	Goldy McJohn
Bob Simpson	Gordon Lightfoot
Bobby Cochran	Günther Schabovski
Cat Stevens (Yusuf Islam)	Guy Mortier
Chantal Pattyn	Hank Snow
Charlie Wolf	Hank Williams
Connie Froboess	Hanz Guderian
Danny Johnson	Harald en Patsy
David Bowie	Heino
Debbie	Heli Hewko
Dennis Hopper	Helmuth Kohl
Dickie Peterson	Henry Kissinger
Dorothy Scully	Hermann Hesse
Ed Sullivan	Ho Chi Minh
Elsbeth Zimmermann	Howlin' Bill
Elvis Presley	Howlin' Wolf

Hoyt Axton
Hugh Hefner
Hugh O'Sullivan
Ian Gillan
Ike Turner
J.F. Kennedy
Jack London
Jack Nicholson
Jacques de Pierpont
James Brown
James Coburn
Jan Palach
Janis Joplin
Jerry Edmonton
Jimi Hendrix
Jimmy Carter
Jimmy Vaughan
Joachim Fritz Krauledat
Joachim von Ribbentrop
Johan Cruijff
Johan Sebastian Bach
John Fogerty
John Kay
John Lee Hooker
John Mayall
John Mooney
Joseph Stalin
Josip Tito
Junior Walker
Jürgen Conings
Jutta Maue
Karl Marx

Kenny Wayne Shepperd
Kent Henry
Kim Jong-un

Klaus
Larry Byrom
Larry Green
Lars Christensen
Laurie Richardson
Lech Walesa
Leigh Stevens
Lester Butler
Lightnin' Guy
Linda Van Gelder
Little Richard
Lyndon B. Johnson
Mao Ze Dong
Marlon Brando
Marshall Rokossovsky
Martin Luther
Martin Luther King
Marvin Gaye
Mathias Greffrath
Marika Rökk
Mark Overbeeke
Marlene Dietrich
Michael Monarch
Michael Wilk
Mikhail Gorbachev
Morgan Cavett
Muammar Gaddafi
Muddy Waters (McKinley Morganfield)
Neil Young
Nick Lowe
Nicolae Ceausescu
Nicolas Kassbaum (Nick St. Nicolas)
Nicolay Enig
Niki Lauda
Noddy Holder
Palmer Brothers

Pat Boone
Patsy
Paul Whaley
Penty Glenn
Peter Alexander
Peter Fonda
Peter Heinz
Peter McGraw
Philippe Menard
Pol Pot
Reb Foster
Richard Burton
Richard Nixon
Richard Podolor
Rick Derringer
Ringo Starr
Rita Coolidge
Rocket Richotte
Rod Stewart
Roger Troch
Roland Van Campenhout
Rolf
Ronald Reagan
Ron Hurst
Rudi Schüricke
Rushton Moreve
Sir Douglas

Scott Mackenzie
Shawn Kay
Son House
Stan King
Steve Fister
Steve Marriot
Sylvain Vanolme
Tania Dexters
T. Lau
Tina Turner
Tom (O'Neal) Gundelfinger
Tom Holland
Tom Jones
Tom Pagan
Udo Jürgens
Vjadjeslav Molotov
Vladimir Lenin
Wally Whyton
Walt Disney
Wayne Cook
Winston Churchill
Wojciech Jaruzelski
Woody Guthrie
Christof Hodgson
Adolf Hitler

Disclaimer

The historical background in this story is completely authentic and based on official archives and history books.

The story of John Kay himself is partly based on some old interviews, magazines and some questions I was allowed to ask him. It is also partly based on some hypothetical feelings. To make it look a bit more like a roman, you can- indeed- smell some author's fantasy between the lines. Some real insiders, who were sometimes at the first row when things happened, may- as a matter of fact- have another opinion about some details...

The photographs in this book are either:

- taken by the author himself,
- provided by and used with the approval of John Kay or Jutta Maue, from the public domain, or
- used with the permission of the author or the copyright holder.

In case of any doubt about copyrights, please contact the author or the publisher.

Steppenwolf - First Period (up to February 1972)

Day By Day. Not limitative calendar list. *(not guaranteed)*

17.03.13	John Kay's father Fritz Krauledat born in Absteinen, East Prussia, Germany, as the oldest of nine children
13.06.13	John's mother Elsbeth Zimmermann born in Malissen, East Prussia, Germany, as one of seven children
07.01.36	Richard Podolor born in Los Angeles, CA
18.03.36	Reb Foster born as James Dennis Bruton in Fort Worth, TX
21.04.43	Mars Bonfire born as Dennis McCrohan in Oshawa, Ontario, Canada
28.09.43	Nick St. Nicholas born as Klaus Kassbaum in Plön, Rosenstraße 13, Germany
16.02.44	Jack London born as Dave Marden in London, England
26.02.44	Jutta Maue born in Langenhorn (Hamburg), Germany
17.03.44	Fritz Krauledat killed in Pleskau, Germany
12.04.44	John Kay born as Joachim Fritz Krauledat in Tilsit, Germany
02.05.45	Goldy McJohn born as John Raymond Goadsby in Toronto, Canada
03.09.45	George Biondo born in Brooklyn, New York City, NY
08.07.46	Pentti "Whitey" Glan born in Finnland
09.09.46	Bruce Palmer born in Toronto, Canada
24.10.46	Jerry Edmonton born as Jerry McCrohan in Oshawa, Ontario, Canada
05.04.48	Kent Henry born as Kent Henry Plischke in Hollywood, CA

06.11.48	Rushton Moreve born as John Rushton Morey in Los Angeles, CA
27.12.48	Larry Byrom born in Huntsville, Alabama
14.10.49	Ron Hurst born in Holyoke, Massachusetts
27.02.50	Steve Palmer born (Year?)
05.07.50	Michael Monarch born in Los Angeles, California
08.08.50 (?)	Elsbeth Krauledat marrying Gerhard Kyczinski in Hannover
30.10.50	Bobby Cochran born
02.05.50	Gary Link born in Pittsburgh, PA
31.03.51	Michael Wilk born
11.12.51	Michael Palmer born (Year?)
19.08.52	Charlie Wolf born
09.04.53	Jerry Sumner born
22.03.55	Rocket Ritchotte born
14.06.55	Danny Johnson born in Lousiana, LA
06.11.56	Doug Adams born
16.03.57	Steve Fister born in Buffalo, NY
22.10.62	Jutta Maue arriving in Canada after emigrating from Germany
09/10/11.04.65	John Kay in concert at the New Balladeer, Los Angeles
04/05/06/18/ 19/20/06.65	John Kay in concert at the New Balladeer, Los Angeles
30.06.65	The Sparrows in concert at the Stratford Arena, Stratford, Ontario, CAN, with The Liverpool Set
15.09.65	John Kay joins The Sparrows
03.01.66	The Sparrows in concert at Chez Monique, Toronto, ON, Canada
28.04.66	The Sparrows recording „Twisted", „Goin' To California" and „Square Headed People" at Allegro Sound Studios, New York, produced by David Kapralik and engineered by Bruce Botnick
05.06.66	The Sparrow in concert at the Arthur, New York City

06.06.66	The Sparrow recording further demos as „Good Morning Little Schoolgirl", „Bright Lights, Big City", „Hootchie Kootchie Man", „The Pusher", „King Pin", Goin´ Upstairs" and „Baby Please Don´t Go" in New York produced by David Kapralik
25.06.66	The Sparrow recording „Tomorrow`s Ship" in New York produced by Kapralik & McCoy
14.07.66	The Sparrow recording further songs as „Goin´ To California" and „Twisted" in New York produced by David Kapralik
06/07/08.08.66	The Sparrows in concert at Charlie Browns' Coffee House Cumberland, IN
14.09.66	Through
24.09.66	The Hard Times still without Larry Byrom opening for the Chambers Brothers at the Whisky A Go Go in Los Angeles, CA
21.10.66	The Sparow recording „Green Bottle Lover" in New York produced by David Kapralik
30.10.66	The Sparrow in concert at the Hullabaloo in Los Angeles, CA
03.11.66	The Sparrow recording „Tighten Up Your Wig" in Los Angeles produced by Stan Freeman
08.12.66	Through
22.12.66	The Sparrow in concert at The Ark, Gate 6, Sausalito, CA, with Sons Of Champlin and Freudian Slips
16/17/18.12.66	The Sparrow in concert at Avalon Ballroom, San Francisco, CA, with Youngbloods and Sons Of Champlin
22.12.66	The Sparrow in concert at The Ark, Gate 6, Sausalito, CA, with Sons Of Champlin and Freudian Slips
13.01.67	Sparrow in concert at Avalon Ballroom, San Francisco, CA, with Moby Grape and the Charlatans

14.01.67	Sparrow in concert at Avalon Ballroom, San Francisco, CA, with Moby Grape and the Charlatans
14.01.67	Sparrow in concert at Goman's Gay, San Francisco, CA (morning show), with Kaleidoscope and Country Joe & The Fish
15.01.67	Sparrow in concert at Goman's Gay, San Francisco, CA (morning show), with Kaleidoscope and Country Joe & The Fish
20.01.67	Sparrow in concert at Avalon Ballroom, San Francisco, CA, with Moby Grape, Steve Miller Blues Band and Lee Michaels
21.01.67	Sparrow in concert at Avalon Ballroom, San Francisco, CA, with Moby Grape, Steve Miller Blues Band and Lee Michaels
03/04/02.67	Sparrow in concert at Avalon Ballroom, San Francisco, CA, with Kaleidoscope and Country Joe And The Fish
10.02.67	Sparrow in concert at Regency Ballroom, Leamington Hotel, Oakland, CA, with Wildflower, The Living Children and The Immediate Family
16.02.67	Sparrow in concert at The Ark, Sausalito, CA, with Moby Grape and California Girls
17.02.67	Jutta Maue arriving in LA by emigrating from Canada
18.02.67	Sparrow in concert at The Ark, Sausalito, CA, with Moby Grape and California Girls
24.02.67(?)	John Kay and Jutta Maue marrying (?)
25.02.67	Sparrow recording „Too Late", „Can`t Make Love By Yourself" und three more tunes in Los Angeles produced by David Rubinson
03/04.03.67	Avalon Ballroom, San Francisco, CA, with Country Joe & the Fish and the Doors
05.03.67	Avalon Ballroom, San Francisco, CA, with Moby Grape, Country Joe & The Fish, Big Brother &

	The Holding Company, Grateful Dead and Michael Mc Clue
16.03.67	Berkeley Community Theatre, Berkeley, CA, with the Charles Lloyd Quintet and Country Joe & The Fish
25.03.67	Santa Cruz Civic Auditorium, Santa Cruz, CA, with Blue Cheer and Quicksilver Messenger Service
30/31.03.67	California Hall, San Francisco, CA, with Hedds, Santana Bluz, Orkustra and The Outcasts
07.04.67	Avalon Ballroom, San Francisco, CA, with Charlatans and Canned Heat
08.04.67	Mt. Tamalpais Outdoor Theatre, Mt. Tamalpais, CA, with Big Brother & The Holding Company, Quicksilver Messenger Service and The Charlatans (afternoon show)
08.04.67	Avalon Ballroom, San Francisco, CA, with Charlatans and Canned Heat
11/12/13.04.67 14/15//16/28/	Matrix, San Francisco, CA, with Jefferson Airplane
29/30.04.67	Matrix, San Francisco, CA
09/10/11.05.67	same
12/13.05.67	Avalon Ballroom, San Francisco, CA, with The Doors
14.05.67	Matrix, San Francisco, CA, show was taped for later LP/CD use
19/20/21.05.67	Matrix, San Francisco, CA
26.05.67	National Guard Armory, San Bruno, CA
28.05.67	National Guard Armory, San Bruno, CA, with Sons Of Champlin
29.05.67	or
30.05.67	Haight Ashbury Karmic Ball Fund, California Hall, San Francisco, CA, with Sandy Bull, Epics, Outfield, Flying Circus, The Loading Zone, The Ancestra Spirits, The Bearing Straight, The Orkestra and others

02.06.67	Fillmore West, San Francisco, CA, with Jim Kwestin Jug Band and Peanut Butter Conspiracy
03.06.67	Fillmore West, San Francisco, CA, with Jim Kwestin Jug Band and Peanut Butter Conspiracy
05.06.67	Whiskey A Go Go, West Hollywood, CA
09/10.06.67	California Hall, San Francisco, CA, with the Steve Miller Blues Band
10.06.67	KFRC Fantasy Fair & Magic Mountain Music Festival, Sidney B. Cushing Memorial Amphitheater high on the South face of Mount Tamalpais in Marin County, CA.. headlined on this first of two days by the Fifth Dimension
17.06.67	Through
27.06.67	The Galaxy, Los Angeles, CA, on the last day with Michael Monarch on additional lead guitar
28.06.67	Oakland Civic Auditorium, Oakland, CA
11/12/13.12.67	Whisky A Go Go, West Hollywood, CA, supported by Topang Canyon and Sweatwater
14.12.67	same but without Topanga Canyon
25/25/27/	
28.01.68	Whisky A Go Go, West Hollywood, CA, with John Mayall & The Bluesbreakers
29.01.68	Steppenwolf's self titled debut album is released in the United States
02.02.68	Steppenwolf in concert at Mass Rally at L.A. Sports Arena, Los Angeles, CA, with Blue Cheer, Nina Simone, Dr. Spock, James Foreman and Peter Torck of the Monkees
16.02.68	Steppenwolf in concert at the Blue Law, Torrance, CA
17.02.68	Velvet Dandelion in concert at St. Mary's Center, Norton, MA
23.02.68	Steppenwolf in concert at the Santa Monica Civic Audithorium, Santa Monica, CA, supporting Cream with The Electric Prunes and Penny Nicholas (2 Shows)

01.03.68	Steppenwolf in concert at Valley Music Theatre At Ventura Bay, Woodland Hills, CA, with The Animals and Sweetwater
08.03.68	Steppenwolf in concert at Cheetah, Venice Beach, Los Angeles, CA, with Quicksilver Messenger Service and Kaleidoscope
09.03.68	Steppenwolf in concert at Cheetah, Venice Beach, Los Angeles, CA, with Quicksilver Messenger Service and Kaleidoscope „Steppenwolf" self-titled first album debuts on Billboard`s LP chart
17.03.68	Steppenwolf in concert at Pasadena Exhibition Hall, Pasadena, CA, with Iron Butterfly, Peanut Butter Conspiracy, Clear Light, Jackson Browne, Penny Nichols, Gordon Alexander, Bluesberry Jam, Alexander's Rag Time Band, The Rockets, The Fields and The Peace Officers
24.03.68	Steppenwolf appear in a benefit show for Radio Strike Fund for KMPX and KPPC DJ's at Kaleidoscope in West Hollywood with Buffalo Springfield, Jefferson Airplane, Tiny Tim, H.P. Lovecraft, Quicksilver Messenger Service, Firesign Theatre, Clear Light, Peanut Butter Conspiracy, Sweetwater and Genesis (featuring Kent Henry)
28.03.68	Steppenwolf in concert at the Fillmore West, San Francisco, with Country Joe & The Fish, Flamin' Groovies
29.03.68	Shawn Mandy Kay born in Los Angeles at UCLA Medical Center Steppenwolf in concert at the Fillmore West, San Francisco, with Country Joe & The Fish, Flamin' Groovies
30.03.68	Steppenwolf in concert at the Fillmore West, San Francisco, with Country Joe & The Fish, Flamin' Groovies

06.04.68	Steppenwolf in concert at Earl Warren Showground, Santa Barbara, CA, supported by Electric Flag and Traffic
07.04.68	Steppenwolf in concert at Swing Audithorium, San Bernandino, CA, with Blue Cheer, Electric Flag and The Drift
10.04.68	Steppenwolf in concert at Earl Warren Show Grounds, Santa Barbara, CA, with Traffic and Electric Flag
11.04.68	Steppenwolf in concert at Anaheim Convention Center, Anaheim, CA, with Blue Cheer and Electric Flag (2 shows)
12.04.68	Steppenwolf in concert at Government Hall, Sacramento, CA, supported by Hamilton Street Car
19.04.68	Steppenwolf in concert at Avalon Ballroom, San Francisco, CA, with Charly Musselwhite, The 4th Way, Indian Head Band
20.04.68	Steppenwolf in concert at Avalon Ballroom, San Francisco, CA, with Charly Musselwhite, The 4th Way, Indian Head Band
21.04.68	Steppenwolf in concert at Avalon Ballroom, San Francisco, CA, with Charly Musselwhite, The 4th Way, Indian Head Band
26.04.68	Steppenwolf in concert at Independence Hall, Philadelphia, PA (2X)
27.04.68	Steppenwolf in concert at the California State Long Beach Men's Gym, Long Beach, A, supported by H. P. Lovecraft and Kaleidoscope
02/03.05.68	Steppenwolf in concert at the Whisky A Go Go, West Hollywood, CA, with Travel Agency and Glad
04.05.68	Steppenwolf makes their first appearance on „American Bandstand" lip synching to „Born To Be Wild"

05.05.68	Steppenwolf in concert at the Whisky A Go Go, West Hollywood, CA, with Travel Agency and Glad
10.05.68	California State College at Los Angeles University, Los Angeles, CA, supported by Peanut Butter Conspiracy and General Store
13.05.68	State Fair Music Hall, Dallas, TX, with The Chessman and American Breed
15/16/17.05.68	LaCave, Cleveland, OH
18.05.68	Chase Park Hotel Ballroom National Guard Armory, St. Louis, MO, supported by the Dead Public Service
21.05.68 22/23/24/ 25/ 26/05.68	University Of Wisconsin, Madison, MI
30/31.05.68	Electric Theatre, Chicago, IL
07/08.06.68	Marine Stadium, Miami, FL
	Fillmore East, New York City, NY, with Quicksilver Messenger Serivce and Electric Flag
09/10/11/ 12.06.68	The Scene, New York City, NY, with Mose Allison and Kenny Rankin
14/15.06.68	Electric Factory, Pittsbourg, PA, supported by Lothar & The People
15.06.68	TV broadcast of "Upbeat" on WEWS Channel 5 from the WUAB-TV Studios with Steppenwolf, Helen Alberth, American Breed, Ronnie Dante, Jay And The Techniques, Robert John, The Robots, Sly And The Family Stone, Blue Cheer and Billy Vera
22.06.68	Velvet Dandelion in concert at Fall River Arts Festival, Fall River, MA
02/03/04.07.68	Fillmore West, San Francisco, CA, with Creedence Clearwater Revival, Butterfield Blues Band and It's A Beautiful Day
05.07.68	Hollywood Bowl, Los Angeles, CA, with the Doors and the Chambers Brothers; Doors Set is filmed for later release

12/13.07.68	Sound Factory, Sacramento, CA, with Ace Of Cups, Initial Shock
19.07.68	Steppenwolf in concert at Rainbow Ballroom, Fresno, CA, supported by Bo Diddley
20.07.68	Steppenwolf appears on „American Bandstand" again
21.07.68	Steppenwolf in concert at the Sanctuary, Lake Tahoe, CA, with New Country Weather, Maggie's Farm, New Bob City Lights
23.07.68	Steppenwolf in concert at Community Concourse Theatre, San Diego, CA, supported by the Brain Police
25.07.68	Steppenwolf in concert at the Portland Civic Audit, Portland, ME
26.07.68	Steppenwolf in concert at the Eagles Auditorium, Seattle, WA
27.07.68	Steppenwolf in concert at the Eagles Auditorium, Seattle, WA
03.08.68	Steppenwolf in concert at the Newport Pop Festival, Orange County Fairgrounds, Costa Mesa, CA, with Tiny Tim, Electric Flag, Sonny & Cher, Chambers Brothers, Canned Heat, Country Joe And The Fish, Butterfield Blues Band and James Cotton Blues Band. Maybe the only gig with Michael "Mike" Port on bass guitar.
08.08.68	Steppenwolf appears in „Playboy After Dark"-TV Show, playing live versions of „Berry Rides Again, „Sookie Sookie" and „Born To Be Wild"
09/10/11.08.68	Avalon Ballroom, San Francisco, CA, supported by Siegel-Schwall, Santana and Jerry Abrams Head Lights. Maybe the first gig with Nick St. Nicholas on bass guitar.
14.08.68	Cellar Club, Chicago, IL
15/16.08.68	in Boston, MA
17/18.08.68	in Gaithersburgh, MD
19/20.08.68	in King Of Prussia, PA

21.08.68	in Savannah, GA
22.08.68	the Palladium, Los Angeles, CA (Teen Tempo Show)
23.08.68	in Charleston, SC
23.08.68	in Charlotte, NC
24.08.68	in Evansville, IN
25.08.68	in Baltimore, MD or Monterey County Fairgrounds, Monterey, CA
26.08.68	in Atlanta, GA
27/28/29/30/ 31.08.68	Fillmore West, San Francisco, CA with Grateful Dead, Staple Singers, Santana & Sons Of Champlin „Born To Be Wild"/"Everybody's Next One" reaches Nr. 2 in the US-Single Charts
01.09.68	Steppenwolf in concert at the Los Angeles Sports Arena, CA, with the Quicksilver Messenger Service, the Buddy Miles Express, H. P. Lovecraft, the Sons Of Champlin, Fraternity Of Man, Three Dog Night and Black Pearl
02.09.68	The Sky River Rock Festival, Sultan, WA
06.09.68	Civic Auditorium, San Jose, supported by Lee Michaels Syndicate Of Sounds
11.09.68	The Avalon Ballroom, San Francisco, CA, with Santana
13.09.68	The Civic Auditorium, Honolulu, MI, with Pulse, Theatre of Madness and Lights by Starchild
14.09.68	The Civic Auditorium, Honolulu, MI, with Pulse, Theatre of Madness and Lights by Starchild
17.09.68	The University of Waterloo, Waterloo, ON, Canada
19.09.68	"Born To Be Wild" certified as a gold single in US
20.09.68	Steppenwolf in concert at the Terrace Ballroom, Salt Lake City, UT, with The Cleveland Wrecking Co. and The Holden Caufield
28.09.68	Sunset Rollerama, Tucson, AZ
01.10.68	"Steppenwolf The Second" released in the USA

05.10.68	"Magic Carpet Ride" debuts on Billboard's single chart "Steppenwolf The Second" debuts on Billboard's LP chart
13.10.68	Steppenwolf in concert at Theatre For The Performing Arts, Hemisfair Arena, San Antonio, TX, with Johnny Winter and New Atlantis
18.10.68	Steppenwolf in concert at Kinetic Playground, Chicago, IL, with Ten Years After (2 shows) Rocket Ritchotte with Velvet Dandelion in concert at Welfare Hall, Attleboro, MA
19.10.68	Indiana State Fairgrounds Coliseum, Indianapolis, IN
20.10.68	Steppenwolf in concert at the Scene, Milwaukee, WI, supported by Country Joe & The Fish (two shows)
26.10.68	Steppenwolf in concert at Woolsey Hall, Yale University, New Haven, CT, supported by Tim Buckley
01.11.68	Steppenwolf in concert at Veterans Memorial Auditorium, Providence, RI Kent Henry with Genesis in concert at the Avalon Ballroom, San Francisco, CA, with Taj Mahal and the Byrds
02.11.68	Akron Civic Theatre, Akron, OH „Magic Carpet Ride" peaks at Nr. 3 in the Canadian single chart Kent Henry with Genesis in concert at the Avalon Ballroom, San Francisco, CA, with Taj Mahal and the Byrds
03.11.68	Steppenwolf in concert at Cincinnati Music Hall, Cincinnati, OH, supported by the Ditallons Kent Henry with Genesis in concert at the Avalon Ballroom, San Francisco, CA, with Taj Mahal and the Byrds
06.11.68	Steppenwolf in concert at The Scene, Los Angeles, CA
08.11.68	Steppenwolf in concert at Fillmore East, New York City, NY, with the Children of God and Buddy

	Rich & His Orchestra
09.11.68	Steppenwolf in concert at Fillmore East, New York City, NY, with Buddy Rich & His Orchestra
15.11.68	Steppenwolf appearing on the „Smothers Brothers Comedy Hour" TV show with „Magic Carpet Ride" and „Rock Me"
15.11.68	Steppenwolf in concert at the Electric Factory, Philadelphia, PA, supported by The Youngbloods an Woody's Truck Stop
20.11.68	Onondago Memorial Auditorium, Syracuse, NY, supported by „Sly & Family Stone"
21/22.11.68	Thee Image Club, Sunny Isles Beach, FL
27.11.68	The Baltimore Civic Center, Baltimore, MD, supported by Iron Butterfly Steppenwolf's self titled debut LP certified Gold
29.11.68	Steppenwolf in concert at the Civic Arena, Pittsburgh, PA, supported by The Turtles, The Grass Roots, The Ohio Express, The New Hudson Exit and The Shadow Of Knight
30.11.68	Westbury Music Fair, Westbury, NY
06.12.68	Steppenwolf in concert at the Quaker City Rock Festival at the Spectrum, Philadelphia, PA with Grateful Dead and Iron Butterfly
07.12.68	„Steppenwolf The Second" reaches Nr. 4 in the US-Album Charts
13.12.68	Steppenwolf in concert at the Anaheim Convention Center, Anaheim, CA, with Black Pearl and Three Dog Night
20.12.68	Film "Candy" premieres at the Beverly Hills Theatre in Los Angeles
20.12.68	Steppenwolf in concert at the Spectrum, Philadelphia, PA, supported by Ten Wheel Drive and Tony Joe White
21.12.68	The San Diego Community Concourse, San Diego, CA, supported by The Brain Police

26.12.68	The San Francisco Holiday Rock Festival, Cow Palace, Daly City, CA with Canned Heat, The New Buffalo Springfield, Spencer Davis Group, Blue Cheer, Three Dog Night, Electric Prunes, Santana Blues Band
27.12.68	Holiday Rock Festival, Tingley Coliseum, Albuquerque, NM, with Grass Roots, Three Dog Night, Spencer Davis Group, Canned Heat
28.12.68	The Curtis Hixon Convention Hall, Tampa, FL
29.12.68	The three day Miami Pop Festival, Hallandale, FL, with Grateful Dead, Marvin Gaye, Chuck Berry, Turtles, Joni Mitchell and others
30.12.68	Atlanta Municipal Auditorium, Atlanta, GA
31.12.68	Arizona Veterans Memorial Colosseum, Phoenix, AZ, with Blood, Sweat & Tears, Three Dog Night and Illinois Speed Press
05.01.69	Steppenwolf appear on „Smoothers Brothers"-TV Show
19.01.69	Steppenwolf in concert at Hilton Hotel for WABC/PAL „Big Break" Concert in New York City, NY
26.01.69	Steppenwolf appear on „Playboy After Dark"-TV Show, miming to „Chicken Wolf" and „Don't Cry"
31.01.69	Steppenwolf in concert at Civic Center Music Hall, Oklahoma City, OK
01.02.69	Montana State University, Montana, MT
02.02.69	University Of Oregon, Eugene, OR, supported by Three Dog Night
03.02.69	Salem Armory, Salem OR
05.02.69	Spokane Coliseum, Spokane, WA06.02.69 Portland Memorial Coliseum, Portland, OR, supported by Three Dog Night
07.02.69	HEC Edmundson Pavilion - University Of Washington, Seattle, WA
08.02.69	Sacramento Memorial, Sacramento, CA

11.02.69	Santa Rosa Fairgrounds, Santa Rosa, CA, supported by Rik Elswit and A Euphonius Wall
12.02.69	„Steppenwolf The Second" is certified gold
21.02.69	Steppenwolf in concert at Civic Center Music Hall, Oklahoma City, OK
22.02.69	Kansas City Municipal Auditorium, Kansas City, MO
23.02.69	Convention Hall, Wichita, KS
24.02.69	Thomas Jefferson Field House, Council Bluff, IH
27.02.69	Fountain Street Church, Grand Rapids, MI, supported by Brownsville Station
28.02.69	Grande Ballroom, Detroit, supported by MC 5, Sun and Three Dog Night
01.03.69	Grande Ballroom, Detroit, supported by MC 5, Sun and Three Dog Nigh Rock Me" debuts on Billboard`s singles chart
02.03.69	Steppenwolf in concert at Music Hall, Cleveland OH, supported by Arlo Guthrie
03.03.69	Steppenwolf appear at the Upbeat Television show
06.03.69	Steppenwolf in concert at Boise State College Gym, Boise, IO, supported by Mark Almond
07.03.69	Eastman Auditorium – C.M.A. "Now Concert", Rochester, NY
08.03.69	Dillon Gymnasium – Princeton University, Princeton, NJ
15.03.69	„At Your Birthday Party" debuts on Billboard`s LP chart
21.03.69	Steppenwolf in concert at Aragon Ballroom, Chicago, IL, supported by Three Dog Night Bangor Flying Circus
22.03.69	Kiel Auditorium, St. Louis, MO, supported by Three Dog Night
23.03.69	Masonic Temple, Davenport, IA, supported by the Pete Klint Quartet Magic Carpet Ride" single certified gold

26.03.69	Steppenwolf in concert at Franklin County Veterans Memorial, Columbus, OH
28.03.69	Fillmore East, New York City, NY, with Julie Driscoll, Brian Auger & Trinity and John Hammond
29.03.69	Fillmore East, New York City, NY, with Julie Driscoll, Brian Auger & Trinity and John Hammond
30.03.69	Syracuse War Memorial Auditorium, Syracuse, NY
01.04.69	Electric Factory, Philadelphia, PA, supported by Aynsley Dunbar Retaliation
02.04.69	Electric Factory, Philadelphia, PA, supported by Aynsley Dunbar Retaliation
03.04.69	Bushnell Auditorium (Memorial Hall), Hartford, CT
05.04.69	Boston Arena, Boston, MA, with Arthur Brown, Youngbloods, Ascenson, The Pack
18.04.69	Memorial Hall, Austin, TX
19.04.69	Will Rogers Memorial Hall, Forth Worth, TX
20.04.69	Corpus Christi Coliseum, Corpus Christi, TX
21.04.69	Steppenwolf appear on the Ed Sullivan Show, New York City, NY
25.04.69	Steppenwolf in concert at Mid South Coliseum, Memphis, TN, promoted by Tom Carr
26.04.69	Independence Hall, Lakeshore Auditorium, Baton Rouge, LA (two shows) supported by The Bored
27.04.69	Long Beach College Gym, Long Beach, CA, supported by HP Lovecraft and Kaleidoscope
02.05.69	Exhibition Center, Tulsa, OK
03.05.69	University Of Arkansas, Fayettville, AR
07.05.69	Sam Houston Coliseum, Houston, TX
08.05.69	Film "Easy Rider" is unveiled at the 22nd Festival de Cannes, South of France
10.05.69	„It`s Never Too Late" debuts on Billboard`s single chart

11.05.69	Steppenwolf appear at the NME Poll Winners concert, Wembley, London, UK
13.05.69	Press Reception at Nash House, Pall Mall, London, UK
14.05.69	TV shooting for Beat Club, Bremen, GER
15.05.69	TV shooting for Top Of The Pops, BBC, London, UK
16.05.69	TV shooting for Joe Brown Show, London, UK
16.05.69	Steppenwolf in concert at Marquee, London, GB, supported by Steamhammer, King Crimson, Terry Reid and Hard Meat
17.05.69	Manchester University, Birmingham, England, UK
18.05.69	Mothers Club, Birmingham, England, UK
19.05.69	Bay Hotel, Whitburn, England, UK
20.05.69	Marselisborghallen, Arhus, Denmark, supported by Daisy
21.05.69	Stockholm, Sweden
22.05.69	Folkoner Centereit, Copenhagen, Denmark
23.05.69	TV shooting in Copenhagen and Brussels In concert at Sport Halle, Mechelen, Belgium, supported by Wallace Collection. Show was filmed for Belgian TV including the songs Born To Be Wild, Chicken Wolf, Hoochie Coochie Man, Jupiter Child, Magic Carpet Ride and The Pusher.
24.05.69	Paradiso, Amsterdam, NL
25.05.69	Gronigen, NL
27.05.69	Through
29.05.69	Germany days off
30.05.69	Lyceum, London, UK
30.05.69	North London Colleges, UK, with Nice and supported by Blossom Toes and Glass Menagerie (Midnight To Dawn)
01.06.69	Steppenwolf returning from 14-day European Tour of England, Scandinavië, Belgium, Holland and Germany

07.06.69	German TV show Beat Club first broadcasts Steppenwolf moving playback to Born To Be Wild, Sookie Sookie and Rock Me
14.06.69	Steppenwolf in concert at Swing Auditorium, San Bernadino, CA, supported by Locomotive, Pepper Tree, Jerome and Grass Roots
20.06.69	Oakland-Alameda County Coliseum Arena, Oakland, CA, with Three Dog Night, Grass Roots and Smith
21.06.69	The Newport Pop Festival, Devonshire Downs, Northridge CA, with Albert Collins, Brenton Wood, Buffy Sainte-Marie, Charity, Creedence Clearwater Revival, Eric Burdon and War, Friends of Distinction, Jethro Tull, Lee Michaels, Love and Sweetwater.
22.06.69	Toronto Rock Festival at Varsity Stadium, Toronto, Canada, with The Band, Chuck Berry, Johnny Winter, Dr. John and Tiny Tim
23.06.69	The Montreal Forum Laugh In, Montreal, Canada, with Robert Charlebois and Triangle
26.06.69	Cow Palace, Daly City, CA
28.06.69	International Sports Arena, San Diego, CA
30.06.69	Oakland Colosseum, Oakland, CA
04.07.69	Hemis Fair Arena, San Antonio, TX, with the Byrds
05.07.69	Sam Houston Coliseum, Houston, TX
11.07.69	Buffalo Memorial Auditorium, Buffalo, NY
12.07.69	Ashton Park Convention Center, Ashton Park, NJ, supported by The Man (2 shows)
14.07.69	Film „Easy Rider" premiers in New York City at the Beekman Theatre
18.07.69	Steppenwolf in concert at Foreman Stadium, Norfolk, VA
19.07.69	Westhampton Rock Festival At Suffolk Raceway, Westhampton, NY
25.07.69	Cincinnati Gardens, Cincinnati, OH, supported by Chuck Berry

26.07.69	Freedom Hall, Louisville, KY
27.07.69	Camden County Music Fair, Cherry Hill, NJ
02.08.69	The Singer Bowl at Flushing Meadows, New York City, NY, supported y Moody Blues and NRBQ
03.08.69	Singer Music Festival at the Pavilion, Forrest Hills, New York City, NY, supported by Rhinoceros and Spooky Tooth
09.08.69	Veterans Memorial Auditorium, Des Moines, IA, supported by Pete Klint Quartet
13.08.69	Film „Easy Rider" premiers in Los Angeles at the Village Theatre
15.08.69	Steppenwolf in concert at the Tuledo Sports Arena, Tuledo, OH
16.08.69	„Move Over" debuts on Billboard's Single Chart
17.08.69	Steppenwolf in concert at Hara Arena, Dayton, OH Steppenwolf guests at Ed Sullivan Show filmed in New York City, NY
22.08.69	Rhode Island Audithorium, Providence, RI
23.08.69	New Heaven Arena, New Heaven, CT Steppenwolf appearing on „American Bandstand" lip synching to „Move Over" and „Power Play"
29.08.69	Edmonton Gardens, Edmonton, Alberta, CAN
30.08.69	Winnipeg Arena, Winnipeg, Manitoba, Canada
06.09.69	Thunderbird Peace Festival, Capilano Indian Reservation, Vancouver, BC, Canada, with Jimy Hendrix, Steve Miller Blues Band, Country Joe & The Fish, The Youngbloods, James Cotton Blues Band, Buddy Miles Express, Collectors, Pacific, Gas & Electric, Southwind an Fields
12.09.69	The Forum, Inglewood, CA, with Three Dog Night and Grass Roots
20.09.69	Honolulu International Center, Honolulu, HI, with by Blue Cheer
21.09.69	Bouck Gym, Cobleskill, NY
12.10.69	Foreman Field, Norfolk, VA

19.10.69	Lyceum, London, GB, supported by „Family", „Spirit Of John Morgan" and „Van Der Graaf Generator"
20.10.69	Photo shooting in front of the EMI building in London, GB
23.10.69	Niedersachsenhalle, Hannover, supported by Jeronimo
24.10.69	Grugahalle, Essen, Germany, supported by Jeronimo
25.10.69	Jahrhunderthalle Frankfurt, Germany (2 shows), supported by Jeronimo
27.10.69	Rheinhalle Düsseldorf, Germany (2 shows), supported by Jeronimo
28.10.69	Messehalle 8, Köln, Germany, supported by Jeronimo
29.10.69	Culturhouse, Helsinki, Finnland (2 shows), supported by Apollo
31.10.69	Falkoner Centeret, Kopenhagen, Denmark, supported by Day Of Phoenix
01.11.69	Tinghallen, Viborg, Denmark (2 shows)
03/04.11.69	Cirkus Krone, München, Germany (2 shows?), supported by Jeronimo
05.11.69	Festhalle Planten + Blomen, Hamburg, Germany (2 shows), supported by Jeronimo
08.11.69	Allen Fieldhouse, Lawrence, KS
12/13.11.69	Thelma, Los Angeles, CA
15.11.69	Albuquerque Civic Auditorium, Albuquerque, NM, supported by Bubble Puppy "Monster" debuts on Billboard's LP chart
22.11.69	Steppenwolf appearing in the German television broadcast of "4-3-2-1 Hot And Sweet" lip synching to "Move Over" on channel 2
27.11.69	Steppenwolf in concert at Civic Center, Baltimore, MD
28.11.69	Calgary Stampede Corral, Calgary, Alberta, Canada

29.11.69	Agrodome, Vancouver, British Columbia, Canada, with Spring
30.11.69	The Palm Beach International Raceway Festival, Jupiter, FL, with Jefferson Airplane, Byrds and others
05.12.69	Las Vegas Convention Center, Las Vegas, NV
06.12.69	Carnegie Hall, New York City, NY, supported by Rare Earth (2 Shows)
10.12.69	The Spectrum, Philadelphia, PA
16.12.69	Winter land, San Francisco, CA as a benefit
17.12.69	Steppenwolf appears on „Playboy After Dark" TV-Show, miming to „Monster" and „From Here To There, Eventually"
19.12.69	Steppenwolf in concert at Kiel Convention Hall, St. Louis, MO, supported by Joe Simon
20.12.69	Steppenwolf in concert at Philadelphia Spectrum, Philadelphia, PA, supported by Ten Wheel Drive and Tony Joe White
26.12.69	Steppenwolf in concert at Wharton Field House, Moline, IL, supported by Chosen Few
27.12.69	„Monster" debuts on Billboard`s singles chart
27.12.69	Steppenwolf in concert at Veterans Memorial Auditorium, Des Moines, IA, supported by The Chosen Few
10.01.70	Atlanta Municipal Auditorium, Atlanta, GA
11.01.70	Shreveport Hirsch Memorial Coliseum, Shreveport, LA
16.01.70	Mid-South Coliseum, Memphis, TN, supported by the Byrds and the Country Funks before 8.000 people
17.01.70	Ottawa Civic Centre, Ottawa, ON, CAN, supported by Leather and Polychromatic Experiment
18.01.70	Roberts Stadium, Evansville, IN
22.01.70	Santa Monica Civic Auditorium, Santa Monica, CA, with Taj Mahal and Flying Burrito Brothers; Steppenwolf show recorded for later LP

23.01.70	Jacksonville Coliseum, Jacksonville, FL
24.01.70	The Armory (Fort Homer Hesterley Armory), Tampa, FL, supported by Tony Joe White
26.01.70	Mid South Coliseum, Memphis, TN
31.01.70	Municipal Auditorium, Nashville, TN, supported by Tony Joe White and Looking Glass
06.02.70	„Rock Stars", hosted by Richard Robinson, interviews John Kay
06.02.70	Steppenwolf in concert Charleston Civic Center, Charleston, SC, supported by Looking Glass and Randall Wray & Heavy Rain
13.02.70	The Indiana State Fairgrounds Coliseum, Indianapolis, IN, with the Byrds and the Soul Messengers
14.02.70	Saint Valentine's Pop Festival, Clemson, SC, with Steam, Pacific Gas & Electric and others
21.02.70	Amarillo Civic Center, Amarillo, TX, supported by Bubble Puppy
22.02.70	Lubbock Municipal Coliseum, Lubbock, TX
27.02.70	The Milwaukee Auditorium, Milwaukee, WI
28.02.70	The University of Maine Ump Gym, Portland, ME, supported by Tony Joe White
07.03.70	Freedom Hall, Louisville, KY, supported by Conception and Rugby's
14.03.70	Agricultural Hall – Allentown Fairgrounds, Allentown, PA, supported by Double Exposure and Rock Island
15.03.70	University of Waterloo, Waterloo, Canada, ON
18.03.70	„Monster" LP is certified gold
20.03.70	Steppenwolf in concert at Memorial Hall, Kansas City, KS
27.03.70	Tulsa Assembly Center Arena, Tulsa, OK
28.03.70	Chicago Civic Opera House, Chicago, IL, supported by The Sun
03.04.70	Philadelphia Civic Center, Philadelphia, PA, supported by Pacific Gas & Electric, Steam and In-Sex

04.04.70	Steppenwolf in concert at the Rhode Island Audithorium, Providence, RI, supported by Frijid Pink
05.04.70	Music Hall, Boston, MS, supported by Frijid Pink
10.04.70	Steppenwolf in concert at the Houston Music Hall, Houston, TX,
11.04.70	Steppenwolf in concert at the Houston Music Hall, Houston, TX, late Hemisfair Arena, San Antonio, TX „Hey Lawdy Mama" debuts on Billboard`s singles chart
16.05.70	Century II Performing Arts & Convention Center, Witchita, KS, supported by Rick Harrison
17.04.70	U.K. Memorial Coliseum – UK's Little Kentucky Derby, Lexington, KY, supported by Don McLean
18.04.70	„Steppenwolf Live" debuts on Billboard`s LP chart Steppenwolf in concert at the Municipal Audithorium, Austin, TX
19.04.70	Steppenwolf in concert at the North Carolina State University, Raleigh, NC
23.04.70	Auburn Memorial Coliseum, Auburn, AL
25.04.70	Steppenwolf appears on ABC-TV`s „Get It Together"
01.05.70	Steppenwolf in concert at TraveLodge Theatre, Phoenix, AZ, supported by John Hammond
06.05.70	Steppenwolf supposed to appear at Berkely Community Theatre, Berkely, CA, with Shades of Joy and Osceola as "Benefit For The Chosen Few", show cancelled
09.05.70	McDonald Gym, Beaumont, TX
14.05.70	Reed Green Coliseum – University of Southern Mississippi, Hattiesburg, MS
16.05.70	Performing Arts & Convention Center, Witchita, KS
19.05.70	Before more than 8.000 supporters of college strike at the University of California's Bovard Field
24.05.70	Fairfield Halls, Croydon, Surrey, England

29.05.70	Aerodrome, Schenectady, NY
30.05.70	South Mountain Arena, West Orange, NJ, last show with Nick St. Nicholas, with Ten Wheel Drive and Genya Raven
05.06.70	Greenville Memorial Auditorium, Greenville, NC, first Show with George Biondo
06.06.70	Dinner Key, Miami, FL
07.06.70	Curtis Hixon Hall, Tampa, FL
12.06.70	Island Garden Arena, West Hempstead, NY, supported by Bush (2 shows)
13.06.70	Hampton Beach Casino Ballroom, Hampton Beach, NH
14.06.70	Blues Image in concert at Anaheim Stadium, Los Angeles, CA, supporting the Who along with Leon Russel and John Sebstian
18.06.70	Steppenwolf in concert at Park Center, Charlotte, NC
27.06.70	Bath-Festival, England, with Led Zeppelin, Byrds, Donovan, Frank Zappa, Santana and others
02.07.70	Royal-Albert-Hall in London, England, supported by Colosseum
11.07.70	Memorial Stadium at Georgia Southern University, Savannah, GA, supported by Strawberry Walrus
14.07.70	„Steppenwolf Live" LP is certified Gold
17.07.70	Steppenwolf in concert at Downing Stadium, Randall's Island, NYC, filmed, with Grand Funk Railroad, Jimmy Hendrix Experience, John Sebastian, Jethro Tull
18.07.70	War Memorial, Rochester, NY
24.07.70	Municipal Auditorium, Nashville, TN, supported by The Gentry's, Teagarden and Van Winkel
26.07.70	Merriweather Post Pavilion, Columbia, MD, supported by Don McLean
31.07.70	O'Keefe Centre, Toronto, ON, Canada, supported by Bush

03.08.70	Atlanta Municipal Auditorium, Atlanta, GA
06.08.70	Summer festival for peace at Shea Stadium, New York City with James Gang, Paul Simon, Janis Joplin, Johnny Winter, Poco a.o.
08.08.70	The Warehouse, New Orleans, LA
09.08.70	Minneapolis Auditorium, Minnesota, MN
14.08.70	Edmonton Gardens, Edmonton, Alberta, CAN
21.08.70	Bush opening for Iron Butterfly at the LA Forum, Los Angeles, CA
22.08.70	„Screaming Night Hog" debuts on Billboard's Single Chart
30.08.70	Steppenwolf in concert at Du Quoin State Fairgrounds, Du Quoin, IL, supported by Smith
??.??.70	Memorial Stadium, Savannah, GA, supported by Strawberry Walrus
04.09.70	Dallas Memorial Auditorium, Dallas, TX, supported by James Gang and Bush
06.09.70	Jacob Brown Auditorium, Brownsville, TX, supported by Flash
12.09.70	Cobo Arena, Detroit, MI, supported by John Mayall & Savage Grace
26.09.70	Taylor County Coliseum, Abilene, TX, supported by Temple
02.10.70	The Forum, Los Angeles, CA, supported by Bush and John Mayall
04.10.70	Houston Music Hall, Houston, TX
17.10.70	Honolulu International Center, Honolula, HI, supported by Sugar Loaf
24.10.70	Civic Auditorium, Albuquerque, NM, supported by Earth
25.10.70	Sports Arena, San Diego, CA, supported by Sugar Loaf and Jo Mama
05.11.70	University Of Athens, Athens, GA
13.11.70	Appalachian State University, Boone, NC
14.11.70	Orlando Sports Stadium, Orlando, FL "Who Needs Ya'" debuts on Billboard's single chart

21.11.70	"Steppenwolf 7" debuts on Billboard's LP chart
27.11.70	Steppenwolf in concert at the Pacific Coliseum, Vancouver, BC, CAN, supported by Savoy Brown
02.12.70	„Steppenwolf 7" reviewed in Rolling Stone Magazine
19.12.70	Steppenwolf in concert at Forum de Montreal, Montreal, QC, Canada, supported by Bush, Soma and Rabble
08.01.71	Fillmore East, NYC, NY, with Spencer Davis Group and Luther Allison
24.01.71	Anaheim Convention Center, Anaheim, CA, supported by B. B. King and Shuggie Otis
30.01.71	Lantz Gym, Charleston, IL, supported by Ned
31.01.71	Kiel Auditorium, St. Louis, MI
01.02.71	University of Illinois, Champaign, IL (?)
04.02.71	Fillmore East, New York City, NY, supported by „Ten Wheel Drive" and „Luther Allison"
05.02.71	Fillmore East, New York City, NY, supported by "Ten Wheel Drive", "Luther Allison", "Genya Ravan" and Joe's Lights
06.02.71	Fillmore East, New York City, NY, supported by „Ten Wheel Drive" and „Luther Allison"
11.02.71	Fillmore West, San Francisco, CA, with Fleetwood Mac
12/13.02.71	Winter land, San Francisco, CA, with Cold Blood, Shivia's Headband and Buddy Guy/ Jr. Wells Blues Band
20.02.71	Ohio University Convention Center, OH, supported by Steel River and Edwin Starr
24.02.71	John Kay appears at the Anaheim Convention Center, Anaheim, CA, as speaker for the panel discussion on rock concerts
26.02.71	Watres Armory, Scranton, PA
27.02.71	Cherry Hill Arena, Cherry Hill, NJ
05.03.71	The Syndrome, Chicago Coliseum, Chicago, IL

06.03.71	Boise State College Gym, Boise, ID, supported by Marc Almond „Gold" debuts on Billboard's LP Chart „Snowblind Friend" debuts on Billboard's Single Chart
13.03.71	Capitol Theatre, Port Chester, NY
15.03.71	The Warehouse, New Orleans, LO, supported by Little Feat
19.03.71	The Armory, Minneapolis, MN
20.03.71	University Hall, Charlotteville, VA
21.03.71	Alexander Memorial Coliseum, Atlanta, GA
26.03.71	Ritchie Coliseum University Of Maryland, Rossborough, MD (2 shows)
02.04.71	St. Johns Arena, Columbus, OH, supported by Pacific Gas & Electric
03.04.71	Miami Marine Stadium, Miami, FL
12.04.71	„Steppenwolf 7" and „Steppenwolf Gold" certified gold
16.04.71	Steppenwolf in concert at Olympia Stadium, Detroit, MI, supported by Alice Cooper
17.04.71	Civic Center Music Hall, Oklahoma City, OK, supported by Zephyr
18.04.71	Steppenwolf in concert at Zembo Mosque, Harrisburg, PA (2 shows)
23.04.71	Villanova Fieldhouse, Villanove, PY, supported by Rags and the Family
30.04.71	Houston City Hall, Houston, TX.
14.05.71	Alexander Memoria Colosseum (Georgia Tech), Atlanta, GA. Last show with Larry Byrom on guitar
15.05.71	Kent Henry joins Steppenwolf
20.05.71	Steppenwolf in concert at the Warehouse, New Orleans, LA, supported by Little Feat Recording sessions for album "For Ladies Only" begin
22.05.71	Steppenwolf performing songs from "Steppenwolf 7" as "Album of the month" broadcasted on TV

28.05.71	Steppenwolf in concert at Knoxville Civic Coliseum, Knoxville, TN Steppenwolf in concert at Charlotte Coliseum, Charlotte, NC, supported by Steel River
30.05.71	Maple Leaf Gardens, Toronto, ON, Canada
05.06.71	Bush in concert at the Bitter End, Los Angeles, CA
06.06.71	Steppenwolf in concert at Boise State College Gymnasium, Boise, ID, supported by Mixed Blood Bush in concert at the Bitter End, Los Angeles, CA
26.06.71	Steppenwolf in concert at Beggar's Banquet Festival, Borough Of York Stadium, Toronto, ON, Canada, supported by Bread, Bloodrock, Beach Boys, Alice Cooper, Lighthouse and Chilliwack
02.07.71	Steppenwolf in concert at Cumberland County Memorial Auditorium, Fayetteville, NC, supported by The Assembly
03.07.71	Scheduled Wolf concert at the Salt Palace, Salt Lake City, UT, is cancelled
10.07.71	Steppenwolf in concert at Soldiers and Sailors Memorial Auditorium, Chattanooga, TN
17.07.71	„Ride With Me" debuts on Billboard`s Single Chart
23.07.71	Steppenwolf in concert at Forum, Los Angles, CA
06/07.08.71	Steppenwolf in concert at the Wildwood Convention Hall, Wildwood, NJ
08/09.08.71	Steppenwolf in concert at Manhattan Center, NYC, supported by Five Dollar Shoes
14.08.71	Steppenwolf in concert at the Edmonton Gardens, Edmonton, Alberta, CAN, supported by Fat Chance
19.08.71	John Kay appears at Hotels Ambassador, Chicago, IL, as speaker with Curtis Mayfield and Peter Yarrrow

21.08.71	Steppenwolf appearing on „American Bandsand" lip synching to „Ride With Me" and „For Ladies Only" (edited version)
27.08.71	Scheduled Wolf concert at Monroe Civic, Monroe, LA, cancelled
02.10.71	"For Ladies Only" debuts on Billboard's LP chart
06.11.71	„For Ladies Only" debuts on Billboard's Single Chart
13.11.71	Steppenwolf in concert at Hollywood Palladium, Los Angeles, CA, in benefit of Hollywood Sunset Free Clinic, supported by Charles Lloyd and String Cheese
20.12.71	„For Ladies Only" reviewed in Rolling Stone
23.12.71	„For Ladies Only"-LP reviewed in „Rolling Stone" Magazine
14.02.72	The original Steppenwolf breaks up Steppenwolf Party Invitation at Jack Ryan's Mansion, Bel Air, CA
15.02.72	**Mayor Sam Yorti declares „Steppenwolf Day" in Los Angeles**

The complete list, 158 pages long and updated until February 2023, is in the hands of Klaus Sander, a very enthusiastic German Wolf packer.